KU-632-749

FOLKTALES

FROM THE GAMBIA

WOLOF FICTIONAL NARRATIVES

**translated and annotated
by
EMIL A. MAGEL**

AN ORIGINAL BY THREE CONTINENTS PRESS

© Emil Magel 1984

First Edition
Three Continents Press
1346 Connecticut Avenue N.W.
Washington, D.C. 20036

ISBN: 0-89410-220-6; -221-4 (pbk)
LC No.: 81-51649

All rights reserved. No part of this book may be
used or reproduced in any manner whatsoever
without written permission from the publisher
except for brief quotations in reviews or articles.

Cover Art by Karen Jurew

For Pat, Laura

and the children of The Gambia

ACKNOWLEDGMENTS

In preparing this collection of Wolof fictional narratives, I have received encouragement and assistance from numerous sources in the United States and The Gambia. Valuable guidance was provided by Bakari Sidibe, the Director of the Gambian National Archives and by Mustapha Ceesay, the Secretary-General of the Gambia-Swedish Red Cross. Momadu Djak and Al Haji Omar Ceesay shared their language and translation skills during the initial recording process. I would especially like to thank Edris Makward in the Department of African Languages and Literatures at the University of Wisconsin for his academic and moral support from the inception of this project to its completion. Finally, I would like to acknowledge my debt to all the Wolof storytellers who graciously shared their values, ideals, and creative talents with me and to the Gambian people who warmly invited me into their lives and made me feel at home.

PREFACE

Dr. Emil Magel has put together here an arresting selection of forty-five oral narratives collected among the Wolof people of the Republic of Gambia, during his field research there in 1973-74.

It is a true delight to read and re-read these lively narratives, for while one cannot deny that verbal oral art always loses a great deal through written transcriptions, let alone through translation into a foreign language, yet Dr. Magel's presentations are made with so much faithful care and intelligence that one is reminded of the famous words of the Senegalese poet Leópold Sédar Senghor in his preface to Birago Diop's second volume of *Tales of Amadou Koumba* (Les Nouveaux Contes d'Amadou Koumba, Paris, 1958). In that now classic preface, the father of négritude, and now retired first President of the Republic of Senegal, wrote that, in spite of Diop's claims at being nothing but "a modest translator of the tales of the griot Amadou, son of Koumba," his renderings of the griot's tales do indeed reveal "the very substance and sap of Negro-African narrative."

It goes without saying that Dr. Magel's ambition and approach here are not those of the creative writer drawing his inspiration from the traditional lore of his people with which he has been nourished since early childhood. Indeed, Dr. Magel is no native Wolof storyteller or writer, nor for that matter, does he pretend to be either. He is not a Birago Diop or a Bernard Dadie.

Yet, his translations of these oral Wolof texts which he taped himself in various hamlets, villages and towns of the Gambia, are definitely not lifeless shadows of the originals. For while we may miss the actual music of the songs, the sounds, the intonation, the gestures, the mimicry, the movements produced by the storyteller, and above all, the spontaneous reactions and the participation of the audience, still *Bouki*, the unworthy and unreliable hyena, *Golo*, the uncouth and noisy monkey, or *Leuk*, the cunning and sometimes helpful hare—to mention only the three most common animal characters of the Savannah tales—do come to life through these pages. Thus, when *Golo*, posturing as a griot, picks up his drum and produces an initial flurry of elementary sounds: "PREPARE TO SHAKE, PREPARE TO TREMBLE!" we share the hilarity of the live audience that is indeed vividly suggested through the vengeful incredulity of the villagers of Jarang in the story *The Monkey Who Claimed to be a Gewel*. Likewise, we can but sympathise with *Lebeer*, the gullible hippopotamus, when he is tricked by treacherous *Bouki*, and then saved by the wily *Leuk* (*The Hare Saves the Hippopotamus*). Also, when some social imperfections constitute the central subject matter of a narrative, such as morbid jealousy in *The Jealous Co-Wife*, or capriciousness in *The Handsome Suitor (I* and *II)*, or greed and gluttony in *The Greedy Father* and *The Mauritanian and His Wealth,* these social shortcomings that are universally frowned upon in Wolof society, are not depicted here through endless and boring abstract moralizing, but through vivid and dynamic characterization.

Dr. Magel brings a sound and rigorous academic approach to his presentations. Moreover, his familiarity with Wolof lore, customs, and history, is convincingly apparent in his excellent introduction, and above all, in the unpretentious but very informative footnotes at the end of each tale. In fact, these footnotes have a double function here. On the one hand, they provide the invaluable cultural background that brings home to the lay reader the robust down-to-earth humor, and the insatiable lust for life that characterize Wolof traditions. In these notes, Dr. Magel shows also that these tales are both general entertainment and popular education. Indeed we laugh wholeheartedly at *Bouki-the-Hyena's* blockheadedness or at *Naar-the-Moor's* self-centered indiscretions, or at the exaggerated greediness of *Ngurmi-the-lazy-husband;* but we should also bear in mind that adultery is a serious crime for all parties concerned in traditional Wolof society *(Two Lovers Punished)*, and that it is not proper to pretend to be what one is not *(The Monkey Who Claimed to be a Gewel)*, or to be too demanding in life *(The Handsome Suitor)*.

This collection is directed both to the scholar and the teacher as well as to the lay reader. For one arresting quality of this little book is indeed the pervading empathy with the culture and the lives of the people involved in these stories. This genuine empathy with the humor and the humanity of the subject matter is communicated to the reader from the outset, and becomes irresistibly contagious as more and more stories are read. The obvious reason for this is that Dr. Magel doubtless relished hearing and participating in these live performances when he witnessed them in their natural context. Then, on reading again his excellent Wolof transcriptions of his tapes, and translating them for the purpose of this book, he appears to be reliving for himself, and sharing with us, the original experience, with almost the same intensity.

Thus, Dr. Magel's translations are not flat word for word renditions of the original Wolof texts into English. Nor are they free adaptations in English, with arbitrary additions and omissions for the purpose of some doubtful embellishment or censure. The latter would have turned his book into just another addition to the now long list of misrepresentations bearing the pretentious name of so-called works of "primitive folklore"; and the former would have proven to be an unnecessarily trying experience for the genuine, curious reader.

Dr. Magel's translations are faithful without being servile and undiscriminating. The dialogues keep much of their colorful flavor in the English; and repetition as a true literary device is truthfully reproduced in the English texts. His approach is illustrated by the Appendix included at the end of the book. It is the transcribed Wolof text of *The Donkeys of Jolof* as told by the skillful young griot of Bati Hai, Lamin Jeng *(Fari Mbam ci Rewi Jolof)*. A Senegalese version of this tale appears as *Fari-L'anesse (Fari the She-Ass* in Dorothy Blair's selection, *Tales of Amadou Koumba*, London, 1966).

In this presentation of his selection of 45 narratives, Dr. Magel has chosen an original form of classification which he calls *thematic pattern* instead of the so-called classification by genres, or thematic affiliations such as is used most frequently by anthropologists and folklorists (see Susan Feldmann's *African Myths and Tales*, New York, 1963, or Paul Radin's *African Folktales and Sculpture*, New York, 1952 and 1972). In this most common form of classification, we find headings such as *The Beginning of Things*, *Trickster Tales, Explanatory Tales, Tales of Human Adventure, The Realm of Man, The Animal and His World, Man and His Fate*, and the like. Such neat classifications may be logically satisfying, particularly when one is dealing with tales from all over the continent. But in the case of the present collection, comprising 45 tales from a comparatively very limited geographic area— basically a cluster of hamlets and villages in one of the smallest independent countries in the world, namely The Gambia—such a classification by genres or thematic affiliations would be inappropriate. Furthermore, while the stories with central animal characters are more numerous here than those dealing strictly with humans, there are indeed no significant thematic or structural differences between the two. Likewise, from the point of view of literary devices used such as characterization, dialogues, humanistic references, songs and refrains, the animal stories presented here cannot be said to be basically different from other stories. In fact, most animal characters embody, above all, human behavior and conflicts.

Thus, Dr. Magel's choice to group these tales according to three basic structural patterns, does have the advantage of a presentation that is much closer to the common African viewpoint vis-a-vis tales and narratives—a viewpoint that implies that all these stories are nothing but pieces of fiction which originate from society's collective imagination and experience, and whose function is basically two-fold: entertaining and edifying for the listeners. One should also never lose sight of the fact that the individual narrators whose stories were expertly taped, transcribed, and translated here by Dr. Magel, are indeed creative artists and performers in their own right—some better than others, naturally—seeking direct communication with their listeners, at each performance. The importance of this communication remains the same even with the incidental presence of a researcher and his tape-recorder. This, fortunately, Dr. Magel is fully aware of; and his awareness is abundantly evidenced in his footnotes.

Finally, it should be noted that while the geographic area covered by Dr. Magel is indeed very limited, the tales collected here reveal a great deal of variety and richness, while suggesting also a definite amount of cultural unity among the Wolof people. This sense of cultural unity is apparent not only among the inhabitants of this comparatively remote and isolated district of Saloum, but it involves also the people of Sine-Saloum, Cayor, Jolof, and Waalo, in Senegal. The different versions of the same stories presented here and performed by different narrators—and in one case by the same narrator—are eloquent illustrations of this unity.

Naturally, it is not surprising that most of the stories presented here were told by griots—Lamin Jeng, his wife Awa Jeng, Momat Sise, Momodou Njay among the best—as they are indeed the undisputed "masters of the spoken word." It is no coincidence or accident that the late Guinean writer, Camara Laye, titled his last book, the story of the great *Sundiata* told by the Malinke griot, Babou Condé, "Belen Tigui"—*Le Maître de la Parole* (Paris, 1978, *The Master of the Word*).

Many of the narratives here can be seen as different versions and performances of the same narratives recreated by Birago Diop in his three collections *(Les Contes d'Amadou Koumba*, Paris, 1948, *Les nouveaux contes d'Amadou Koumba*, Paris, 1958, and *Contes et Lavanes*, Paris, 1963). There is also an interesting comparison to be made between the stories presented here in English, and those collected in Senegal and translated into French, by two young French researchers, Jean Copans and Philippe Couty (*Contes Wolof du Baol*, Paris, 1976). Marcelle Colardelle-Diarrassouba's vigorous essay, *Le lièvre et l'araignée dans les contes de l'Ouest Africain*, Paris, 1975 (The Hare and the Spider in the Tales of West Africa) could also serve as an invaluable reference work in this context.

Edris Makward, Professor
University of Wisconsin-Madison
January, 1981

TABLE OF CONTENTS

PART ONE: INTRODUCTION   7

PART TWO: STORIES
THEMATIC PATTERN:
STATEMENT-ANALOGY-REFUTATION-CONCLUSION
Tumani and His Mother's Promise   25
The Child in the Silk-Cotton Tree   28
The Jealous Co-Wife   33
The Guardian Sheep   37
The Handsome Suitor, I   40
The Handsome Suitor, II   45
The Passion of the *Gewel*   50
The Hyena Engages the Hare as a *Gewel*   53
The Hyena and the Hare Search for Wealth   59
The Hyena Engages a Strange-Farmer   62
The Lion's Treasured Goat   66
The Elephant and Blackbird Court the Same Girl   70
The Monkey and the Dog Court the Same Girl   75

PART THREE: STORIES
THEMATIC PATTERN: STATEMENT-ANALOGY-CONCLUSION
The Young Man and the Talking Skull   81
The Koranic Teacher   85
Kumba the Orphan Girl   90
The Brothers Samba   96
Sidi Ngali and His Traveling Companions   100
Samba the Satan and Omadi the Righteous   104
Two Lovers Punished   107
The Bag of Money   109

Ngurmi the Lazy Husband, I   116
Ngurmi the Lazy Husband, II   119
The Greedy Father   123
The Mauritanian and His Wealth   126
The Hyena Wrestles the *Konderong*, I   128
The Hyena Wrestles the *Konderong*, II   132
The Hyena Eats the Ostrich's Eggs   134
The Bearded Rock   137
The Dog Captures the Hyena   139
The Dog and Monkey Build a Town   141
The Courtship of Yasin   144

PART FOUR: STORIES
THEMATIC PATTERN: STATEMENT-REFUTATION-CONCLUSION

The Eternal Lovers   151
The Donkeys of Jolof   154
Samba's Wife   159
The Marriage of Two Masters of the Wolof Language, I   163
The Marriage of Two Masters of the Wolof Language, II   168
The Mendacious Child   172
The Search For a Friend   175
The Hare Seeks Endowments From Allah   179
The Hare Saves the Hippopotamus   182
The Hare and Hyena in the Well   185
The Hare Makes the Hyena His Riding Horse   189
The Pilgrimage to Mecca   192
The Monkey Who Claimed to be a *Gewel*   196

BIBLIOGRAPHY   199

APPENDIX   203

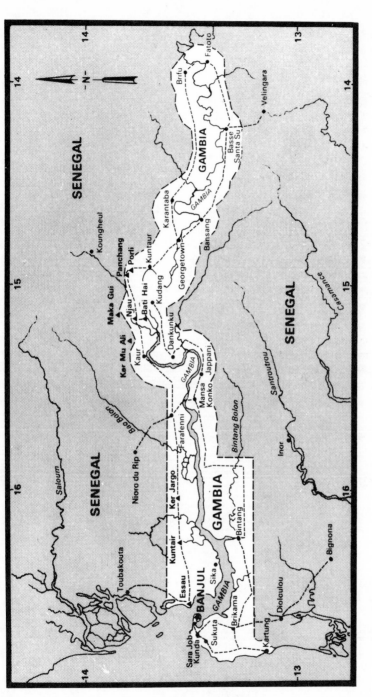

GAMBIA

— — — NATIONAL BOUNDARY
★ NATIONAL CAPITAL
— — — — ROAD
▲ TOWNS IN WHICH TALES IN THIS COLLECTION WERE COLLECTED

MILES

0   10   20   30

0 10 20 30

KILOMETERS

PART ONE
INTRODUCTION

Like the majestic baobab, with its bark taut and twisted in reconciliation with the sun, Wolof fictional narratives stand as monument to the dignity and determination of a people living on the periphery of their cultural core. Residing primarily on the Northern bank territories of the Gambia River, in the Salum, Badibu and Niani regions, the Gambian Wolof represent the southernmost settlers of the Wolof expansion under the traditional *Burba Jolof* before the sixteenth century. After the 1566 revolt of the Senegalese Wolof of Kayor from the *Burba Jolof,* the Wolof of the north bank of the Gambia River acknowledged the *Bur Salum* as their titulary ruler. Historical narratives and genealogical accounts, however, consistently trace the origins of these people to the ancestral state of Jolof in Senegal. The Anglo-French boundary dividing The Gambia and Senegal was drawn through the traditional Wolof territory, artificially distinguishing inherently related families.

Gambian Wolof live in close proximity to Mandinka, Fula, Jola and Serahuli ethnic groups. Recent demographic surveys of The Gambia estimate its total population at 493,197. The Wolof comprise twelve percent of this figure, or 59,183. Eighty-five percent of these live in rural areas in community settlements averaging one hundred residents. The urban Wolof live predominantly in Banjul, capital of The Gambia, and its suburban communities. The cultural strains resulting from close, inter-ethnic relations make them extremely sensitive to preserving their distinct cultural traditions. Four centuries removed from their frontier days, they have maintained their cultural outpost. Like the resilient baobab, it has turned and bent with the external pressures of Islamic and European colonialism, yet it has succeeded in maintaining its essential core of ideals and values. These have remained vital and effective through various instruments of cultural preservation and regeneration.

Although they are not the primary means of cultural maintenance, Wolof fictional narratives, *leb,* embody those ideals and values in an esthetically pleasing and entertaining manner. The popularity of the narrative performance experience, at all levels of the society without caste, age, or sex barriers, defines it as a powerful influence on an individual's world perspective and his/her daily inter-personal behavior. The frequency of narrative story-telling likewise contributes to their social and cultural importance. The exchange of stories between adults and/or adults and children is virtually a daily activity. Although not scheduled into their normal routine, some time from each day is devoted to fictional narration. This may occur during the daylight hours at the village square, at the well, out in the agricultural fields or within the family compound during the evening and night hours when domestic chores are completed. The commonly accepted premise that tales are only told at night around a glowing campfire is not adhered to in practice by the Wolof. Wherever and whenever two or more people are gathered together, the possibility exists for an informal narrative exchange. As such, the forty-five fictional narratives presented in this collection offer dramatic insights into those ideals and values which are fundamental to Wolof cultural and personal survival.

FICTIONAL NARRATIVE FORMULA

Wolof *leb* constitute one of six oral literary genres. The others are: *chosan,* historical narratives; *lebatu,* proverbs; *chax,* riddles; *woy,* songs; and *bida,* folk beliefs and pre-Islamic superstitions. Each of these genres is defined by its form and content.

Leb are circumscribed by a relatively fixed opening and closing formula which mark its formal parameters. In the Upper Salum, where most of the narratives for this collection were recorded, the following initial formula was observed. In formal narrative sessions the storyteller increases the volume and raises the pitch of his/her voice and intones:

leb-on. . . . . there was a story,

which immediately sparks the audience to respond with normal volume and pitch:

lup-on. . . . . our legs are crossed (i.e. we are sitting down and ready).

The alternating pattern is repeated with the narrator's:

am-on a fi. . . . . it happened here,

and the audience's reply:

da na am. . . . . it was so.

The storyteller then begins his/her chosen narrative. When more than one *leb* is to follow, the opening dialogue may not be included for each. The audience, understanding that the next performance will also be a fictional narrative, accepts the contextual parameters introduced by the first as continuing throughout the next.

The closing formula, signaling the end of the *leb,* is provided solely by the narrator. Rarely does a narrative fail to be followed by one of several variant closings.

1. Fi la leb dohé tabi ca gec... This tale passed here and entered the sea.
2. Leb dohé nonu tabi gec... The tale passed in this form and entered the sea.
3. Leb dohé fofu tabi ajana... The tale passed by here and entered heaven.
4. Nonu la leb tabi ajana... In this form the tale entered heaven.
   Bakan bu ko jeka fon... Whoever first understands it,
   tabi ajana... (will) enter heaven.

THEMATIC PATTERNS

The form is also distinguished from other oral literary genres in their patterns of thematic development. Although Wolof fictional narratives are entertaining and relaxing, they are fundamentally presentations of abstract concepts in oral/aural disguise. The themes evolving from the arrangement of their constituent elements follow three basic developmental patterns. Viewed in terms of Statement, Analogy, Refutation, and Conclusion, the narratives are intellectual arguments in artistic form which support specific cultural beliefs and behaviors. The universal thematic movement from conflict to resolution is achieved through one of the following patterns:

1. Statement-Analogy-Refutation-Conclusion;
2. Statement-Analogy-Conclusion;
3. Statement-Refutation-Conclusion.

Each of the stages can be detailed, expanded and/or repeated as often as the narrator deems appropriate for the explication of his/her theme. Pattern number one represents the complete pattern. However, not all narrators utilize the four stages in their thematic development. But there is the potential within each tale for a four stage expression. The choice belongs to the narrator in the selection of appropriate stages for the presentation of his/her argument.

Each of the forensic patterns begins with a presentation of the Statement. This is often developed in terms of a conflict between an individual and his/her society or between two individuals. Ultimately one of the individuals represents the society's position or point of view. In the opening narrative sequence the initial action or attitude attributed to a given character is usually intended to be understood by the audience as contradictory to accepted social and cultural values. The character expressing this view or performing this action will thus be seen against a negative background. The character, animal or human, becomes the implication of the action or attitude as a symbol of negative behavior. The conflict sets up the initial Statement against which the narrator will argue in his/her subsequent development. The actual Statement is rarely declared directly by the narrator. Rather, he/she relies on the familiarity of the audience with the implied meaning of the action/attitude or he/she develops the initial sequence so as to highlight the conflict and render the antagonist's anti-social position clear. The Statement is the definition of the antagonist's viewpoint in relation to a given social/behavioral code.

The initial conflict is often not immediately apparent to non-Wolof audiences. But characters have a narrative history of acting/speaking in certain well-defined manners. For example, the hyena always acts shamefully and the monkey is always dishonest in tales. When these feature in narratives, their behavior is assumed to imply the negative so that the narrator can rely on the audience to supply the justification for the negative interpretation in the conflict. The actions of such fixed symbols in the tradition do not need overt explanation or dramatic rendition.

In the narrative "The Young Man and the Talking Skull" the Statement evolves out of the young man's conflict with his father regarding his choice of a marriage partner. The young man states that he must marry the girl he himself has chosen regardless of his father's admonitions against her. The young man's position vis-a-vis his father's represents his stated position. The thematic Statement stage of the narrator's argumentation relies on this young man's stated objective. It forms the premise against which the storyteller will develop his/her argument.

In the narrative "Samba's Wife" the female hyena is introduced without any stated description of her character or behavior. Yet she is interpreted by the audience as a negative, anti-social creature because she is a hyena, the commonly accepted symbol of shame. The narrator does not need to develop the how or the why by which she is so viewed. She accepts and relies on the convention and proceeds with the development of the tale. The forensic Statement thus evolves out of the implied conflict between the man who married the hyena and his society. The man has chosen to marry outside the accepted bounds of intermarriage rules, represented symbolically by his marriage to the hyena. His selection connotes an anti-social, anti-traditional perspective. This view represents the thematic Statement upon which the storyteller will formulate her argument. The narrator and the tale become advocates for the society, arguing for its defense and support.

In thematic patterns one and two, an Analogy forms the second discursive stage of the narrative. The Analogy stage is an extended comparison with the initial conflict/statement stage which is designed to heighten the contradiction presented by it. It is a comparison of actions/behaviors/attitudes essentially different from the initial conflict stage but strikingly alike in one or more pertinent aspects. This stage is intended to clarify some particular dimension of the conflict which the narrator wants to stress in the narrative.

The Analogy repeats the conflict although with different actions and/or different situations and characters. It presents another narrative episode as metaphor to the opening Statement stage. The idea contained in or produced by the incidents and/or characters is viewed as analogous to that effected by the initial conflict. It can be understood as a repetition of the initial conflict on another level, a repetition which advances it a step further. The Analogy further illustrates the conflict between the individual and society or between two individuals.

In "The Koranic Teacher" the Analogy stage is presented in a series of events which repeat the initial conflict between the Koranic teacher and his community. That conflict highlights his janus-like, hypocritical attitudes and behaviors. Outwardly religious and forthright, he secretly violates many social and religious codes. He is introduced as a teacher who had murdered several of his former students. This contradiction between appearances and reality forms the background against which the subsequent episodes are equated. Through the analogous behaviors of a precocious child, the narrator examines the peculiar character of the teacher and his effect on the society.

Just as the Koranic teacher must lie to carry out his religious charade, the child is also presented with this fault. He lies to the teacher about the source of his laughter as he lies to the people of the teacher's girl-friend's village. He greedily demands more food at breakfast time and an extra bowl of food at dinner telling his hosts each time that his teacher instructed him to ask for more. Like the teacher who misused the trust and faith of the people, the student abuses the teacher for his own personal satisfaction. When he accidently loses control of his excretory system, the student invites all the people into his sleeping quarters to view the abomination. As a literary convention of Wolof oral narratives, excrement is employed as a symbol of humiliation and defeat. Although normally protected from scandal and shame by his religious position, the young student humiliates the teacher by exposing his faults to the people.

In the final episode, when the teacher attempts to kill the child, the roles are reversed as it is the child who succeeds. The murder is drawn out in more detail than is common in Wolof narratives in order to highlight the gruesomeness which probably surrounded the circumstances of the teacher's reported slayings. After extorting numerous cattle, goods and the location of his secret cache of money, the devious child cuts the last remaining swatch of grass that his victim holds and forces him into a deep pit where he eventually dies. The child, like his own teacher, has no regard for human life except as it benefits himself. The teacher is assaulted and humiliated just as his former students, their families and the community were misused by the Koranic teacher. This series of analogues forces the audience to view the religious leader's initial characterization in terms of the student's behavior. They clarify the contradiction by pointing out in greater detail the implications of such attitudes/behaviors.

In the narrative "Sidi Ngali and His Traveling Companions" the Analogy stage is presented in the series of incidents which capture the meetings of Sidi Ngali and his friends. In the initial conflict stage Sidi had been characterized as a fiendish monster-child who had killed many of his own brothers and sisters. After having been evicted by his father, he encounters three other creatures who resemble him. Samba Hurr and Samba Tongo are presented as vicious brutes while the traditional symbol of evil, the *konderong*, is shown in all its imagined horror. The three-fold confrontation with Sidi Ngali is analogous to that initially established between Sidi and his father. Through these situations and characters the full dimension of Sidi's evilness is presented. Sidi Ngali's behavior is seen through the filter of his traveling companions' behaviors, attitudes and statements. Being associated with these obviously anti-social, anti-human creatures, his own actions must be judged and interpreted accordingly.

Thematic patterns one and three utilize Refutation in the presentation of their argument. The Refutation stage provides images which contradict the error of judgement/anti-social behavior and/or negative attitudes expressed by the antagonist in the initial conflict of the tale. This stage argues against the initial negative Statement by presenting characters/behaviors/attitudes which demonstrate the society's position regarding the conflict. The actions of human or animal characters stress the benefits of a unified, cohesive society; they reaffirm the social basis for the particular belief/attitude/custom in question. The initial Statement is shown to be false and untenable in Wolof society. The Refutation stage of narrative argumentation can bring forward as witness, as testimony, particular actions of other characters which contradict the efficacy of the initial statement and thus reinforce the society's viewpoint. These characters are typically exemplary models of good social behavior and staunch supporters of its cultural ideals and values. This stage can also feature actions by the antagonist which refute his/her own initial claim or Statement. These activities demonstrate why the character is mistaken. Typically the character shows that he/she does not have the internal qualities and/or physical skills required to substantiate the original claim. By demonstrating these weaknesses, the character reinforces the commonly accepted beliefs and practices. Thus either through direct example or indirect confirmation, the

Refutation stage of narrative argumentation establishes the social perspective against which the antagonist's initial Statement/claim is contradicted.

In the tale "Tumani and His Mother's Promise," Tumani's heroic behavior in ridding the village of a dangerous lion rebuts his mother's earlier statements. She promised to give her unborn son to the lion if he aided her at the well. Her disregard for the importance of Tumani's life reflects a blasé attitude to life in general and her role in particular. She is willing to exchange her son's life for a meaningless, instantaneous satisfaction. Her attitude is contrasted by the storyteller with that of Tumani himself who, when he grows up, risks his own life protecting the lives of the people of his village. His behavior reflects the social ideal: a willingness to sacrifice oneself for the protection of others. The narrative presents him as a model of good behavior, the exemplar of social ideals and values while exposing his mother as an example of imperfection and shame. Tumani's action and subsequent honorific reception by his neighbors provide testimony to his perception of his role in maintaining life. When his mother chokes on the lion's claw in her food, her punishment provides negative reinforcement as a deterrent to similar anti-life attitudes/activities.

"The Hare Seeks Endowments" provides an example of an antagonist refuting his own initial Statement or claim. In this tale the hare shows himself to be of superior intelligence and a master of finesse as he successfully accomplishes three impossible tasks Allah sets out for him. The hare eagerly and effortlessly performs them because he desires to have Allah bestow more intelligence on him. When initially questioned by Allah, the hare claims to be mentally deficient. This assertion conflicts with the commonly accepted narrative conventions regarding hare. Allah himself reflects the society's viewpoint towards his claim when he tells him "I have never actually counted you among fools." Hare however disagrees; his statement is interpreted by the audience therefore as excessively greedy and in direct conflict with the social codes. The hare's own subsequent actions displayed in accomplishing Allah's directives refute his claim of stupidity and verify the society's original position regarding his sufficient intelligence. The Refutation stage of narrative argumentation provides evidence which both contradicts the original premise and affirms society's position regarding it.

The final stage of argumentation shared by each of the three thematic patterns is Conclusion. This stage presents the consequences which result from the initial conflict situation. The resolution typically features the punishment of the anti-social and/or the reward of the socially committed character. The Conclusion applies the narrator's final stamp of approval or disapproval to the antagonist's initial actions/behaviors/attitudes regarding the selected topic. In the majority of narratives the conclusion reinforces the social codes of behavior by providing episodes which aim at the amendment or reformation of the offender. Corporal chastisement, loss of wealth, loss of status, loss of family and even death are representative judgments meted out to recalcitrant characters. The Conclusion is the final proof of the narrative argument against the anti-social behaviors/attitudes in question because it is a verification of the logical consequences which result from them.

The Conclusion stage of "The Young Man and the Talking Skull" validates the culture's warning against marrying without regard to custom. The young man, who selected his own wife and secured her parent's consent through his own efforts, lost both his wealth and his status. He returned home to his family a much wiser but poorer child because of his doubtful future.

Sidi Ngali, in the tale "Sidi Ngali and his Traveling Companions," is killed by the fierce *konderong*. His death is treated by the narrator in the same casual manner as Sidi himself viewed the deaths of his three brothers and sisters. Sidi is thrown into the air by the *konderong* and, after flying in the sky a great distance, lands in a millet field where a blindman mistakes him for a stone. The blindman slings his body like a stone at the weaver birds eating the grain. The body flies a great distance only to land in a pail of milk. The owner in turn flicks it out of the way until it lands in the eye of a young child. The child cries a moment and then stops. The fleck of dust has disappeared. The narrator, in selecting an appropriate punishment for Sidi Ngali's actions, applied the same trivial attitude to his death as Sidi himself displayed. Sidi's death means nothing to the blindman, the herdsman, nor the child. As representatives of society, they treat him with the same degree of insignificance as he displayed in handling the death of his siblings.

In "Samba's Wife" the Conclusion stage of the tale closes on Samba, a lonely, disheartened father. As he watches his wife and children run away from the village with the pride of hyena, the full weight of his original mistake burdens him. He is left without family precisely because he did not follow the traditional advice regarding the selection of a marriage partner. He married someone he did not really know from a distant land he knew nothing about. Although not specifically elaborated in the opening episode of the tale, the conflict between his actions and the cultural practice is significant. The narrator concludes the tale by directing his chastisement precisely towards the area of conflict. Samba's loss of family becomes the narrator's verification of the social dictum against the disregard of marital rituals and practices. Samba, like other social offenders, finally realizes the logical consequences of his decision.

The four stages of narrative argumentation enable a storyteller to discuss areas of social tension which are of particular interest to him/her in a conventionally acceptable medium. Behind the mask of entertainment and relaxation, the narrator presents a form of discourse which aims at proving to an audience the efficacy and accuracy of his/her own beliefs and values. Although they can be particular to certain individuals, these generally conform to those which are also socially and culturally approved.

Confirmation of this view of narrative is evidenced by the subsequent audience-narrator-audience discussions which frequently follow the tale presentations. Like 'dilemma tales' which propose questions at their conclusion, Wolof *leb* also promote debate. Similarly, one narrative will often spark the telling of another by a member in the audience who believes there is another perspective on the topic. The exchange of stories which results often exhibits an atmosphere reminiscent of that created by wrestling matches, where audiences take sides and support their favorite with verbal encouragement. At these performances audiences usually talk in terms of winners and losers in order to acknowledge the narrative and argumentative skills of the competing storytellers.

The narratives in this collection are arranged according to these thematic patterns in order to facilitate the appreciation of narrative argumentation. The annotations provided after each are intended to enhance the cultural, thematic and linguistic details, often obscure to non-Wolof audiences which do not have the background information required for accurate interpretations.

FICTION AND SOCIAL REALITY

The fixed formulaic openings and closings and the standard thematic patternings introduce a degree of distinctness from conventional speech and conceptual norms which is likewise reflected in narrative content. Although *leb* have a direct relationship to reality, they are spoken of primarily as fiction. This distinguishes them from *chosan*, which are considered by Wolof to be true and realistic. *Leb* contain elements adapted directly from reality, combined and blended with entirely fictitious characters and situations. Within them *rab*, animals, *doma,* witches, *pica,* birds, and *konderong,* deformed, magical creatures, interact with *nit,* human beings in the universal struggle for self-actualization.

Presented as fiction, the tales explore the significant tensions within a given family or community in extreme terms. The reality of daily social interaction is examined in the context of the unreal world of *leb*. The characters created by the storyteller embody extreme positions of a given tension in a dramatic presentation and resolution of that stress. Their behavior exhibits either the positive or the negative dimension of the social code pertaining to the selected issue. The resolution of the stress is inherently bound up with the success or failure of the characters regarding it. In general, the good/right/ honorable characters vindicate the social code and are rewarded. The opposing characters concomitantly enforce the codes through their subsequent defeat and/or punishment.

The fictional dimension of these presentations also lies in the very extremes of the 'pictured' dilemma. The choices between good/bad, honorable/shameful are obvious and clear. Although the selected tensions being presented are real and contemporary, the dichotomy offered in extreme is fictional. Real life choices between right/wrong are rarely as simplistic and one-dimensional as those facing the tale characters. Life in a Wolof community is more complex and ambiguous.

The entertainment value of the narratives in part depends upon this lucidity and unreality. The vicarious experience of the good and the mockery of the bad characters' behaviors can be shared with other members of a group. Within the reality of the narrative context, an individual's commitment to upholding and confirming the social codes can be realized without actually experiencing the conflict/tension simultaneously in reality. Membership in a family/ community is affirmed and experienced by participation in and a sharing of values and ideals with other members of the audience. With an additional awareness of the timelessness of the tales, the shared experience transcends the contemporary and firmly roots the audience in an experience shared with former family and community members. The resulting satisfaction from experiencing the positive confirmation of one's values and ideals in the resolution of the narrative contributes to the popularity of the medium.

The narratives refrain from becoming unrestrained flights of fantasy through a close reflection of social, economic, and political realities. Within the tales it is apparent that Wolof society is traditionally organized into endogomous, vocational communities each of which has its own distinct sub-culture, its own professional beliefs and secrets and a considerable degree of internal self-regulation. The society is usually described in academic literature as a hierarchy of three groups: *jambur*, nobles; *nyenyo*, artisans; and *jam*, servile bondsmen.

The artisan castes are composed of the *tega*, smiths, *ude*, leatherworkers, *laobe*, carpenters, and *gewel*, bards. Their services are essential to the proper functioning of the community. They are organized into client-patron relationships with the *jambur* families, forming a mutually dependent system. The nobles provide financial and material support for their artisan families while they in turn act as their host's blacksmiths, tanners, cobblers, weavers, musicians, historians and entertainers.

Traditionally the most skillful *nyenyo* families are attached to the personal service of the kings and leading noblemen. Lesser-talented casted persons serve lesser noble families in a corresponding, hierarchical system. For the *gewel*, in particular, those who are clients of royal nobility have a higher status than the wandering minstrels of the countryside who are not attached to any specific *jambur* family.

The third group of Wolof are the servile bondsmen or slaves. These are also distinguished according to the status of their masters. The royal slaves, like the royal artisans, had a higher status than the slaves of the lower nobles. In pre-colonial times it was from this caste that the Wolof royalty chose their soldiers, law enforcement officers, tax collectors and minor bureaucrats.

Within this hierarchical social structure, each member of the community finds his/her social position according to the heredity position of the family. Even if a child does not perform the traditional role of his/her parents, the child's status remains as theirs. Intermarriage between the castes does not normally take place.

CONCEPT OF HONOR

Although caste membership stratifies the Wolof according to hereditary birth and occupational craft, the system achieves conformity to its basic ideals/precepts of society because Wolof culture provides each member considerable avenues to a high level of personal and group dignity and satisfaction. The potential for this achievement is viable in every caste in spite of the apparent contradictions within the hierarchically determined ideological system.

The existence of a social hierarchy of castes among the Wolof has given rise to an acute awareness of honor. Within the hierarchy each caste occupies a certain role to which is attached a specific status or rank. Each member of a caste is aware not only of his/her role and status in the social structure but also the social rankings of others. Furthermore, everyone strives to uphold that status through behavior attendant to that rank. Honor provides the link between the values and ideals of Wolof society and its individual members who are attempting to personify them. Each member establishes a certain social identity by following the cultural definition of honor for his/her particular caste. The society, in turn, confirms special social status, treatment, and honor for such achievements within each caste.

Although each caste maintains particular forms for the achievement and recognition of honor, the general outlines of honor are evident across caste bounderies. The Wolof proverb *Nit ku amul jom, amul dara* (The person who does not have honor does not have anything) expresses the Wolof ideal of the determining quality of humanity. Leopold Senghor has defined *jom* as being "the feeling that one has of his own personal dignity." It is the value of a person in his/her own eyes as well as in the opinion of others. It is the estimation of his/her own worth, the right to one's own honor; but it is also the acknowledgment of that right as demonstrated by the members of society.

The constituent elements of the concept of honor are founded upon the overruling principle of control, *reytal.* It incorporates the control of one's internal motivations as well as the control of one's external movements. *Jom* denotes a disposition toward self-restraint and control over one's thoughts and actions. *Gace*, shame, denotes the opposite; it is a disposition toward unrestrained and excessive emotion and movement. For a person to be recognized as 'honorable' he/she must demonstrate the following characteristics: self-respect; composure; courage; integrity; truthfulness; generosity; sociability; reserved speech; and intelligence. Each of these qualities is manifest through concrete behaviors in daily activities. They must be translated from the abstract to the practical to validate one's claim to honor in one's caste.

Although the awareness of honor is very developed among the Wolof it is only acknowledged in inter-caste public gatherings among the *jambur*. Those who dominate the social, political and economic structure only recognize honor among themselves and their equals. This recognition is affirmed in public by the *gewel* who are responsible for confirmation of individual and family honor in their oral presentations. The actual honor of lower caste members, who are greatly influenced by the upper caste model, is not acknowledged at such gatherings. To claim such would be considered shameful for it would undermine the ideological system which equates the upper caste, noble families as *a priori* the good while the caste and servant families are perceived as bad. Just as Friedrick Nietzsche traced the origin of the concept of 'good' in German culture to the concept of 'noble', the Wolof identify the concepts of goodness, beauty and nobility as inherently related. This prohibition has not however prevented lower caste members from aspiring to incorporate the ideals of the honorable person in their own lives. A cursory reading of *leb* collected from members of all Wolof castes reveals a consistent pattern of behavioral modeling. Those activities deemed honorable for upper caste members are, with some caste determined exceptions, generally perceived as worthy of emulation among the lower castes. The constituent elements of honor are valid across caste lines as each member seeks to realize the moral foundation of his/her caste rank.

STRUCTURAL PATTERNING

These cultural ideals and their negative counterparts are experienced in the tensions presented in the tales themselves. Thematic intensity is achieved through a structural patterning which highlights this positive/negative behavioral polarity.

The honorable/shameful structural polarity is most dramatically evident in the narrative "Kumba the Orphan Girl." In this tale two main characters embody positive or negative attitudes/behaviors. Kumba the orphan girl represents the ideal Wolof young woman, one who is hospitable, respectful, obedient, religious, courageous, self-controlled and taciturn. Her behavior demonstrates in an objectified manner her personal honor and dignity even though, as the tale emphasizes, she no longer has living parents. Her antithesis is represented by her half-sister, also named Kumba, whose mother still influences her daily activities and shapes her social perspectives.

The first half of the narrative illustrates the orphan's personal characteristics as she travels from her own village to the Sea of *Denyal* (disappearing) and back again. Each episode along the way proves her worthiness and regard. When Kumba the orphan is first introduced, her identity as an honorable person is established through her hospitable concern for two passing travelers. She provides them with water and utensils with which to quench their thirst. This action clearly follows the Wolof ideal regarding foreign visitors, for whom special care has always been forthcoming. Kumba is courteous to these guests just as she is polite to the deformed old woman she meets soon afterward. She respects this lady even though the elder's outward appearance is abnormal. Her one leg, one hand and one ear do not distract Kumba from extending the required respect. As if to intensify the level of her achievement of the ideal, the narrator indicates that Kumba also got down on her knees as an additional sign of deference. She also demonstrates here, as she does in the subsequent three encounters with strange beings and events, that she can maintain control over her emotions, thoughts and tongue. Confronting bizarre situations (two coconuts cracking into each other, a cloth laundering itself and two cows attempting to carry each other) she does not lose her composure or grasp of proper behavior. She always displays deportment worthy of honor even in the face of the apparently illogical and meaningless. When she finally arrives at the Sea of Denyal and meets the mother of all the wild animals, she obeys her seemingly ridiculous commands. She willingly cooks the elder's meals in spite of being given only one piece of wood and a match stick for the fire and one grain of rice and a year-old bone for the ingredients. Kumba accepts her charge as a demonstration of her obedience and respect for the elder's judgment. She remains quiet and reserved through these trying circumstances. Courageous behavior is also modeled when she sleeps in the same room at night with a lion, a tiger and a hyena. Hiding under their bed without exhibiting fear or loss of control in any manner, she exactly carries out the old woman's orders.

Because her behavior/attitude approaches the 'honorable' ideal throughout her traumatic experience, Kumba is rewarded by the old woman. She is given the commonly accepted symbols of wealth and high status in Wolof society of numerous cattle and servants. Her reward is affirmation of her worthiness of these goods and consequent status as well as confirmation of the efficacy of her attendant conduct.

Kumba the orphan's activities become significant in comparison to those displayed by her negative counterpart. This young woman progresses along the same path forged by the first. Yet in each episode along the route, the second Kumba demonstrates exactly the opposite character traits. These negative responses to the same stimuli present the contrast and provide easy recognition of right and proper deportment.

Encountering the two travelers, this Kumba refuses to aid them with water and prohibits them from using her drinking utensils. In addition she is disrespectful to them and chastises Kumba the orphan for acting hospitably. Farther along the journey to the Sea of Denyal, Kumba loses control of herself as she exclaims in horror at the various strange sights she encounters. She is neither quiet nor reserved in speech, preferring to externalize her every thought and emotion. Against all cultural norms, she insults the one-earred, one-handed and one-legged old woman and humiliates her for her impairment. She likewise speaks harshly and impudently to the owner of the Sea of Denyal. Showing no respect for her age, she refuses to follow the woman's command to immediately cook her a meal. Instead, Kumba decides to refresh herself after the long eventful journey. When she begins to cook, she questions each of the old woman's materials for the fire and the ingredients for the meal. She complains about their meagerness and the hopelessness of her assigned task. Her inability to correctly carry out orders is also pictured while she hides under the bed of animals at night. There she violently stabs them in direct opposition to the elder's directions to only gently prick them with a sewing needle. In the morning when greeted amiably, she demands to be given the mysterious eggs, completely ignoring proper social etiquette and respect. Her pride and contempt for other people and her lack of self-control illustrate her as a negative/shameful model of behavior. She acts as counterpoint to Kumba the orphan and serves to intensify her efforts and qualities.

The confirmation of this character as a negative model by the narrator is realized with her subsequent punishment. After again failing to follow directions exactly, Kumba breaks the mysterious eggs and is consequently attacked and eaten by the carnivorous animals within. Thus her own mistakes and personality shortcomings bring about her own destruction. The contrast with the positive reward assigned to her half-sister emphasizes the role each individual plays in his/her own destiny. Each character is rewarded according to his/her own merits as they are objectified in daily activities. Self regard without concommitant respectable behavior is self-indulgent pride. Kumba, with all the support of a mother and a community, demonstrates a too high regard for herself without the accompanying required demonstrations to actually merit such self-esteem. The Wolof concept of honor as an active pursuit is confirmed through the narrative of the two Kumbas. Other tales in this collection similarly support this thesis.

A second structural design commonly employed by narrators to highlight the behavioral polarity focuses on one main character as he/she/it is engaged in a series of events. Each episode emphasizes the character's good/bad orientation as if in a repeated chorus or refrain. Most frequently this pattern accentuates the negative perspective of a character without the corresponding positive model being included for contrast and comparison. The negation of the appropriateness of the assigned behaviors/attitudes is effected through the subsequent punishment of the offending participant.

This pattern can be recognized in the narrative "The Young Man and the Talking Skull." After the initial confrontation between the father and the son over the proper procedures for engaging a wife, the tale presents nine episodes which repeat the negative behavior exemplified in the first. In each of the encounters the young man is forced by the skull to violate the norms of his society in increasingly extreme proportions. The skull becomes a symbol of the young man's egocentricity urging him, as it did in the opening conflict, to ignore the other members of his society for his own sake. The nine episodes become metaphors for the exploration of the initial conflict. In these the effects of the young man's refusal to marry a girl from his own village according to Wolof custom in his community and culture are externalized. His negative behavior shocks the essential core of Wolof values and ideals. Respect for elders, sharing of food, division of labor according to sex, sanctity of Islam and its places of worship and respect for truth are ignored. The girl's community is outraged by his behavior and faces him as a threat to their continued security. They subsequently repeal their former stamp of approval and refuse to allow him to marry his betrothed. Since the young man induced the divorce proceedings with his behavior he cannot legally claim the return of his bride-price. The community protects itself from further damage to its ideals and punishes the outcast at the same time. The young man's loss of wife and wealth is viewed as just reward for his behavior. Like Kumba, the spoiled young woman in the previous example, he becomes an exquisite example of a negative role model. The absence of a counter-balancing positive character in this tale allows the narrator to build up his case against the antagonist and persuade the audience through the accumulation of metaphorical evidence. Emphasizing the negative insures that the antagonist and his statements will be rejected while that of the narrator will be endorsed. After the nine-fold repetition of cultural violations, no member of the audience identified with the young man and perceived him as forthright and honorable. Thus the narrator's argument was validated.

Although presented in terms of fantasy, the fictional narratives are rooted in Wolof social reality. The imagined world is explored against the background of the real as if holding out the possibility of the former influencing the latter for the benefit of all. The interplay of fiction and reality is an attempt to correlate Wolof values and ideals with contemporary realities. As the closing formula of *leb* indicate, they endeavor to encourage real people along a path towards an earthly paradise *(leb dohé tabi ajana)*.

PART TWO
STORIES
Statement—Analogy—
Refutation—Conclusion

TUMANI AND HIS MOTHER'S PROMISE[1]

There was a story . . .
Our legs are crossed . . .
It happened here . . .
It was so . . .

There was a young woman who was pregnant. One day when she went to the well to draw water, the well was dry. Since there was no water at her home, she had to leave her village and walk out into the bush in order to fetch some. She had to go into the bush to reach the nearest well. So she set out one day heading for that well.

After a while she arrived at the well with her water jar. She filled it up. But when she attempted to lift the water jar and set it on her head, she found that she could not lift it up. She looked around for someone to help her lift it but she did not see anyone around. She became very confused. She said, "Now what am I going to do? I cannot lift this up but I need the water. I cannot wait here for someone to come by because I have plenty of work to do at home. What *can* I do?"

She stood beside the well crying until a lion passed by there. He saw her crying and asked her, "Why are you crying?" When she saw the lion she became very frightened and increased her wailing. The lion said to her, "Do not be frightened. I will not hurt you. I have only come here to help you." She said to him, "I have no one to help me lift up this water jar. I need the water because there is no water at my home." The lion said, "I will help you."

As they were lifting the water jar onto her head the lion said, "Wait! What are you going to give me for helping you lift this jar?" She stopped and said, "Ah, what can *I* give to you? What do I have that you could want?" He said, "Just look around for something you can give me. You can give me that which is in your stomach. When you deliver your child, you can give it to me. Just promise to give it to me when you give birth. It does not matter whether it is a boy or a girl." She replied, "Alright, I promise." The lion then helped her to lift

25

the jar onto her head. When it was done the lion left and the woman began her journey home.

She walked and walked and walked until she reached her home. When she arrived there she said, "Now, how will I get this water jar off of my head? Who will help me put it down?" The lion again heard her question and came to her. He said to her, "I will help you." She said to him, "No. I do not want your help again." The lion said, "I only came here to help you. I do not want anything else. Remember you have already promised to give me your child when you give birth." She said, "Yes." So she allowed the lion to help her remove the water jar from her head. Then he left.

The woman took some water and washed her rice with it. Then she poured the water for her chickens to drink. The goats also came and drank. Then her children came and drank. Then she drank some of the water.

She remained in her village for a long time until finally her child was born. Her young boy grew up very quickly. He grew up to be very strong and fierce. He defeated all the other boys in the village at wrestling matches. Soon everyone grew to fear him. When his mother needed some water, he would pick up two water jars and carry them to the well. He would put one jar on each shoulder after he had drawn water from the well and carry them both back home. None of the other children were like him. All the people talked about how strong and brave he was.

One day all the trees began to shed their leaves. The wind began to blow fiercely. The people became very frightened. They said, "What is happening?" It was the lion who was coming to the village. When the lion approached the gate to the village he sang out:

>TUMANI, YOU WERE BEQUEATHED TO ME!
>TUMANI, YOU WERE BEQUEATHED TO ME!

When Tumani heard the lion's voice, he saw the leaves of the trees and their branches shaking. The people around advised him, "Do not go near the lion. Run away like us." He said to them, "I will not run away." Everybody else ran away and hid in their safe places. When the lion approached him it sang out:

>TUMANI, YOU WERE BEQUEATHED TO ME!
>TUMANI, YOU WERE BEQUEATHED TO ME!

The young boy said, "Mother and Father, listen to what the lion is saying. He said that Tumani was bequeathed to him?" They did not answer him.

The lion came closer to him until they could see each other clearly. Tumani said to the lion, "I am not running. I will not be frightened. I am not running away from you. You do not frighten me." The lion sang:

>TUMANI, YOU WERE BEQUEATHED TO ME!
>TUMANI, YOU WERE BEQUEATHED TO ME!

Then the lion attacked him. Tumani moved out of his path and the lion lost his balance and fell to the ground instead. Tumani quickly grabbed the lion's head and opened his mouth. He ripped the lion's jaws open and proceeded to tear the lion into halves. Tumani fought with the lion until it was killed.

Tumani's mother had seen what her son had done. She ran throughout the village shouting, "Tumani, my son, has killed the lion. Tumani has killed the lion. My son is a hero, a very brave person. My son is a hero, he killed the lion." All the people came out of their hiding places. They said among themselves, "Tumani is *indeed* a hero. He killed the lion."

Then they went and assembled all the cows they could find. They killed them and prepared them for a big celebration. They also cooked a big bowl of *chere*[2] for everyone to eat. After it was prepared they all sat down to eat.

While Tumani was eating, he put one of the lion's claws into his bowl of *chere* and took it to his mother. He gave it to her to eat. The woman was very happy. She took the *chere* and began to eat it. She ate and ate until she swallowed the lion's claw. When it stuck in her throat, she ran off to the washroom to try to vomit whatever was stuck in her throat. Some women saw her running and followed her. They said, "What is the matter with you?" She could not speak because the lion's claw was stuck in her throat. The women ran to her son. They said to him, "Tumani, your mother is in the washroom. She is vomiting something that is caught in her throat."

Tumani walked to the washroom and saw his mother choking. He hit his mother very hard on the back until the lion's claw finally popped out of her mouth. When it was out, Tumani said to his mother, "The next time that you are expecting to give birth to a child, when going to the well, do not promise to give that child away."[3]

[1] Narrated by Yasy Djak, age 43, in Banjul, The Gambia, on November 7 at 8:00 p.m. in her own compound before 4 young men and one child. Only one of the members of the audience was related to her. The others were neighbors who often visit her to hear her stories.

[2] Traditional dish made of steamed millet and baobab leaf. It is often accompanied with a meat or fish sauce made with tomatoes, ground nuts, pumpkins and/or beans. It can also be served with milk and sugar and eaten at breakfast time.

[3] The mother's irrational promise to the lion exemplifies her casual attitude to her new-born's life. Instead of caring for the unborn child, she gives it away for an insignificant reason. This does not mean that a drought is not serious; it does, however, highlight the primary responsibility of the mother, regardless of circumstances: nothing is more important than protecting the life of one's child. This narrative is not merely a statement of the mother's role. It also provides justification for that thesis. Yasay Djak specifically draws a positive picture of Tumani. He grows up to be a real hero, a protector of his people. His courage and self-sacrifice identify him as a potential honorable man. His mother's careless regard for his life might have destroyed this remarkable young man. It is significant that Tumani saves his mother's life. Had he been as flippant about her life as she was about his, she would have choked to death.

THE CHILD IN THE SILK-COTTON TREE[1]

There was a story . . .
Our legs are crossed . . .
It happened here . . .
It was so . . .

In one compound there were two co-wives. One of the women could bear children while the other one was barren. As a result, the childless woman envied the fruitful one.

Through Allah's will the fertile wife gave birth to a new baby.

One day the barren wife went to fetch some water at the well. When she returned, she sought aid of the new mother in lowering the water jug from her head. After helping her, the new mother took some of the water from the jug and walked to the washroom to shower.

When she left, the barren woman went and snatched up the new baby. She took it, threw it into a deep hole and covered it with soil.

While she was burying the baby, a wild duck[2] was circling in the sky and just happened to see what the woman was doing. So the bird landed and dug the baby out of the hole. Then it took the baby to her own nest on the banks of a nearby river.

There she fed the baby and brought it water to drink. She fed the baby and took care of it until it became as grown up as Fatu Kinneh.[3] When the baby smiled, her teeth were as white as milk, shining with their beauty.

It happened one day that a hunter, who roamed about in the bush quite often, was out searching for some animals to shoot. He walked and walked and walked until he reached the banks of the river. There he saw the baby high up in the branches of a silk-cotton tree.[4] He saw the baby up in the tree and looked and looked and looked at her until he was sure that it was a human being. Then he went back to his village and rushed to visit the village chief.

There he told the chief what he had seen. The chief ordered the drums beaten. All the inhabitants of the village gathered together to be addressed. He

28

then told his people, "This hunter saw a child sitting up on top of the silk-cotton tree and did not know what or who put her up there."

Then he proposed a plan to find a means of cutting down the tree so that he could determine who the child's parents were. The chief took out a large amount of money from his purse and gave it to eight carpenters.[5] He ordered them to go and cut the silk-cotton tree down.

On the next morning the eight woodcutters went to the tree and began to chop and chop and chop until there was just a very thin sliver of wood holding up the tree. It was then the child sang:

> OH, WILD DUCK, OH, WILD DUCK!
> THE SILK-COTTON TREE IS BECOMING THIN.
> OH, IT IS BECOMING THIN.

Whereupon the wild duck sang back:

> TREE TRUNK ENLARGE! TREE TRUNK ENLARGE!

When the duck sang, the silk-cotton tree assumed its original form. When the men saw what had happened they exclaimed, "Ah, what is going on?" They wondered how they were going to cut down the tree. So they began to chop and chop and chop until the tree was on the verge of falling down. Then the little girl sang out again:

> OH WILD DUCK, OH WILD DUCK!
> THE SILK COTTON TREE IS BECOMING THIN.
> OH, IT IS BECOMING THIN.

Whereupon the wild duck answered:

> TREE TRUNK ENLARGE! TREE TRUNK ENLARGE!

And the silk-cotton tree returned to its former shape. They said, "Hey... Hey... Hey...! We cannot cut this tree down." All day they tried to cut it down but they could not do it. When they were exhausted, they returned to the chief. They said to him, "Whenever the tree was about to fall over, the child in the tree would cry and she was answered by something near the river which caused the tree to return to its original shape. The tree would not fall down."

The chief then gave the wood cutters some magic powders. He ordered them to split up into two groups. Four of them would chop the tree and the other four would go down to the river. In that way when the child's cries are answered, they will know the direction the answer comes from. The chief said to them, "If the answer comes from the river, sprinkle the magic powder there so that when it drinks the water, it will die." The men replied, "Yes."

The next morning they went to the tree and began to chop and chop until the tree was about to fall. The girl then said:

> OH, WILD DUCK, OH WILD DUCK!
> THE SILK-COTTON TREE IS BECOMING THIN.

OH, IT IS BECOMING THIN.

Whereupon the wild duck sang back:

TREE TRUNK ENLARGE! TREE TRUNK ENLARGE!

The tree then returned to its original shape. The men quietly and secretly went to the river where the wild duck was drinking. They poured some of the magic powder into the water. When the wild duck flew away and disappeared from their view, the men returned to the tree.

They chopped and chopped and chopped until the tree was about to fall down. Then the child cried out:

OH, WILD DUCK, OH, WILD DUCK!
THE SILK-COTTON TREE IS BECOMING THIN.
OH, IT IS BECOMING THIN.

Whereupon the wild duck responded:

TREE TRUNK ENLARGE! TREE TRUNK ENLARGE!

The tree then returned to its original shape. They said, "Hey! The wild duck has not yet drunk from the magic water yet." They began to chop and chop and chop at the tree again. When it was about to fall the child cried out:

OH, WILD DUCK, OH WILD DUCK!
THE SILK-COTTON TREE IS BECOMING THIN.
OH, IT IS BECOMING THIN.

Whereupon the wild duck responded:

TREE TRUNK ENLARGE! TREE TRUNK ENLARGE!

The tree then returned to its original shape. They could not cut the tree down. The men returned to their chief.

This time he gave them another magic powder and told them to divide the group in half as they did before. One group would cut the tree and the other would pour the powder into the water where the wild duck had relocated.

The next morning they all went to the tree. Four of them remained to chop the tree until the tree was about to fall. Then the child sang out:

OH, WILD DUCK, OH WILD DUCK!
THE SILK-COTTON TREE IS BECOMING THIN.
OH, IT IS BECOMING THIN.

Whereupon the wild duck responded:

TREE TRUNK ENLARGE! TREE TRUNK ENLARGE!

The tree then returned to its original shape. But the four men at the river had located the wild duck when it replied, so they poured the magic powder into the water. It waited there until the men left. Then it returned.

The four men at the tree began to chop again. They chopped and chopped and chopped until the tree was about to fall. Then the girl sang:

OH, WILD DUCK, OH WILD DUCK!
THE SILK-COTTON TREE IS BECOMING THIN.
OH, IT IS BECOMING THIN.

Whereupon the wild duck responded:

TREE TRUNK ENLARGE! TREE TRUNK ENLARGE!

This time only a portion of the tree assumed its original shape. They said, "Ah, it must have drunk some of the water with the magic powder in it." So they again began to chop and chop and chop the tree. When it was almost about to fall the girl sang out again:

OH, WILD DUCK, OH WILD DUCK!
THE SILK-COTTON TREE IS BECOMING THIN.
OH, IT IS BECOMING THIN.

Whereupon the wild duck responded:

HUM-HUM-HUM-HUM-HUM-HUM!

They said, "Now we will soon know who the girl belongs to." This time only a small portion of the tree returned to its original shape. The men began to chop and chop and chop. When it was almost about to fall the girl sang out again:

OH, WILD DUCK, OH WILD DUCK!
THE SILK-COTTON TREE IS BECOMING THIN.
OH, IT IS BECOMING THIN.

Whereupon the wild duck responded:

HUM-HUM-HUM-HUM-HUM-HUM!

But the tree fell down. They caught the child and took her to the village.

There the drums were beaten to call all the inhabitants together. The men assembled on one side and the women on the opposite side. One by one the men came forward and the child refused to go to any of them. The girl's real father at this time was absent from the village on a long journey. Then the women came forward in single file. The girl refused to go with all of them except the last woman who was her real mother. As she came forward the child ran to her and hugged her tightly.[6]

[1] Narrated by Alison Jalo in Porli, The Gambia on November 20 in the compound of Bessi Njay before 31 men, women and children at 10:35 p.m.

[2] In Wolof, *Jime*. Alison Jalo could provide no reason why a wild duck appeared in this tale. Since this animal did not appear in any other recorded narratives its significance remains obscure.

[3] This is a reference to a two year old girl in the village who was being held by her mother during the narration of this story.

[4] In Wolof, *benteg*. The wood of this tall, straight tree is very light and subsequently used in the construction of dug-out boats.

[5] In Wolof, *Laobe*. This caste of men is responsible for construction of tools and other objects out of wood.

[6]Alison Jalo's emphasis on the repeated activities of the people of this village establishes a counter-weight to those of the barren co-wife. The people of this village expend tremendous energies to save the life of the girl in the silk-cotton tree. The nine-fold repetition of the tree chopping image establishes the deep commitment of the community to life. The girl is viewed as precious and deserving of this effort to return her to her family. Their example sets up the background against which the motives and actions of the barren mother are to be judged. In this comparison, her behavior is seen as anti-social, contrary to that idealized by the other members of the society. The final image emphasizes the joy and love between mother and daughter that the community struggled so hard to preserve.

THE JEALOUS CO-WIFE[1]

There was a story . . .
Our legs are crossed . . .
It happened here . . .
It was so . . .

There was a young man. He had no mother. Only his father was still living. They lived in the same compound. The father only had this one child.

The young man's step-mother also had one son.

This father had a very large herd of cattle, which his eldest son one day would inherit.

The step-mother did not like this young man at all. Every day she would try to do things that would kill him. She wanted to get him out of the compound, but she did not have the power to accomplish it. Every day she would devise a new plan to force the young man to leave.

There was a river out in the bush where only the wildest and meanest animals lived.

One day the step-mother called her husband and said, "Samba[2] must take the herd out to the Jeri[3] river today." The husband said, "Really?" She replied, "If he does not go to the river today, I will pack up my belongings and leave you."

The young man's father then called Samba and said to him, "Tomorrow you will lead the cattle to Jeri. If you do not take the cattle to Jeri then your step-mother will leave my compound." He replied, "Yes."

In the morning Samba first milked the cows as he always did. When he was finished, he went to his father and said to him, "I will not go to Jeri. Anyone who goes there will surely die." His father said, "You *must* go there!" He replied, "No!" His father said, "If you do not go there, your mother will leave me." Samba replied, "Alright."

You know, anyone who ever went to that river with his cattle never came back home. But the step-mother persisted in her attempts to kill the young man in some way.

Then the young man returned and untied the cattle. As he prepared to leave home he sang to his cattle:

> MOTHER TOLD ME TO HERD THE CATTLE AT JERI;
> FATHER TOLD ME TO HERD THE CATTLE AT FUTA.[4]

The largest bull in the herd replied:

> MY CROWN OF HORNS; MY CROWN OF HORNS;
> SAMBA, IF YOU HERD AT JERI, I WILL PROTECT YOU.

They walked and walked and walked towards the river. When they reached the middle the the bush the young man sang out again:

> FATHER TOLD ME TO HERD AT FUTA.
> MOTHER TOLD ME TO HERD AT JERI.
> FATHER TOLD ME TO HERD AT FUTA.
> MOTHER TOLD ME TO HERD AT JERI.
> FATHER TOLD ME TO HERD AT FUTA.
> MOTHER TOLD ME TO HERD AT JERI.

The bull replied to him:

> MY CROWN OF HORNS, MY CROWN OF HORNS;
> BUBU NGARI, BUBU NGARI.
> SAMBA, IF YOU HERD AT JERI, I WILL PROTECT YOU!
> BUBU NGARI, BUBU NGARI,
> SAMBA, IF YOU HERD AT JERI, I WILL PROTECT YOU!

They walked on and on until they were very near to the river Jeri. They were able to see lions, tigers, leopards, hyenas and all the other animals there. All the animals stood up TEM[5] staring at the large herd of cattle that had just arrived. The young man became very frightened. He could not move but stood very still. He began to sing:

> FATHER TOLD ME TO HERD AT FUTA.
> MOTHER TOLD ME TO HERD AT JERI.
> FATHER TOLD ME TO HERD AT FUTA.
> MOTHER TOLD ME TO HERD AT JERI.

Then the bull replied:

> MY CROWN OF HORNS, MY CROWN OF HORNS,
> SAMBA, IF YOU HERD AT JERI, I WILL PROTECT YOU!

The young man then took shelter behind the bull. The lion approached them. Just as he was about to jump on the young man, the bull intercepted him in the air and pierced the lion in the stomach with his sharp horns. The lion died. Then the tiger attacked. He jumped in the air. As he was about to land on the young man, the bull caught him with his horns and stabbed him in the stomach. The tiger died. The bull acted like this, until he had killed two lions and three tigers. The other bulls had killed all the rest of the wild animals there.

The young man then went and cut off a few of the lions' tails, their legs and their manes. Then he went over to the tigers. He cut off a few of the tigers' tails, their legs and their hair. He placed all of these into his bag. He did that to show the people in his village that he had actually traveled to the river. When they were finished drinking, they prepared to depart.

As they were walking back home the young man sang out to his cows:

> MOTHER TOLD ME TO HERD AT JERI.
> FATHER TOLD ME TO HERD AT FUTA.
> FATHER TOLD ME TO HERD AT FUTA.
> MOTHER TOLD ME TO HERD AT JERI.

Then the bull replied:

> MY CROWN OF HORNS, MY CROWN OF HORNS,
> SAMBA, IF YOU HERD AT JERI, I WILL PROTECT YOU!

They walked and walked and walked for a long time. When they were in the middle of the bush, the young man stopped and sang out again:

> FATHER TOLD ME TO HERD AT FUTA.
> MOTHER TOLD ME TO HERD AT JERI.
> FATHER TOLD ME TO HERD AT FUTA.
> MOTHER TOLD ME TO HERD AT JERI.

Then the bull replied:

> MY CROWN OF HORNS, MY CROWN OF HORNS,
> SAMBA, IF YOU HERD AT JERI, I WILL PROTECT YOU!

When they reached their compound the young man then tied up all of his cows. Then he went to his father and said, "My father!" and he replied, "Yes?" "I have gone to Jeri and now I have returned!" His father said, "Hunnh, how *could* you go to Jeri and return?" Then the young man took out his sack and opened it. He showed his father all the parts of the lions and the tigers. The father said to him, "It is true, you *have* been to Jeri! Here are legs, tails and hair to prove it."

When the woman heard what the young man had done, she became very angry, but she could not do anything about it. She remained in her house, remained in her house until her anger cooled off. Everything that she had attempted to do to kill the young man had failed. The young man always escaped her traps, without any harm being done to him.

One day the step-mother prepared some sour milk for the young man. She put poison into it. She set it down where the young man always sat and ate his morning meal. When the young man finished milking his cows, he went home to eat his breakfast.

After he sat down, he began to drink the sour milk. But before he could drink it, the bull approached him and kicked the calabash of sour milk onto the ground. The young man said, "Hey, what are you doing?" He grabbed a stick and began to beat the bull. The bull picked up the young man with his horns. Then he set him down again and said, "The sour milk, which your step-mother had prepared for you, was poisoned. If you would have finished it, you would have died." The young man then went and milked four cows and drank the milk until he was satisfied.

Everything that the step-mother tried to do to kill the young man had failed. Soon afterwards the woman collected her belongings and left his father's compound.[6]

[1] Narrated by Malik Boye in Porli, The Gambia, in the compound of Bessi Njay on November 1 at 8:15 p.m. before 53 men, women and children.

[2] The eldest son's name.

[3] A river said to flow through the territory of Walo in Senegal.

[4] Refers to the Futa Toro area in Senegal which is in Walo.

[5] Onomatopoetic expression recreating the sound of the animals rustling to attention as they become alert.

[6] For a comparative tale see "The Guardian Sheep."

THE GUARDIAN SHEEP[1]

There was a story . . .
Our legs are crossed . . .
It happened here . . .
It was so . . .

There was a young woman whose husband hated her. She left in anguish, separating from her husband, and abandoning her son.

When this boy grew up, he became a shepherd. He guarded a large flock of sheep and a herd of cattle.

There was among the flock of sheep one that was extremely beautiful. The boy took extra care of this animal. He was very particular about his sheep and loved it very much. He would never allow any harm to endanger its life.

Now his mother's co-wife was always trying to discover a method of getting rid of him. With her first plan, she prepared some poisoned *lax*[2] for him, blended with some sour milk and a little sugar. When it was prepared, she set off to deliver it to her step-son.

At that time the boy was seated in the shade under a tree. It was midday and he was resting. Like all shepherds, he was sitting there with his favorite sheep from among the flock beside him. The boy sang to his sheep:

HARME,[3] HARME, HARME! WHATEVER I ASK YOU,
YOU ARE BOTH MOTHER AND FATHER!
WHATEVER YOU KNOW,
YOU MUST TELL YOUR SON.

The ram replied:

KODO,[4] KODO
THE *LAX* AT HOME, DO NOT EAT IT!
THE *LAX* AT HOME IS POISONED.
DO NOT EAT IT, KODO.

Soon the co-wife arrived. She brought the boy's *lax*. She said to him, "My son, I am very proud of you. You have been working very hard all day tending the animals. I have brought you your lunch. Now I must go and look for some firewood." After she had set out searching for firewood, the young boy quickly began to dig a deep hole. When it was finished, he acted just as if he had eaten the whole lunch. When his mother returned, he said to her, "Mother, take the bowl back home, I am finished." She said, "Yes?" He replied, "Yes." She said, "That is how a man should eat, especially with *lax*. It should not take very long." Then she gathered the bowls and returned home.

That night, as she was preparing supper, she pounded some millet and mixed some poison into it for the boy's morning meal.

The next morning the boy awoke and went to his favorite sheep and sang a song to it as he tied up all the animals with rope:

> HARME, HARME, HARME! WHATEVER I ASK YOU,
> YOU ARE BOTH MOTHER AND FATHER!
> WHATEVER YOU KNOW,
> YOU MUST TELL YOUR SON.

The sheep replied:

> KODO, KODO, SOMETHING HAS BEEN MIXED WITH YOUR FOOD.
> THE *CHERE* AT HOME IS POISONED.
> THE *CHERE* AT HOME, DO NOT EAT IT!
> DO NOT EAT IT, KODO!

That morning his step-mother arrived and brought him the couscous. She said to him, "My son, you must eat your morning meal before you go out to tend the animals." He replied, "Yes." When the woman went to collect some firewood, the boy dug another hole. When it was deep enough, he poured the *chere* into it and covered it with sand. Then he went to his herd and milked some of the animals. He drank this milk instead of eating the *chere*.

When he returned, he acted as if he had eaten all the *chere*. He called out to his mother, "Mother, come and carry away the bowls, I have finished eating." "Have you eaten all of this food already?" she asked. He replied, "Yes." Then she left and returned home.

In her mind the woman thought to herself that the boy would probably die out in the bush since he had eaten so much of the poison. There was poison in the *lax* and poison in the *chere*.

The boy went into the bush and tended the animals. He watched them for the whole day until he was prepared to return home.

In the boy's village, the woman had been digging a deep hole about forty meters deep. She dug this hole at the exact spot where the boy always sat whenever he was milking his animals before his meal. After she dug the hole, she went out into the bush and looked for the deadliest, most poisonous snake she could find. When she caught the snake, she brought it home and threw it into the middle of the hole. It stayed there at the bottom of the pit. The woman had tried to kill the boy twice, using food, but she was not successful. Each time the sheep warned him that the food was poisoned.

As they were returning home the young boy sang to his favorite sheep:

HARME, HARME, HARME! WHATEVER I ASK YOU,
YOU ARE BOTH MOTHER AND FATHER!
WHATEVER YOU KNOW,
YOU MUST TELL ME.

The sheep sang back to him:

KODO, KODO. IT IS DANGEROUS AT HOME!
THERE IS A HOLE IN THE YARD.
WHEN YOU GO HOME,
DO NOT SIT NEAR IT.

When he returned home, his mother called out to him, "My son! Come over here and eat your dinner." She started to place the bowl of food next to the deep pit where the boy would certainly fall into it. The boy called out to her, "Mother, place my food in front of the tethering posts because that is where a cow just gave birth." Since a cow just then gave birth, the woman placed the bowl on the other side, away from the hole.

It happened that the woman's own son, who was very spoilt, was answering a call from the step-son. As he approached the deep hole his mother shouted out, "Don't go over there. Stop! Wait! You will surely die." But the young boy could not hear what his mother was saying. The woman was too late. The boy fell into the hole, was bitten by the snake and died. What this woman had planned for the step-son happened to her own child.[5]

[1] Narrated by Bessi Njay in Porli, The Gambia on November 20 at 11:45 p.m. in his own compound before 20 adults.

[2] Boiled millet mixed with sour milk, sugar and baobab fruit. It is a food commonly eaten as the morning meal.

[3] The special sheep.

[4] The young boy's name.

[5] The opening image of this narrative establishes the emotional groundwork on which its theme turns. The image is one of an abandoned child; he has been left in a household without love or protection. His mother left home because her husband did not love her; the step-mother is jealous and wants to kill him. Being denied love in his family, the boy finds it among his flock of animals. His relationship with one sheep reflects a mutual love based upon care and protection. The repeated choral sequence of the young boy requesting advice and the sheep warning him of impending danger focuses on the paternal relationship between this youth and his animal friend. The three-fold repetition provides direct contrast between the human and animal worlds. At home there is hate and danger while the opposite exists among the sheep. Since the boy has been abandoned by his mother and father, he looks to the sheep as surrogates. This does not mean, however, that the human world should model their family relationships according to an animal model. Rather, it underscores the low level of family life exhibited by the human family. It is a derogatory statement about this type of human family more than a prescription for family harmony. By nature, humans are esteemed because they are better than animals. This family is not; consequently, they suffer the loss of a beloved son. In this comparison, they have been humiliated and judged inferior. This literary convention bears strong resemblance to that observed in the use of precocious children surpassing adults in social and moral behavior.

THE HANDSOME SUITOR, I[1]

There was a story . . .
Our legs are crossed . . .
It happened here . . .
It was so . . .

Once there was a beautiful girl. She stated that she would never marry a man with a scar on his body. Whenever a man approached her father about marriage, she would send a fly to inspect the prospective suitor to see if he had any scars on his body. The flies would always report back to the girl, "Ha, Ha! That one has scars on his body." The beautiful girl would then send the man away. He would be rejected.

The girl carried on in that manner for a long time until a snake heard about her beauty and decided that he wanted to marry her. But first he changed himself into a very handsome man with a body that had no scars. Then he changed the tree in which he lived into a horse. Thus he started on his journey, to see the girl.

The snake-man rode on his horse and every tree that he passed changed into a horse with a rider on top of it. He passed many trees on his way and every one turned into a horse with a man on it until there was a very large procession of horsemen following him. This man then ordered his praise-singer to proceed ahead of the entourage to proclaim his intentions of marrying the girl and her family. When the praise-singer arrived before the girl's father's compound he sang, "I am coming. I come to marry your daughter. I do not have any scars on my body." The inhabitants said, "That is very good."

Soon afterwards the man arrived. He greeted them, "Salaam Alekum!" and they replied, "Alekum Salaam." The girl informed all her friends that her suitor had arrived. They assembled and cooked a large meal in honor of the man's arrival.

The girl then ordered a fly to inspect the man's body just as it had done to every other prospective suitor. It reported back, "Ah, your husband has no

40

scars. Not one scar. His body has no imperfections." The girl said, "That is very good. Now *this* is the right man to be my husband."

The girl went to her father and said that this man was the one she wanted to marry. When the man approached the father to ask his permission to marry his daughter, the father consented to the marriage. In time the young man performed all the necessary marriage rites and was soon given the girl as his wife. The man then asked her father for permission to take his wife back to his own house. The father said, "That is alright. Take her."

That same day the handsome man with his new wife and entourage mounted their horses and began their return journey. But the farther they traveled, the less numerous were their attendants. The farther they went, the more their followers disappeared. They traveled . . . Their followers disappeared . . . They traveled . . . Their followers disappeared. The girl questioned her husband, "Ah, Uncle?[2] What has happened to all our companions?" He replied, "When we arrive near their homes, they just leave us." "But why are we all alone here in the bush?" asked the wife. "Because there is no one around here who doesn't have scars. You said that you did not want to marry anyone who had scars. I am the only person who doesn't have them," explained the husband. So they rode on and on until they reached the place where the husband made his home.

When they arrived, the horses on which they were riding changed into trees. The woman asked him, "What has happened to your horses? Where did they go?" But the man did not answer her.

He led her towards a large baobab tree[3] which was his home. He commanded, "Open up," and the tree opened itself. Then they entered the tree.

Inside the tree they sat down. The woman became terrified and asked, "Hey, what is this place? Look, take me to your home. How can I live in a tree?" The man responded, "Here, this is where I live. You, as my wife, will also live here with me."

They sat in the tree for a long time until suddenly the man transformed himself back into a snake. This startled the woman who screamed out, "What is this? What is going on?" "I am your husband," answered the snake. "You stay inside the tree while I go out into the bush to hunt for something for us to eat." Then he went out hunting.

He was gone a long time. When he returned he brought back a man's corpse. He said to his wife, "Here, cook it." But she refused saying, "NO, I will not cook it. This is a dead man." The snake became angry and left the tree again. At that time the girl decided to run away. She knew the secret and cried out, "Open up," and the tree opened. She ran and ran into the bush until she approached a group of people who were carrying some merchandise to sell at a distant market. She cried out for help:

> MY HUSBAND IS NOT A MAN,
> THAT ONE IS REALLY A SNAKE.
> HE BROUGHT ME A CORPSE TO COOK.
> MY HUSBAND IS NOT A MAN:
> THAT ONE IS REALLY A SNAKE.
> WE LIVE IN A TREE,
> LIKE THE SNAKES OF THE BUSH.
> MY HUSBAND IS NOT A MAN.

But the people ignored her cries for help. They kept carrying their goods as they said, "You are a liar."

The girl sat down near the road and cried and cried. After a while she got up and went back to the tree. When her husband arrived, he saw her crying so he said to her, "You said you wanted to marry a man without a scar. Now you have it. Keep it."

The next morning, the snake again went out to hunt for food. The girl stood inside the baobab tree and said, "Open," and it opened up. She again ran to the road and sat by the side of the road. She saw another group of people traveling by and she cried for help:

> MY HUSBAND IS NOT A MAN;
> THAT ONE IS REALLY A SNAKE.
> HE BROUGHT ME A CORPSE TO COOK.
> MY HUSBAND IS NOT A MAN;
> THAT ONE IS REALLY A SNAKE;
> WE LIVE IN A TREE,
> LIKE THE SNAKES OF THE BUSH.
> MY HUSBAND IS NOT A MAN.

These strangers passing by said to her, "What is wrong with you? Why are you crying?" She answered, "Me, I married a man who changed himself into a snake. He went hunting and brought home a dead man for me to cook. He wanted me to eat it." They said, "Kumba,[4] you must leave him; run away. Take your child in the middle of the night after the snake goes into the bush to hunt and travel across the river." She thanked them for their advice and returned to the tree.

In the middle of the night, Kumba strapped her child to her back and left the tree-home. She ran to the edge of the river. There she entered into a boat, a small river-crossing craft, and fled across the river with her child. After she crossed, she proceeded to her home. She entered her compound and at every corner of it she spit 'Tuh' here and 'Tuh' there.[5]

When the snake returned to his tree-home and did not find his wife there, he immediately set off to find her. He directly returned to her village and quickly entered her compound. Whenever he called out her name 'Kumba' the spit would answer, "UMM?" . . . "KUMBA!" . . . "UMM?" He looked everywhere but he could not find her. He did not see anything. He called out, "KUMBA," but only "UMM" was the reply. He did not see anything or anyone, so he returned to his home.

Then a chicken,[6] who was heading straight for the mortar, approached nearby. The snake saw it and asked it if it had seen his wife. "Your wife left you," said the chicken, and pecked and pecked at the ground until its stomach was full. After eating, it said, "Your wife left and rested by the side of the road. Then some people passed by and saw her crying but they kept on walking. She returned to the tree-home but left again crying. When another group of men passed by, these asked her, 'Why are you crying?' She told them her husband was a snake. They told her, 'Leave your husband. Take your child and cross the river. Look for a river raft and cross the river.' 'How can I do that?' asked the girl. 'If I cross the river I will sink, sink down to the bottom.' They said to her, 'Go to the river and look for a crossing place. Draw some water from the river and then sit along the bank. When a boat arrives near there, enter it and cross with him.' That is what your wife did. That is the reason she is not here."

So the snake traveled the same road as before to his wife's house. He went to the river and was transported across. When he arrived in the compound, he called out for his wife, "KUMBA." When she heard this again, the people of her village rushed to her compound; they captured the snake and killed it.[7]

---

[1] Recorded in the compound of Mariamu Sinyam on November 12, in Banjul, The Gambia, at 8:30 p.m. before 2 men and 3 women. Mariamu Sinyam, age 48, belonged to the caste of smiths. Her father was a silversmith and her husband is a welder.

[2] The Wolof term *nijay* refers specifically to the maternal uncle. It is employed as an expression of respect by Wolof women to their husbands. The use here reflects the young girl's Islamic upbringing and provides an ironic contrast to the evil of the snake.

[3] *Gui*, a large tree with a hollow core, often large enough for a person to stand up in. Traditionally, it was the burial ground for some member of the *gewel* or griot caste. In the oral narratives, unexplainable, supernatural events occur there and powerful beings inhabit them.

[4] Kumba is a very common female name among the Wolof. It is consistently used in the narratives as a literary convention designating the female character. The use of this name masks the individuality of this woman while emphasizing the behavioral type.

[5] This is an accepted escape device used in many narratives allowing the intended victim flight from a seemingly overwhelming oppressor. In some narratives, feces replace the talking spit.

[6] The chicken is a conventional character who represents a person who cannot keep secrets, the proverbial tattle-tale.

[7] It is significant that the young girl returns home where she is saved by her people. It was these very people to whom she refused to be married. Her refusal to marry any man who had a scar is an exceptional demand, one entirely divorced from reality. It is unrealistic and dangerous. As she pursues her self-centered dream, she further jeopardizes her own life. Since the snake eats human beings, he might one day decide to eat her. When she returns to her village, she brings with her a

realization that safety can only be secured within her society. By calling out to her people for help, she demonstrates a need for them which she had originally refused to acknowledge. In the narrative, the snake becomes a metaphorical extention of the egotistic and dangerous practices followed by the young girl. Just as the snake could have destroyed her, the rejection of her prospective suitors could also have proved fatal.

THE HANDSOME SUITOR, II[1]

There was a story . . .
Our legs are crossed . . .
It happened here . . .
It was so . . .

Once there was a beautiful young girl who vowed that she would never marry a man who had a scar on his body. She did not want a husband who had a scar.

One day her uncle's son, whom they call Mbonat,[2] approached her father about marrying the beautiful girl. Mbonat was a very courageous man. It was Mbonat who would go and fight against his relative's enemies. You know, courageous men have many scars. Mbonat had scars all over his body, so the girl refused to marry Mbonat.

Other prospective suitors called upon the girl. Before she would accept them, however, she ordered one of her father's many servants to attend to them while they washed their bodies. Whoever came only had to wash and they saw that he had scars.

The girl acted like that for a long time until one day a *konderong*[3] heard about this girl. He changed himself into a human being. He passed a tree on his way to the girl's village and it changed into a man. All the leaves he passed, changed into money. He passed another tree and it changed into a man. The leaves on that tree also changed into money. All these men then collected the money and traveled together.

When he arrived at the girl's compound he said, "Salaam Alekum" and all the people there responded "Alekum Salaam." Then he went up to the beautiful girl and said, "It is you. You are the only reason for my coming here." The girl then ordered one of her father's slaves to go with this man while he washed. But the *konderong* told the girl, "I want you to look at me so that there will be no mistake." She did not see one scar on his body.

The girl then ran to her father and said, "Father," and he answered, "Yes?"

45

"Father, a man has come to our village to marry me. Since he has no scars on his body, I want to marry him."

The girl's father owned a large herd of horses. It was his custom to give a horse as a wedding present to every one of his daughters. When this girl went to the horses to choose her one horse, each of the horses the girl picked refused to go with the girl. They would not go with her. Only the oldest and ugliest horse would consent to follow the girl. She grumbled about taking that horse. She did not want it because it was not as beautiful as all the others. She refused to accept the horse as a wedding gift. The *konderong* heard what was happening and approached the girl. He offered to let her ride on his horse which, you know, was the tree in which he lived before it was changed into a horse. Allah forbid, this *konderong* changed into a human being only to win the young girl in marriage.

After the marriage, they started on their journey riding the horses that had been transformed from trees. When they passed a place where the tree belonged, it changed back into a tree again. This happened until there remained only the two of them. When the girl did not see any other people, she said, "Samba,⁴ where are you going?" He replied, "Far, far away to the place with the crooked tree." The horse traveled on and on until they arrived at his home. When they reached there, he used magic and got off of the horse just as the horses changed back into trees. They had stopped right in the middle of the bush. The girl did not see anything familiar. Up until that day she did not know that her husband was a *konderong*.

She then said to him, "Samba, what is all this?" He replied, "Now, then, whoever marries outside his clan will soon regret it, because you will not know him. Me, I am a *konderong*. Unless you marry within your clan you will not know what you are entering. Me, I am a *konderong*. I will not kill you; I will not do anything to hurt you. You said that you would not marry a man with a scar. Any man who is living only ten years has scars. If he works in his fields, he wounds himself with his knife. If you look at anyone among your relatives, you will see that they all have scars. All humans have scars."

They lived there together for a very long time until one day Samba went hunting but he was not able to catch anything. He returned without anything. The next day he went hunting again but captured nothing. Again he went hunting but caught nothing. The next day as he was hunting, he spotted a Mauritanian⁵ walking through the bush. The *konderong* followed the Mauritanian for a short time until he was able to kill him. He brought the Mauritanian home and said, "Cook it." She replied, "Me, I will not cook it, nor will I eat it. I do not eat human flesh." Then the *konderong* said, "I will cook it for myself." The girl ran behind their tree to her herd of cows and said, "If I ever see a man who is a hero, that hero I will marry."

When she had said that some flies overheard her. They flew to the house of Mbonat and said to him:

QUICKLY, QUICKLY TO YOUR UNCLE'S CHILD
KONDERONG HAS NOT KILLED HER.
KONDERONG HUNTED AND KILLED A MAURITANIAN.

The flies buzzed around and added:

QUICKLY, QUICKLY MBONAT
WE WILL TAKE YOU TO YOUR WIFE.

When Mbonat heard these words he gathered up his horses and prepared them for a journey. He rode his horse in the brush-lands until he reached her home. When she saw him approaching, she ran out to meet him; "I am here," she called out. "Mbonat, I am here." "I too am here," answered Mbonat. "Oh my Mbonat, when you first came to my father's house, I did not want to marry you. If you take me away from here, I will marry you," she said. "Ah, but you refused to marry anyone from your clan. You know that anyone who leaves his family should stay away," he responded. "But what am I to do here?" she asked urgently. "Let us go away right now," she urged. He replied, "Me, I came here; I will not run away from your husband. I will wait until he returns. I came here; I will not run away."

After he had said that, Mbonat decided to set a trap for the *konderong*. He went into the bush and collected two *kereny*[6] fruits which *konderong* love. He placed them in the middle of the open courtyard in front of his house. He then waited for the *konderong*.

Some flies were sitting on top of the *konderong's* head singing:

QUICKLY, QUICKLY MBONAT WILL TAKE YOUR WIFE.

They said, "He has set a trap with *kereny* fruits." The lion then sang:

KERENY, KERENY I WILL REFUSE THEM.

Then he sang:

MBONAT AND I.
HIDING WITH MY WIFE AT MY HOME.
I WILL REFUSE THEM BEFORE I MEET HIM.
MBONAT AND I.

The *konderong* paced back and forth . . . back and forth . . . until his eyes saw the *kereny* fruits. Then he said:

KERENY, KERENY I WILL REFUSE THEM.

Then he sang:

MBONAT AND I.
HIDING WITH MY WIFE AT MY HOME.
I WILL DESTROY HIM.
MBONAT AND I.

He behaved that way for a long time until you know he found himself under the palm tree where the fruits were set. He said:

KERENY, KERENY I WILL REFUSE THEM.

Then he sang:

MBONAT AND I.
HIDING WITH MY WIFE AT MY HOME.
I WILL DESTROY HIM.
MBONAT AND I.

He then approached the place where Mbonat was hiding. He ran faster and faster until you know their eyes met face to face. Mbonat then shot his gun and the powder charge exploded. It entered the paws of the lion and entered his chest. It spread the lion out on the ground.

Mbonat then took the girl back to her father's compound. He asked him to marry his daughter. The father said, "Take her." Mbonat took the girl; he rode his horse with her to Chan.[7] He rode with her to Chan.

---

[1]Narrative recorded by Bessi Njay in the village square of Porli, The Gambia, on October 18, at 1:30 p.m. before 38 men, women and children. Bessi Njay's reputation as an excellent storyteller extends throughout the Lower Saloum region. A professional griot, he had, as an apprentice, his 8-year-old nephew, Serin Sise, from Senegal, under his tutelage (see narratives "The Dog Captures the Hyena" and "The Bearded Rock").

[2]This praise name literally refers to a land tortoise *Mbonat* with its thick, hard protective shell. A land tortoise is strong and tough, admired by the Wolof for its ability to endure the extreme environmental conditions of this territory on the fringes of the Sahara desert. On close examination, the land tortoise exhibits numerous cuts and gashes upon its shell. Identifying the soldier as Mbonat attributes the qualities of the tortoise to this prospective suitor. He is thus a most unlikely suitor for the girl who refuses to marry a man with a single scar.

[3]This dwarf-like mysterious creature is a frequent character employed by Wolof oral narrators. It is often described as having a long white beard that wraps around its crooked, skinny body and substitutes for clothing. Its feet point backwards yet do not hinder mobility nor agility. Their small size disguises their tremendous strength. They demonstrate remarkable control over the spiritual and physical environment, transforming plants, animals and themselves into other shapes, sizes or forms of life. They are both instruments for reward as well as punishment. They often carry with them a small calabash which can be the source of unlimited wealth and material goods. When the *konderong* feature in stories they are reflections of the mental attitudes of particular characters in the stories. They interact in such contexts with humans and animals alike ensuring the realization of the logical consequences of the given behaviors.

[4]This is a very common name among the Wolof. Its use in the stories fixes the character as a type. The individual and his name are not as important as is the behavior and/or mental attitude of the character.

[5]The use of the character from Mauritania here reflects the traditional animosity that is directed at Mauritanians in Wolof areas. The position of the Mauritanian in Senegal and The Gambia is transient. They enter the countries as small shop owners in similarly small towns and villages. After a year or two of working and saving, they return home with their wealth. The Wolof dislike the high prices they charge for their canned foods and dry goods but, more importantly, they resent the

apparent aloofness and exclusiveness of their behavior. See also "The Mauritanian and His Wealth."

[6]A poisonous fruit that grows on a small bush. The statement that the *konderong* loves this fruit indicates its strength and power over the natural surroundings. Its strength, however, is also its weakness, for Mbonat uses his desire for *kereny* as a trap with which to undermine its normal advantage.

[7]An imaginary term often referred to in the stories. Chan is located somewhere towards the East of the Wolof area. It was from this direction that the Wolof ancestors originally came conquering and settling the land now held. Mbonat, the soldier, is identified as a direct descendant of those original ancestors, sharing their honor and courage.

THE PASSION OF THE GEWEL[1]

There was a story . . .
Our legs are crossed . . .
It happened here . . .
It was so . . .

Our *gewel* clan assembled one day to discuss future plans. At this meeting some people said, "We should try very hard to build our own town. All the other clans have their own towns. Therefore, let the *gewels* have their own town too." Everyone agreed and said, "Praise be to the name of Allah."

They searched around the country for a Marabout[2] who would bless their plans. When they found the Marabout, he wrote them a *tere*[3] and gave them an animal horn. He said to them, "If you go into the bush where you want to build your town, you must put these amulets into the hollow of the biggest tree. Then you must cut down all the other trees around it and use that place as your village square.

These *gewels* walked and walked until they came to a place where the biggest tree was growing. They chose that spot and tied the amulets to the tree. They selected that spot as their village square. They also decided that on Sunday[4] they would cut down all the other trees. When Sunday arrived, all the people from all over the country came to help. They began to cut down the trees.

They started to cut and said, "In the name of Allah." They chopped CHAK[5] and a tree fell down. When they chopped at it again, millet began to pour out of the tree JURU-TUT-TUT . . . JURU-TUT-TUT-TUT . . . JURU-TUT-TUT.[6]

This town could only be ruined by overzealousness.[7] If the town leader became overzealous, the town would be ruined. They said to themselves, "In the name of Allah, this town is *so* good. We only have to cut the trees and millet comes out of them. This town is good; may no evil mouth ruin it."

They cut the *laube*[8] tree. When it fell, they collected two big sacks of millet. They said, "In the name of Allah, let us cut down the *mbeb*[9] tree." They jumped

50

on the *mbeb* tree and began to cut it down. They only chopped twice when the millet began to flow out YUR-YUR-YUR-YUR-YUR-YUR.[10] When the tree fell down, they collected three big sacks of millet. They had only begun to fell the trees.

Later they began to cultivate the farms. They hoed them all. When they cut the trees from their farms, they used the wood to build their town. When they built their town, they grew *suna* here, *sep* there, *bessi* there and *sanyo* there.[11] Then it rained. It was a very good rain. The whole rainy season was good. When the small grains that were sowed in the fields matured, they collected a huge sack at harvest time. They said, "Yes! Yes! Thanks be to Allah. Praise be to Allah. May our town remain in peace till it is old." They all said, "Amen."

Thereafter the fences that they erected between the houses even began to produce millet. When this ripened, they cut it and collected two more huge sacks. They said, "In the name of Allah." They stacked the millet. When they stacked the millet, it was the most beautiful millet stack. The *sep* grew on every side of the millet.

There was a woman. She picked up her child and began to sing to him:

AH, WE ARE ABOUT TO HAVE A TOWN.
OUR TOWN IS VERY GOOD AND PERFECT.
BECAUSE A PLANT OF *SEP* YIELDS A BARREL;
A PLANT OF *SUNA* YIELDS A SACK;
ONLY SIX BEAN PLANTS YIELD A SACK.

A man rushed to her and said, "No! No! We do not allow that. We do not want overzealousness in this town."

The woman remained quiet for a while. Then the child cried. She said, "Shh . . . Shh . . . Be quiet child! Be quiet!"

WE ARE ABOUT TO HAVE A TOWN.
A VERY GOOD TOWN.
BECAUSE IN THIS TOWN WHEN WE STACKED THE MILLET AND COLLECTED IT
EVERY *SUNA* PLANT WAS A SACK;
EVERY *SEP* PLANT WAS A BIG BARREL;
A *SANYO* PLANT WAS A SACK;
ONLY SIX BEAN PLANTS YIELD A SACK.

The woman continued singing.

Another man heard the song and he thought it was beautiful. The first man ran from the village square and told the people that he was going to beat the woman unless she stopped singing. "Stop. Do not ruin our town." "I cannot resist singing this song," said the woman. She began to sing again:

MY UNCLE, THIS TOWN IS VERY GOOD.
EVERY *SEP* PLANT MAKES A BARREL;
EVERY *SUNA* PLANT A SACK;

ONLY SIX BEAN PLANTS YIELD A SACK.

The man said, "Oh, *HA-HA-HA-HA-HA*. Come on child let us sing,

MILLET HAS COME TO US,
MILLET HAS COME TO US,
MILLET HAS COME TO US.

He continued to dance with the child. All the *gewel* danced and sang this song. Soon the town fell into ruins. The *gewel* lost their good town.[12]

[1] Narrated by Lamin Jeng in Bati Hai, The Gambia, on November 2 in his father's compound before 32 men, women and children at 10:15 p.m.

[2] In Wolof, *seriny,* a man versed in the Koran.

[3] A short selection from the Koran written on a small piece of paper or animal skin, folded up and enclosed in leather pouches to be worn around the body or hung at significant locations (i.e. homes, cemeteries, etc.)

[4] In Wolof, *dimase,* from the French, *dimanche.*

[5] Onomatopoetic expression recreating the sound of the *jasi,* machete, and the *semeny,* iron axe, as they hack into the wood of the trees and bushes.

[6] Ideophonic expression creating the image of the grain dripping out of the tree. From the words *Jur,* riches, and *tut,* a little bit.

[7] Excessive demonstration of emotion is contrary to the Wolof behavioral ideal. Any uncontrolled activity precipitates more uncontrolled behavior. This leads inevitably to the destruction of the original cause for the excitement. Control must be exercised if the good fortune is to be maintained.

[8] Hardwood tree from which carpenters construct mortars, small bowls and pestles.

[9] Another hardwood tree.

[10] Ideophonic expression creating the image of the fall of large amounts of millet. From the word *yur,* hail.

[11] These are types of locally grown crops. *Suna* is an early ripening variety of millet; *sep,* beans; *bessi,* sorghum; and *sanyo,* millet that grows in tassles surrounded by hair-like filaments which discourage birds.

[12] The good fortune of the *gewel* is presented in the numerous images of almost effortless bountiful harvests. By merely cutting into a tree or clearing away the undergrowth, they harvest sacks of millet. Even the millet stock fences grow at their new town and miraculously produce grain. But their cornucopia images are doomed to evaporate. *Gewel,* according to caste stereotypes, do not have the requisite internal moral characteristics for wealth and success. In this narrative, their lack of control over their emotions prevails; they give way to the dancing and singing associated with the frivolous life. They show themselves unworthy of their new-found wealth. Their uncontrolled passion eventually leads to the destruction of their perfect, bountiful town. With fatalistic resignation, the protesting elder in the final image invites the young *gewel* to join him in the dancing and singing. His laugh is an acknowledgment of an acceptance of the *gewel* caste stereotype.

THE HYENA ENGAGES THE HARE AS A GEWEL[1]

There was a story . . .
Our legs are crossed . . .
It happened here . . .
It was so . . .

One day a hyena went out into the bush in order to establish his own village. Since he founded this village, he was also the one who administered it. He was the master of it all. He went and built his village together with his wives, his children and his nephews. At that time the hyena was very young and strong; he was in the prime of his life.

Only five days later, after the hyena had accomplished that task, the hare arrived and introduced himself to the hyena in the center of the village. The hare greeted him. *"Bisimilahi,"* replied the hyena. "I heard that you constructed your own village here," stated the hare. "I have my drum. Today I also heard that you are a good man who truly loves himself." The hyena replied, "Very much so!" He asked the hare, "Do you see this area?" "Yes," answered the hare. "That is where you can set up your own compound today. Where is the rest of your family?" The hare replied, "They are following right behind me with all of our baggage." Just then the hare's family arrived and carried all of their possessions into the compound.

Afterwards, the hyena sat down and said, "Hare, you are a *gewel*." "That is right," replied the hare. "That is perfect. Now, since this is my village, I will give you this commission: whenever I have the occasion where I want a *gewel*, you will do the drumming for me. In turn, I will provide all of the food for you and your family. I will kill all of the meat that your family needs and provide your wives with their millet." The hare responded, "That is very good."

After some time, the hyena's power and stamina began to deteriorate. The hyena's strength was finished.

One day the hyena returned from the bush without a second catch for the hare and his family.

It happened that the hyena had originally instructed the hare saying, "You are my guest. Whenever you hear my voice, you should all come directly to my compound. I will then give you your provisions. Then you can take them to your compound."

On this day, when the hyena entered the compound, the hare also followed him there. The hyena called out to his wife, "Korku, come here!" The hare rushed up to him. He said to the hare, "Hey! What is your great rush? Whenever I say anything, you suddenly appear. You know, I built this village. It is mine. After today you are not to enter my compound. If you enter it, I will kill you." Then he called for his cousin. When he arrived he was told, "My cousin, take this one here and put him in his compound. Then barricade his door shut with a large log." "That is the place where you will die," he told the hare. "This is my village and I own it." The hare only answered, "Alright."

The hare remained inside his compound for three days because his doorway was barricaded. He stayed with the compound.

It happened that during those three days in which the hare was imprisoned, he began to grow very weak. He felt he might soon die. He had become very thin. It was then that he saw smoke clouds nearby. He knew that they were from a field fire because they were dark and very thick.

That day he left his compound through a small hole in his back fence. He immediately traveled to the king's town which was about the distance between Njau and Guijanxa.[2] He went to Guijanxa.

There he found the king saying to his people, "Bring me the person who ignited the field fire in my country. Look for him for me and bring him here." While the drums were still beating, the hare arrived. He said to the king, "King, what have you been saying?" The king responded, "Young man, ever since the reign of my grandfather, and his grandfather before him, no one has ever burned the fields in my country. I have been established here as king, and now someone wants to burn the fields in my kingdom. Whoever burned them, I want him. I own him. Whoever even tells me about that one, I will give that person one hundred cows, one hundred goats and one hundred sheep." The hare said, "King?" and he replied, "Yes?" "Call all the men in your village together. He called them and they assembled. The hare continued, "No one is to do anything. Just remain seated here. I myself will bring back the one who set fire to the fields."

It so happened that he wanted to return the hyena to the king, but he realized that he was too little.

He ran back to the compound and re-entered it through the hole in the back fence. When he reached his room, he picked up his *tama*³ so he could play it. He went out into the compound and began to beat very loudly on the drum.

NDON, DON, DON, DON, DON, DON, DON, DON, DON, DON.⁴
LISTEN EVERYONE! THIS IS GOOD NEWS!
THE KING HAS DECLARED THAT THE ONE WHO IGNITED THE FIELD FIRES,
AS I HAVE LEARNED, WILL BE GIVEN
ONE HUNDRED COWS, ONE HUNDRED GOATS,
AND ONE HUNDRED SHEEP.

The hyena said, "Hai! Listen everyone, to what the hare is saying. Praise be to Allah, my children!"

The hare repeated his message drumming,

NDON, DON, DON, DON, DON, DON, DON, DON, DON, DON.
LISTEN EVERYONE! THE KING HAS SAID
THAT WHOEVER BURNED THE FIELDS,
AS I HAVE LEARNED, HE WILL PAY HIM
ONE HUNDRED COWS, ONE HUNDRED GOATS,
AND ONE HUNDRED SHEEP.

The hyena then approached the compound and stood directly before the compound door which was blocked. A big log was blocking the entrance. They had barricaded it. He called out, "Hare?" and he answered, "Yes?" He asked him, "Who has blocked this door?" He replied, "In the name of Allah, you gave the order to barricade my door until I died!" The hyena said, "Hai! I said that only the back door should be barricaded. That is what I said. My cousin did not do what I told him. HUNH! Clear away this barricade!" The cousin then removed the barricade.

Then he entered into the compound and shook the rabbit's hands using both of his hands.⁵ Then he asked, "You, what have you been saying about the king?" "The king has decreed that from the time of his grandfather and his grandfather's father until now, no one has ever burned the fields in his kingdom. Now that the fields have been burned, if he learns who is responsible for it, he will pay him one hundred goats, one hundred sheep and one hundred cows." The hyena said, "Go tell him that I did it." He answered, "Yes!"

So the hare went to the king and told him, "King, I have seen the one who has done it." The king responded, "Then go and tell him that I want him to come here with his whole family. Tell him that he should come here with drums, having his wives and cousins singing an appropriate song." "Yes," replied the hare. The king responded, "That is good."

When he returned to his compound, the hyena met him and asked, "Did you go to the king?" He replied, "Yes." "What did the king say?" "The king said that in the morning you should come with all of your wives and relatives dressed up in your finest clothes. You too should dress in your finest outfit. You must arrive with the *tama* beating and your people singing a song which, you know, tells of your burning of the fields." The hyena replied, "Since you are a *gewel*, you have much more knowledge about that than I. When we prepare to go, you will be my *gewel*." He replied, "Yes."

The following morning the wives prepared themselves. The cousins prepared themselves. The *tama* were readied. The hyena dressed in his finest long robe.

They all set out for the king's village. On the way, the hyena turned towards his wives, who were following him, and said to them, "Young ones, the brush fire, I burned it! The brush fire, I burned it!" They replied, "The brush fire, you burned it." They sang:

> THE BRUSH FIRE, I BURNED IT.
> THE BRUSH FIRE, YOU BURNED IT.
> LAST YEAR'S BRUSH FIRE, I BURNED IT.
> THAT BRUSH FIRE, YOU BURNED IT.
> THE PREVIOUS YEAR'S FIRE, I BURNED IT.
> THAT BRUSH FIRE, YOU BURNED IT.
> THE BRUSH FIRE BEFORE THAT, I BURNED IT.
> THAT BRUSH FIRE, YOU BURNED IT.

They sang that song as they walked along.

When they reached the village of the king, the king said, "I say, that one is *really* bold. He is the one who burned the fields. He is coming here with all his wives and drums singing, 'I am the one who burned the fields.' Ah, that one is *really* bold."

When the hyena reached the king, he greeted him, *"Salaam Alekum."* He replied, *"Alekum Salaam."* He said, "All of you, listen." They listened. He called out, "Hare?" And he replied, "Yes?" He said, "Stop drumming! Set it down because the king must hear what I have to say." The hare said, "Alright." The king said, "Listen, all of you!" They listened. The hyena then turned to his wife and said, "Korku Hyena, tell them!" She then sang:

> UNCLE HYENA, YOU BURNED THE FIELDS.
> I BURNED THE FIELDS
> LAST YEAR YOU BURNED THE FIELDS.
> I BURNED THE FIELDS.
> THE PREVIOUS YEAR, YOU BURNED THE FIELDS.
> I BURNED THE FIELDS.
> EVERY YEAR YOU BURN THE FIELDS.
> I BURN THE FIELDS.

The king exclaimed, "You, Ahaai, are the one whom I have been looking for." The hyena agreed, "Now you know that I have arrived."

The hyena and the king then sat down. The king said, "This eldest one is the one whom I am looking for." Then he commanded, "Seize this one for me! Take him and tie him up behind the compound. Then kill him!" The hyena screamed, "HAI! HAI! Kill me?" "Kill him!" ordered the king. "From the beginning of my kingdom until now, from my grandfather's time till my father's time, no one has burned the fields. Whoever burns the fields is executed."

The hare then said to him, "Hyena?" and he replied, "Yes!" "You know in your village, the one which you have established?" He said, "Yes?" "You locked me up in my compound. You wanted to kill me. You planned to kill me but your plan failed. Today, my plan is successful, so you shall die."[6]

[1] Narrated by Keba Hadi Sise in Njau, The Gambia, on October 31 at 9:00 p.m. before 3 men and 2 women.

[2] A small village located 2 miles from Njau.

[3] A small underarm pressure drum held under the left arm and beaten with the fingers of the right hand.

[4] Onomatopoetic expression recreating the repeated sounds of the drum.

[5] A sign of especially warm greetings used by close friends. Its use by the hyena is an attempt to demonstrate to the hare that he was not the cause of his imprisonment.

[6] This narrative is significant for its positive identification of the caste membership of the hare. He is a *gewel;* his drumming and singing mark his caste affiliation. He employs his skills as griot in the service of his community. By leading the hyena to the king, he insures the implementation of social justice. The hyena, meanwhile, claims a significantly higher order to which he has no inherent right. When he establishes his own village, it is not something that he can naturally sustain. He does not have the moral nor physical requirements necessary to master a village throughout his lifetime. When his youthful strength diminishes, he has nothing to support him; his hereditary characteristics are not suited for leadership. This is the role which *jambur,* nobles/high-caste persons, fulfill. He becomes frustrated when he cannot meet his responsibilities to the hare and his family. His death results from his ignorance of his own position in society. Throughout the tradition, the hyena is described as a character outside the caste system; he does not belong to any one caste, and consequently, he is outside of society, unfit to be accepted by any caste. As in the narrative, "The Hyena and the Hare Search for Wealth," the hare knows his caste affiliation and lives according to its guidelines. By helping the king render justice, he demonstrates his commitment to the established social order.

THE HYENA AND THE HARE
SEARCH FOR WEALTH[1]

There was a story . . .
Our legs are crossed . . .
It happened here . . .
It was so . . .

The hyena and the hare traveled in search of wealth. The hyena wanted silver and gold; the hare wanted a flute.[2] They set out on this journey together.

They traveled for a very long time until they reached a village. They entered it and there saw an old man. They called out to him, "Old man!" He replied, "Yes?" They asked, "Does the king live far from here?" "No, he does not live far from here. You can leave and be there in a very short time." They replied, "That is good!" When the old man left, the hyena said, "Look at the way the old man walks, with a limp. Maybe we should follow him?"[3] The hare replied, "Let us go on our way. Leave the old man alone." The hyena replied, "Alright."

They walked again until they arrived at the king's village. When they met the king they exchanged their greetings. Then the king asked the hyena, "Since you are the oldest, tell me, what is your purpose for coming here?" The hyena responded, "As for myself, I want riches. I don't know what this young man who accompanied me wants for himself. All I want is silver and gold. If I get them now, I will go back to my house immediately." The king acknowledged his request replying, "Yes!" Then he asked the hare, "What do you want from me?" "All I want is a flute." The king replied, "Alright."

Then the king said to them, "Since it is so late you should spend the night here." They said, "Yes." The king dispatched a servant to prepare rooms for them. They were taken to their rooms. The hyena was given an animal skin to sleep on during the night while the hare was given a reed mat. After they had both fallen asleep, the hyena awoke and completely devoured the animal skin on which he had been sleeping. Then he went back to sleep on the ground.

In the morning the hare awoke and returned his mat to the king. When the hyena met the king he was asked, "Where is your sleeping mat?" The hyena softly replied in his very nasalized voice,[4] "I ate it last night. I didn't have any dinner so I ate it instead."

After a while the king ordered ten cows to be brought to him. These he gave to the hyena. The hyena got ten cows. Then he called the hare to him and said, "You, hare, all you want is a flute. Here it is." After they were given their gifts, they left that village altogether.

They traveled a very long time until they were out in the middle of the wilderness. On this journey they became very hungry. They did not have anything to eat. The hare said to the hyena, "Uncle Hyena, we do not have anything to eat. I am very hungry." The hyena said, "Let us have a taste of your flute." The hare agreed and began to play:

> PROTI NDOTI, NDOTI PROTI;[5]
> I ACCOMPANIED THE HYENA, PROTI;
> HE WAS GIVEN TEN COWS, PROTI;
> I WAS GIVEN A FLUTE, PROTI;
> UNCLE HYENA WILL SOON KILL A COW, PROTI.

After the hare had played this song, the hyena could not restrain himself. They killed a cow and prepared it for eating. They ate it until they were completely satisfied. There were nine cows left. After that they left there.

They walked and walked until the hare began to play his flute again:

> PROTI NDOTI, NDOTI PROTI;
> I ACCOMPANIED THE HYENA, PROTI;
> HE WAS GIVEN TEN COWS, PROTI;
> I WAS GIVEN A FLUTE, PROTI;
> UNCLE HYENA WILL SOON KILL A COW, PROTI.

The hyena could not resist the song. He went and killed another cow. Then they ate it. When it was finished, they continued on their journey.

They walked again until they were half-way to their village. The hare told the hyena, "Ah, I am very hungry. We do not have anything to eat." Then he began to play his flute. It said:

> PROTI NDOTI, NDOTI PROTI;
> I ACCOMPANIED THE HYENA, PROTI;
> HE WAS GIVEN TEN COWS, PROTI;
> I WAS GIVEN A FLUTE, PROTI;
> UNCLE HYENA WILL SOON KILL A COW, PROTI.

When the hare finished playing his flute the hyena felt very hungry. He said, "Since we are traveling together, I will feed you." Then he killed another cow and they both ate it. When it was finished they left.

The hare and the hyena continued to act like that until only one bull remained from the original ten. It was the biggest and the strongest of them all.

There was only one bull left. The hare said, "Ah, I am very hungry but there is nothing left to eat." The hyena said, "Yes." So the hare began to play:

> PROTI NDOTI, NDOTI PROTI;
> I ACCOMPANIED THE HYENA, PROTI;
> HE WAS GIVEN TEN COWS, PROTI;
> I WAS GIVEN A FLUTE, PROTI;
> UNCLE HYENA WILL SOON KILL A COW, PROTI.

The hyena became very angry. He went up to the bull. He tried to grab it by its horns but the bull threw him over his back. The hyena landed on the ground and said, "HUUNNH," and remained seated on the ground. The hare began to play again:

> PROTI NDOTI, NDOTI PROTI;
> I ACCOMPANIED THE HYENA, PROTI;
> HE WAS GIVEN TEN COWS, PROTI;
> I WAS GIVEN A FLUTE, PROTI;
> UNCLE HYENA WILL SOON KILL A COW, PROTI.

The hyena said, "How can I kill that bull? He is so strong that he will kill me instead of me killing him. I will just leave him alone." Then the hare began to play his flute:

> PROTI NDOTI, NDOTI PROTI;
> I ACCOMPANIED THE HYENA, PROTI;
> HE WAS GIVEN TEN COWS, PROTI;
> I WAS GIVEN A FLUTE, PROTI;
> UNCLE HYENA WILL SOON KILL A COW, PROTI.

The hyena rose and said to the hare, "I do not want to eat this bull. I can't kill him like I killed the other cows. I will just leave him alone. I don't want him." The hare replied, "Uncle Hyena, why do you not just shoot the bull? That way you can easily kill him." "No, I don't want to shoot the bull. If I shoot at the bull, I might be the one to die. If you want the bull you may have it. I don't want it." So the hare took the bull and his flute. When he arrived at his own compound he tethered it to a post.

After a very long time the hyena became very hungry. He was not able to catch anything to eat for many days. So he returned to the compound of the hare and said to him, "Do you remember when we were traveling together?" "Yes," replied the hare. "I gave you a bull to keep for me. You said that you would care for it until it became very fat." The hare said, "Yes?" He said, "Now I have come to ask for the bull back." He said, "What?" "I want to take my bull back and eat it." The hare repeated. "What?" The hyena said, "Is this the bull we had when we were traveling together?" He said, "Yes, that is the bull." "What are you going to do with it?" The hare replied, "I am just going to leave it here." The hyena said, "Ah, you can't do that. You must slaughter it now." He said, "Alright. I will call you when it is ready to eat."

The hare then went and shot the bull. He cut it up, cooked the meat, and stored it in some food pots. After a while the hare ate some of the meat. Then he ate more of it until it was all finished. When it was completely gone he called the hyena, "Hey hyena, come here." The hyena had been waiting for a very long time. He was extremely hungry. As he ran into the hare's compound he heard the hare say, "Hey Uncle Hyena, show your teeth . . . show your teeth!" As the hyena entered the gate, the hare threw him the last remaining bone. The bone struck the hyena on the teeth and they began to bleed. When the hyena tasted his own blood he began to suck it into his mouth EESSHH . . . EESSHH . . . EESSHH . . . and said, "I got more than you. I got more than you. I got more than you."[6]

[1]Narrated by Malik Boye, age 30, in Porli, The Gambia, in the compound of Besi Njay before 53 men, women and children. Porli is a village composed of members of the griot caste. The head of the village and the religious leader are also griots.

[2]Only members of the griot caste are recognized as musicians. The hare's request for a flute and his subsequent productive playing of it identify the caste membership of the hare.

[3]The suggestion by the hyena underscores his general lack of respect for older people and his carnivorous appetite. His intended behavior marks him as anti-social. He suspects that the old man, who is having difficulty walking, might in fact fall down. There he would be vulnerable to the hyena's attack and easily overcome. The hare provides external control over the hyena's activities. He divorces himself from such ideas and behaviors by scolding the hyena and forcing him to change his mind about the old man.

[4]The hyena's speech is usually narrated with exaggerated nasalization. This adds to the humorousness of the character by presenting him with what is recognized as sloppy, lazy, and mispronounced diction. Often the sounds uttered by the hyena are entirely unintelligible. This dimension in character development allows for artistic variation. As such, it is a mark of virtuosity that audiences respond to with spontaneous laughter. The hyena's speech thus reinforces the description of his being a totally shameful creature, the epitome of the anti-social model.

[5]These sounds imitate the melody played by the hare. Since this chorus is repeated many times, it is frequently sung by the entire audience. The ability to involve one's audience in the participation of such songs enhances the reputation of the storyteller who has turned a story-telling session into a memorable family or community event.

[6]The relationship between the hare and the hyena that is established in the initial sequence is the model that is followed through the subsequent image sets. The hyena's anti-social behavior described in notation number three followed by the hare's exercise of control is the pattern for the later exchanges. The central action sequence involves the hare's request for food and the hyena's denial of it. In order to obtain food, the hare must exercise control over the hyena through musical suggestion. Only after the hare plays his flute does the hyena agree to share. The hyena's refusal to share his food is a mark of shame, for sharing is one of the most important Wolof social values. His denial of the hare's request is uncivilized and dishonorable. This behavior is parallel to that exhibited by him in the initial sequence. The hare forces the hyena to comply with the social code through the exercise of his traditional caste role: musician, entertainer, and social conscience. The final narrative sequence views the hare inflicting pain on the hyena for a similar infraction of the social code. When the hyena could not kill the last bull the king had given him, he in turn gives it to the hare. When the hyena returns to the hare's compound and demands its return, he is reneging on his previous offer. While this *is* typical behavior for the hyena, it is not admired by the Wolof. The hare is thus completely justified in punishing the hyena.

THE HYENA ENGAGES
A STRANGE-FARMER[1]

There was a story . . .
Our legs are crossed . . .
It happened here . . .
It was so . . .

There was a day, like the day when the rainy season approaches, when everyone hires a strange-farmer. The hyena took a strange-farmer. He took on a toad.[2] When it was lunch time, food was prepared for the workers to eat. The hyena called out to the toad, "Come and eat!" So the toad went and washed his hands. Then he approached the bowl of food. When he arrived, his hands had become very dirty. The hyena said to him, "Hey, go back and wash your hands. You know that you can't put those dirty hands in here." So the toad went away, trotting, *mboti-mboti-mboti.*[3]

The rest of the day, they all sat around the compound until it was supper time. The hyena called out to the toad, "Toad, come and dine!" The toad washed his hands and proceeded to the place where the meal was being served. But the hyena said to him, "Man, go and wash those dirty hands of yours. You can't put those in here. Those dirty hands can't get into *my* bowl." So the toad went away.

The next morning at breakfast time, the toad was again called, "Toad, come and eat breakfast!" The toad washed his hands and came trotting, *mboti-mboti* on the ground towards the bowl of food. He was very skinny now. When he reached the serving area, the hyena told him to go back and wash his hands. The toad again left without eating.

Afterwards he encountered the hare hopping down the road, *pohet-pohet-pohet-pohet* until he reached the toad. The hare asked him, "Toad?" and he replied, "Yes?" He said, "You, when I saw you last, you were very fat and fresh, but now you are extremely thin. What has happened to you?" He replied, "My landlord, whenever he calls me to go and eat, if I come, he says that my hands are too dirty. I better go back and wash them again. Now I cannot eat any of the three daily meals. I cannot eat because it is my custom to walk with both hands and feet on the ground. Whenever I go, he always says that my hands are dirty. That is what is troubling me."

The hare proposed to him, "Let us change landlords. You go to my landlord's compound. I will go to your landlord's compound." The toad replied, "Hare, my landlord needs a very quick worker." He replied, "That is what I like, someone who wants a smart man."

The hare arrived at the hyena's compound and said, "Salaam Alekum," and he replied, "Alekum Salaam." Then he said, "Uncle Hyena, I am looking for a landlord." The hyena asked, "Are you swift?" He replied, "Yes, I am very swift." He asked, "What is your name?" The hare answered, *Bisimilahi*[4] is my given name and *Wahumala*[5] is my surname." At that time it was approaching twilight.

In the morning, the hyena's wives prepared breakfast. Then he called him, *"Bisimilahi,"* and he replied, "Yes!" The hare came and ate up all the food very quickly by himself. Then he said, "Uncle Hyena, where am I to put the empty bowl?" The hyena said, "Yes, this is the type of strange-farmer that I want. You see, the toad was here but I could not live with him." The hyena then told him to put the bowl anywhere he wanted. Afterwards they rested until it was lunch time.

He called again, *"Bisimilahi,"* and he replied, "Yes!" He ate up the food very quickly and asked, "Uncle Hyena, where will I put this bowl?" He said, "Ah, this is what I want. It is now that I have my servant. When the rainy season starts, you will farm for me." Then they rested until supper time.

At supper time he called him, *"Bisimilahi,"* and he responded, "Yes!" Then he ate the food quickly and asked the hyena, "Uncle Hyena, where should I place the bowl?" The hyena responded, "Hang it on your ass!"[6] They remained there until the next day.

The hyena went to his wife and said, "You know what we must do?" She replied, "Hunnh?" He said, "Now we must do something. I see that if this guy remains with us for a long time, he will bring about our deaths. From now on you should set aside an extra bowl of food for me every meal. When he comes to eat, he will satisfy himself and then leave. Then I will come and eat the extra bowl of food." So the woman set aside this extra bowl at each meal. They slept until it was breakfast time.

In the morning he called out, *"Bisimilahi,"* and he responded, "Yes!" He ate the food very quickly and then asked, "Uncle Hyena, where shall I place the bowl?" He replied, "Place it on your mother's ass." The hare said, "Ah, Uncle Hyena, did you not say that you wanted a swift servant?"

Afterwards the hyena went behind his house to eat the food from the reserved bowl. He placed it down on the mat. You know, when you are eating, you get used to saying *Bisimilahi* before you begin to eat. The hyena only whispered, *"Bisimilahi,"* and the hare came and said, "Yes!" Then the hare ate that food quickly and asked, "Uncle Hyena, where shall I put the bowl?" He said, "Place it on your father's ass."

After that, he waited until the hare went to the village square. He called all of his wives, Toj Geda, Wida Nyamul Saket and Kumba Kengun. They replied, "Yes?" He told them, "Leave what you are doing and come here. Take whatever grain is in the storage bins and put it into sacks. We must go away from here. This man is going to kill us. He is not a strange-farmer." After that they pounded all their millet and placed it into sacks. They each carried one sack.

They all set out walking on their journey. They walked and walked unaware that the hare had cut a hole in one of the sacks and was inside the last wife's sack of millet. He ate the millet. He ate all of the millet so that the sack became very light; it was completely empty.

After a long time the last wife said, "Uncle Hyena," and he replied, "Yes?" She said, "My load is very light." He told her, "We are in the forest of lightness. I used to carry one hundred and fifty bags of millet here and I didn't even feel it. Let's go on now."

They continued to travel onwards until they squatted down to urinate. It was then that the hare cut a hole in the other wife's sack of millet. He got inside it and began to eat. That wife walked for a very long time and then said, "Uncle, my sack is also very light." He replied, "Listen to what I'm saying. We are in the forest of lightness. I used to carry one hundred and fifty bags without feeling it."

They continued traveling for a while until they decided to rest. At that time he got into the first wife's sack and began to eat until it was nearly empty. The first wife said, "This can't be the forest of lightness only. There is nothing in my sack. It is *too* light." The hyena said, "Look! Listen to what I say. If you are accustomed to carrying a heavy load and you rest, when you pick up the load again, it will feel lighter."

They walked until it was time to rest again. The hyena had been carrying a sack too but he had put *mudaka*[7] inside it. Then the hare entered inside the sack, the one belonging to the owner of the compound, and began to eat it. After they walked a very great distance they decided to prepare their breakfast. They said, "Let us have our breakfast now."

When the hyena untied his sack he said, *"Bisimilahi,"* and then the hare replied, "Yes!" He ate that food quickly and then asked, "Uncle Hyena, where shall I put this sack?" The hyena replied, "Oh, hev. *Bisimilahi! Bisimilahi* and I!

What can I do with this *Bisimilahi?*" He stood up and screamed, "That's it! That's it! That's it! That's it!" as he ran and ran until he collided with a baobab tree and died. That was the last time that the hyena had a strange-farmer.[8]

[1]Narrated by Bessi Njay in Porli, The Gambia, on November 20 at 10:00 p.m. in his own compound before 18 men, women and children
compound before 18 men, women and children.

[2]In Wolof, *mbota.*

[3]Ideophonic expression creating the image of the hopping toad. From the Wolof for toad; in the manner of a toad.

[4]"In the name of Allah," from the Arabic.

[5]"I am not talking to you," from the Wolof.

[6]The hyena is beginning to become disturbed with the activities of the hare. He senses future trouble with him.

[7]Steamed millet flour mixed with roasted ground peanuts and sugar. Usually eaten either as a snack or for the early morning meal.

[8]Death, as a literary convention, signals the ultimate social punishment and rejection of a character and everything it represents in a particular narrative. In this tale the hyena's dishonorable behavior is condemned and repudiated. This narrative illustrates a particular dimension of dishonorable behavior by focusing upon the hyena's relationship to migrant laborers. The hyena demonstrates a sharply tuned sense of selfishness in his treatment of his first job applicant and his stated job qualifications. The initial sequence does not signify the hyena's preoccupation with cleanliness but his unwillingness to provide food for his worker. He only uses this as an excuse to renege on the socially accepted contractual arrangement between Wolof farmer and migrant. His behavior is life-threatening: the toad is described as very skinny and confused. This behavior thus forms the basis for the hare's subsequent punishment of the hyena. The hare's punitive actions focus on the very issue of the contractual agreement which the hyena failed to honor: food. The hare punishes the hyena when he is most deserving. The hare's action is thus not perceived as unjust and cruel; rather, it is fitting and right. The hyena's attempted escape is thwarted because the narrative tradition does not allow for the release of such anti-social characters. His death is a confirmation of the society's system of values.

THE LION'S TREASURED GOAT[1]

There was a story . . .
Our legs are crossed . . .
It happened here . . .
It was so . . .

There was a lion who owned a goat. He loved this goat very much. No matter how hungry the lion became, he would never eat the goat. He kept it tethered at his home and saved it.

It happened that one day the hyena's son, who was called Dulangi,[2] one day passed by the lion's house. There he saw the goat. When he returned home, he said to his father, "I saw a goat at Uncle Lion's house today." The hyena replied, "Yes?" and he said, "Yes!" Hyena asked, "A goat?" and he replied, "Yes!" He said, "A goat at the lion's house . . . do you think that it is possible to get the goat out of there?" He said, "I saw it with my own eyes." "Ah, Dulangi, Dulangi! If I go there and I don't find anything, I will return and kill you."[3] He said, "Father, I swear to you that I saw it."

The hyena went and saw the goat. When he returned home, he called all of his wives together and said to them, "There is a great crisis at hand. A thief wants to steal from another thief. I want each of you to go out and bring back your grandmother's sheepskin." After they had each brought the sheepskins of their grandmothers, he covered himself up with them.

Then the hyena sneaked over to the lion's house and stole the goat. He took it home and killed it. He called his wives, Kumba and Wida Nyamul Saket, and said to them, "Now you must cook this meat quickly." So they cooked it. After it was prepared they all ate it.

The lion soon arrived looking for his goat, but he did not find anything. He saw the hyena's footprints and said to himself, "Ah, that scoundrel!" Then the lion began crying and crying. He cried until the hare approached him and asked, "Why are you crying, Uncle Lion?" He replied, "That hyena stole my goat." Hare asked, "Did he steal it?" and he answered, "Yes!"

The deer also approached him and asked, "Why are you crying, Uncle Lion?" He answered, "The goat that I was depending on has been stolen by that hyena." He asked, "Really?" and he replied, "Yes!"

The deer who had been traveling with the hare said, "I know a song, in addition to all the stratagems of the hare, that will surely force the hyena to reveal himself to us." The lion had already looked all over the bush, searching for the hyena, but he had had no success. Then the hare asked the deer to sing his song for the lion. The deer began:

> ANTELOPE, ANTELOPE,[4] THE RASCAL HAS MUDDIED IT FOR ME.
> ANTELOPE DID NOT DIG THE WELL,
> THE RASCAL HAS MUDDIED IT FOR ME,
> STOP DRINKING, WE DUG THE WELL,
> THE RASCAL HAS MUDDIED IT FOR ME,
> STOP DRINKING, WE DUG THE WELL,
> THE RASCAL HAS MUDDIED THE WATER.
> HE WAS THE ONE, THE RASCAL DIRTIED THE WATER,
> HE WAS THE ONE, THE RASCAL DIRTIED THE WATER.[5]

After the deer had finished singing, the hare said, "Uncle Lion, deer and I will bring the hyena back to you." He said, "Really?" and he replied, "Yes!" He said, "Uncle Lion, if we bring him back to you, what will you grant us?" The lion said, "I will protect you from all the hyena's threats." You know, whenever the hyena goes without eating, he always attacks the hare. The hare then asked the deer to sing his song again. He began to sing:

> ANTELOPE, ANTELOPE, THAT RASCAL HAS MUDDIED IT FOR ME,
> ANTELOPE DID NOT DIG THE WELL,
> THE RASCAL HAS MUDDIED IT FOR ME,
> STOP DRINKING, WE DUG THE WELL,
> THE RASCAL HAS MUDDIED THE WELL,
> STOP DRINKING, WE DUG THE WELL,
> THE RASCAL HAS MUDDIED THE WATER.
> HE WAS THE ONE, THE RASCAL DIRTIED THE WATER,
> HE WAS THE ONE, THE RASCAL DIRTIED THE WATER.

After the deer finished, the hare said, "Uncle Lion, now we are going to use the deer in a trap. He will lay down and pretend that he is dead. Assemble all of the animals you can and tell them to lay down in the middle of the bush as if they too were dead. When you do this, I will bring the hyena back to you."

The lion then went and assembled all the animals: deer, jackal, and all other kinds of animals. They lay down on the ground and pretended that they were dead.

The hare then left, going towards the village as he sang this song:

> ALL THE ANIMALS ARE DEAD. ALL, ALL, ALL, ARE DEAD!
> THEY SAY I SHOULD INHERIT ALL OF THEM,
> BUT I CANNOT INHERIT ALL OF THEM,

SINCE UNCLE HYENA IS THE OLDEST.

The hyena heard this song and said, "UNGH? UNGH?" When his son, Dulangi, began shouting, the hyena jumped on top of him and said, "Hey Dulangi, shut up and listen! I want to hear that song again." Then the hare began to sing the song again:

> ALL THE ANIMALS ARE DEAD, ALL, ALL, ALL, ARE DEAD!
> THEY SAY I SHOULD INHERIT ALL OF THEM,
> BUT I CANNOT INHERIT ALL OF THEM,
> SINCE THE HYENA IS THE OLDEST.

Immediately the hyena jumped up and said to Kumba and Wida Nyamul Saket, "Gather up all the pots for cooking and all the sacks and get ready to leave." When they left their compound, they soon encountered the hare. The hyena asked him, "Where are all of them?" The hare told him, "They have all died." The hyena rushed towards his inheritance with his wives, their cooking pots and sacks.

When they arrived at the place where all the animals were laying down, they did not know where to begin eating. The hyena asked Kumba, "Who do we eat first?" The wife answered, "Let us start with the lion." So the hyena approached the lion and placed his hand on top of the lion's chest. He felt the beat of his heart TIP . . . TIP . . . TIP! The hyena was so frightened that he farted BIPP. They said to him, "What are you doing? Let us begin!"

Then the hare began to sing:

> ALL OF THE ANIMALS ARE DEAD, ALL, ALL, ALL, ARE DEAD!
> THEY SAY THAT I SHOULD INHERIT ALL OF THEM,
> BUT I CANNOT INHERIT ALL OF THEM,
> SINCE THE HYENA IS THE OLDEST.

The hyena said, "I am not sure I want to go first." Wida Nyamul Saket said to him, "Go ahead Uncle Hyena." He replied, "Ah, you come and see for yourself."[6] She approached the lion and touched his chest. She too felt his heart beating. Then she farted BIPP. When she farted, the hyena attempted to run away from the side of the lion. But he arose, seized hold of his leg, and killed him. He also chased after all of the other male hyenas and killed them. He did not destroy any of the female hyenas because there were no male hyenas left around there.[7]

---

[1] Narrated by Malik Boye in the compound of Bessi Njay in Porli, The Gambia, on November 20 at 10:45 p.m. before 28 men, women and children.

[2] Literally *dul*, excrement-*angi*, here is. This name reveals the parental antagonism that is believed to exist within the hyena's family. As anti-social beings, they symbolize a counter-value system. This behavior is important to understand for it is the converse of the Wolof ideal.

[3] Such a statement reinforces the audience's realization that the hyena does not love or respect his own offspring. His behavior strengthens his negative role model image, for parents are

expected, naturally, to love their children.

[4] In Wolof, *kewel.* A type of antelope with two stripes, one white and the other black, along each side of its body.

[5] This chorus appears in other narratives involving the hyena and the antelope. These narratives present the antelope deceiving the hyena and escaping from his grasp. The hyena is subsequently beaten by the other animals for his failure to guard the antelope. The chorus is used here to remind the audience and the hyena of that mutual antagonism. When the hyena spies the antelope on the ground, his desire for revenge leads him to drop his defenses and fall into the trap.

[6] The male hyena is too much of a coward to lead. He would rather turn over his male role of strength and courage to his wife. This behavior is opposite the ideal. Wolof men direct their family through positive example, not by word alone.

[7] This narrative focuses on the negative role-model of the hyena as parent and husband. As a symbol of shame, he exemplifies the opposite behavior and attitudes expected of Wolof fathers. He treats his son with contempt, endorses theft of personal wealth, encourages disrespect for authority (symbolized by the lion), exhibits poor social etiquette, abdicates his dominant position in the family to his wife, and humiliates himself as a weakling and a coward. In the final narrative sequence, the lion destroys all the male hyenas. The negative role-model provided by the father has prohibited any possibility of behavioral change in his sons. The narrative, thus, emphasizes the responsibilities of Wolof fathers to their sons and to the community.

THE ELEPHANT AND BLACKBIRD
COURT THE SAME GIRL[1]

There was a story . . .
Our legs are crossed . . .
It happened here . . .
It was so . . .

An elephant[2] and a blackbird[3] were courting. When they were courting, the blackbird approached a girl first and said to her, "I love you and I want you to be my wife." The girl answered, "I hear what you are saying. If you love me I will know it." He visited her until their conversation was finished. He went home.

The elephant also approached her and greeted her. He said to her, "I love you and I want you to be my wife." The girl said, "Yes, if you love me I will know it." They courted until their conversation was finished. He went home.

On the following day, the blackbird returned and saw the footprints of the elephant. He greeted the girl and asked, "What is this footprint that I see here. It is like the imprint from a mortar. What is it?" She replied, "It is from an animal which they call an elephant. He also told me that he loves me and that he wants to marry me, just like you do." He replied, "Yes? And what was your response to him?" She said, "What I answered him was the same as I answered you. I told him that if he loved me, I would know it. If you love a woman you will serve her well." He said, "Yes, that's good." She said, "What are you going to do for me? If you love me, you will give me something!" They discussed this for a while until their conversation ended. He returned home.

The elephant then came to her village and said, "What is this footprint. It is like the imprint of a cane mat."[4] She replied, "It is the footprint of an animal which they call blackbird. He said that he loves me." He said, "Now I will not stay here any longer. I am going home." When he was going out of the house he defecated in the doorway until there was no longer an open passageway. Then he left.

70

Soon afterwards the blackbird entered the courtyard. He saw the shit that blocked the doorway and he did not know where to walk. He called out to the girl. The girl answered him. He said, "What is this in the doorway of the house?" She said, "The animal whose footprint you were asking about put it there. It is his. He said, 'If you cannot put an equal amount of it there, then do not bother to come here anymore!' " The blackbird replied, "Then I cannot enter here. I am returning home." He took out one of the feathers from his tail and stuck it into the middle of the mound. He said, "I am putting my feather there. If he does not have one of these on his ass he must not come here again." Then he left.

A short while later the elephant arrived. He said, "What is this on my shit? Who put it there?" She replied, "That animal which you were asking about did it. He said, 'If you do not have one of those in your ass, then you better not come back here again.' " "Then I will not enter. I will return home now but you can tell him to assemble all of his relatives, his whole clan, all those birds in the whole world. We will fight. Whoever wins the battle will take you." She replied, "Yes."

As he was leaving, the blackbird arrived and called out to the girl. He said, "What did the elephant say?" She replied, "The elephant said that on Friday you are to meet each other at the big baobab[5] tree, the biggest baobab in the world, the baobab that is as big as this town. All of your relatives, all the animals that fly, call them to join you. He likewise will call all the animals that walk on the ground and they will meet you at the mighty baobab tree. There you will fight. He who wins the battle, takes me." He said, "That is good."

The elephant went and called on the lion,[6] the panther,[7] the leopard,[8] the big scorpion,[9] the little scorpion,[10] and all the snakes.[11]

The blackbird went out and began to call the swallow,[12] the turtle-dove,[13] the marabout bird,[14] the little red bird,[15] and all the other flying ones, the large red hornet,[16] the large black hornet,[17] and all the bees.[18]

When the appointed Friday came, the elephant's army marched to the tree and began to fill up the area. The tree had very big leaves which made it pitch black. They camped there all morning until around ten o'clock but still they saw nothing. They stayed until eleven o'clock and saw nothing. They even stayed till twelve o'clock. The elephant said, "Where is blackbird's army? We have not seen them and now it is getting late. Since it is already twelve o'clock the day is over. Now you, squirrel, you who can climb, climb up this tree and scout around for us." The squirrel climbed up to the top of the tree and raised his head to look around. Just then a hawk swooped down *CHOW*[19] and struck him *CHOWIT* and the squirrel fell to the ground and died.

The hyena said, "Allah is good, Ho! That one has been knocked down by the wind. I will pick him up." The elephant said, "Hyena!" and he replied, "Yes?" He said, "Stop! Do not ruin my battle. What has knocked down that animal?" The hyena replied, "It was just the wind." They did not see the hawk because it was so very fast. He said, "Do not spoil it, hyena." The hyena said, "Yes, but I am just going to pick up the squirrel and eat it."

The elephant called out, "Oppossum!"[20] The oppossum said, "Yes?" and he said, "Go climb up the tree." The oppossum replied, "Since the time before my grandparents, we have not climbed up trees." He said, "Then you must *try* it." The oppossum climbed up into the leaves of the tree. He raised up his head to only look around, when the hawk swooped down *CHOW* and struck him. He too fell to the ground *FAAT.*[21]

The hyena said, "Humm. Praise be to Allah, the wind has knocked down two of us and yet we haven't seen anything." The elephant said, "Do not ruin the battle." But the hyena went, carried off the oppossum, and then ate him.

Then the elephant called out, "Weasel!"[22] The weasel answered, "Yes?" He said, "Climb up," but he said, "Let us wait a little while. They have just killed two of us and yet we have not seen anything." He said, "Just climb." He climbed up. He reached the top and only lifted up his head when the hawk swooped down *CHOW* and knocked him *CHOWIT.* He too fell to the ground *FAAT.*

The hyena said, "Praise be to Allah! Hey, elephant, tell us why we have three dead, yet we have not seen any of blackbird's army?" He said, "Be quiet! Do not spoil the battle." The hyena went, picked up the animal, and ate it.

After that the hawk flew to the blackbird and said, "Me, I have killed three and they are very afraid because I killed them without them even seeing me. They think the wind did it." The blackbird said, "Alright, who is going next?" The screech-owl[23] said, "Let me go." The screech-owl looked and looked as he approached the tree. The elephant's army was discussing the battle. When they were all quiet the screech-owl said, "I cannot fit up in the air and I cannot fit on the ground *BIP-BIP-BIP-BIP.*"[24]

The hyena said, "Elephant, listen to what he says. He said that he is so big that he can't fit in the air or on the ground. He stays in the middle saying *BIP-BIP-BIP-BIP.* Will that thing confront us here?" He replied, "Hey, do not ruin my battle." All the animals were now afraid. The screech-owl returned to the leader and said, "Blackbird, all of them are afraid now. I went up to them. They did not see me and I said, "I do not fit in the air and I do not fit on the ground; I must remain in the middle *BIP-BIP-BIP-BIP.* They all got up and stood huddled together." The blackbird said, "Good! Now, who will go?" The eagle said, "I want to go next."

The eagle[25] went up to the tree and said, *"HUWK,"*[26] as he spit on the ground. The hyena laughed, *"HE-HE-HE-HE* that spit, if it only touches you, you will surely die." The elephant said, "If you talk like that you will ruin the battle." But the lion said, "You must talk like the hyena. If that spit lands on any of us, we will die."

The eagle returned and said, "The elephant himself is very afraid; he is defecating." He said, "Now I will take my anchor." It happened that he had brought along a rope and attached an anchor to it which he had kept in mud until it too became red. He moved forward with all the birds until they were up in the tree. He put it on top of a branch. The elephant's army were all lying down asleep. He threw down the anchor on top of the elephant's stomach. The rope entangled him. The hyena said, "Hai, what is this? Are these the intestines of the elephant?" He yelled over to his wife, "Kumba, Kumba give me my spear!" She replied, *"KORKO KANDEMDEM,* [27] kill him and make him into a bag and then we will run away with it." The hyena laughed, *"HE-HE-HE* the leader of the army, the elephant, is to be made into a bag."

Then all the animals began to run away. They left that baobab tree.

A yellow oriole[28] landed on top of the elephant. The elephant ran in fright down to the town of Kaur.[29] The yellow oriole screeched "He is here . . . He is here!" The elephant then ran back to the tree and then to the town of Balanghar.[30] The oriole screeched, "He is here . . . He is here . . .!" In this way, it was the blackbird who won the beautiful girl.

---

[1] Narrated by Amat Konte, age 53, in his own compound in Njau, The Gambia, on December 15 at 9:00 p.m. before 5 men, 2 women, and 3 children. Although Amat Konte's parents were Mandinka, he has lived all his life in the Wolof town of Njau. He has served the chief of the village, Alhaji Omar Sise, as a military advisor, *farba ju rey.*

[2] In Wolof, *nyei,* no longer found in Senegambia.

[3] In Wolof, *gulagul,* metallic plumed blackbird.

[4] In Wolof, *basang.* A floor mat woven from thin palm leaves, marsh grasses or weeds.

[5] In Wolof, *gui.* This tree, *Andansonia digitata,* has a trunk up to thirty feet in diameter with large white flowers and a hard-shelled, fleshy fruit. Its leaves are used as condiments and its bark is twisted into rope.

[6] In Wolof, *gaende,* no longer found in Senegambia.

[7] In Wolof, *tenew,* reportedly still living in wilderness regions.

[8] In Wolof, *sanfando,* reportedly still occasionally sighted.

[9] In Wolof, *janKalar,* quite common and dangerous.

[10] In Wolof, *jit,* very common.

[11] In Wolof, *jan,* general term for serpent.

[12] In Wolof, *Mbelar.*

[13] In Wolof, *sab leka,* type of bird which changes size before it eats. From the verb *sab,* cry, and *leka,* eat.

[14] In Wolof, *mpica seriny. Mpica* is the general term for bird; *seriny,* for Islamic teacher.

[15] In Wolof, *ramatu.*

[16] In Wolof, *jula.*

[17] In Wolof, *jahtadem.*

[18] In Wolof, *yamba,* common term for bee.

[19] Onomatopoetic expression for the swooping downward flight of a bird.

[20] In Wolof, *njahat,* a type of small wild hog with a long tail and claws that lives in a den.

[21] Onomatopoetic expression for the sudden impact of something onto the ground: thud. From the verb *fat,* to make a noise when falling.

[22] In Wolof, *mber.*

[23] In Wolof, *harjet.*

[24] Onomatopoetic expression recreating the sound of the screeching-owl.

[25] In Wolof, *jahay.*

[26] Onomatopoetic expression recreating the sound of spitting.

[27] Untranslatable; said to be in the language of the hyenas.

[28] In Wolof, *nduh.*

[29] This riverfront town is 12 miles east of Njau where the action of this narrative is set.

[30] This large village is 8 miles east of Kaur, down the Gambia River towards its mouth.

THE MONKEY AND THE DOG COURT THE SAME GIRL[1]

There was a story . . .
Our legs are crossed . . .
It happened here . . .
It was so . . .

A dog and a monkey[2] were both courting the same girl. Both intended to marry her. The dog lived on one bank of a river while the monkey lived on the other. Now their prospective in-laws both liked to chew tobacco. They both chewed tobacco.

One day the monkey walked to the river bank and climbed into his boat. He began paddling JABASHE . . . JABASHE . . . JABASHE[3] . . . until he reached the opposite bank. There he tied up his boat and walked towards the girl's compound SEKEMTALI-JEKEMTALI . . . SEKEMTALI-JEKEMTALI[4] . . . When he finally arrived there, he sat down *MAHABOMBOL.*[5]

Then he took out his tobacco tin and put it in his hand NOFUM . . . NOFUM TEI.[6] He pinched some tobacco and inserted in under his lip, SI-NO-TOT . . . SI-SONET . . . SI-NO-TOT . . . SI-SONET.[7] When the tobacco was settled in his mouth he said, "Ah my daughter-in-law, where is that dog? When did he last come here?" The girl replied, "He left here just now." The monkey boasted, "Honestly, if I ever meet him here, I will kill him. You know his ass looks like a bitter tomato.[8] He has absolutely nothing and yet he wants to be engaged to you. If I ever meet him here . . ."

After the monkey left her compound the girl said to her parents, "I want that monkey and the dog to come face to face one day so that the strongest one can defeat the weakest. Then we will know. Their continual rivalry is too much for me to stand."

The next day when the dog returned she said, "Dog," and he replied, "Yes?" "You know, the monkey said that if he had met you here the other day, he would have fought you. He said, your ass was like a bitter tomato." The dog then responded, "Is that what he said? If only our eyes meet, something fierce is going to happen."

Soon after the monkey prepared to go to the girl's place. When he reached his boat he untied it. He got inside and began rowing JABASHE . . . JABASHE . . . JABASHE . . . until he reached the opposite shore of the river. There he secured the boat and started towards the girl's compound SEKEMTALI-JEKEMTALI . . . SEKEMTALI-JEKEMTALI . . . until he arrived there. Then he sat down like this *MAHAMBOMBOL*. He immediately took out his tin of tobacco and put it in his hand NOFUM . . . NOFUM TEI. He pinched some tobacco and inserted it under his lip SI-NO-TOT . . . SI-NO-TOT . . . SI-SONET . . . SI-NO-TOT . . . SI-SONET. After he did that he said, "My daughter-in-law, hasn't that dog been here yet with his ass like a bitter tomato?" She replied, "He left just now." Then the monkey said, "My tobacco is all used up today. Haven't you any left here?" She said, "Oh yes, I keep it under the wash basin for use after dinner. I did not want any of the children to touch it. That is why I put it there."

The monkey then went to the wash basin and turned it over. His eyes immediately met those of the dog . . . making four. He said, "I think I will put the cover back . . . back . . . back . . . back. I will replace the cover back . . . back . . ."

They ran and ran, racing towards the river. As soon as they reached the river, the monkey climbed into his boat and began rowing quickly JABASHE . . . JABASHE . . . JABASHE. The dog meanwhile clung to the stern of the boat. When they reached the other side of the river, the dog caught the monkey and lifted him up and kicked him with his knees. He continued to beat him very badly.

Later that day, the monkey returned to the girl's compound and said to her, "That dog has disturbed my life so much today when I came to see my bride. I beat him badly until he was defeated." The girl responded, "Well, since that is how it is, I will give you a special powder which if you sprinkle it on the excrement of the dog, he will certainly die." The monkey said, "Yes, let us do it. If we go, I will show it to you."

They walked until they saw some feces. The girl untied her powder bag but the monkey said, "Do not be too quick. Here. The dog knocked me down with his knees, but I knocked him too. He tackled me and threw me down. I fell backwards and felt my ass. These feces might be mine, let us go forward a little." They proceeded to another spot. She then untied the bag again and was about to pour the powder there when the monkey again said, "Here I tripped him up and tossed him down. Then he overturned me and I felt my ass. This feces might be mine but that other up ahead is not mine. Let us go there." To the last mound the monkey said the same thing each time until the wife said, "Shit! All this excrement belongs to you. You shit all of this."[9]

[1] Narrated by Bessi Njay, age 32, in Porli, The Gambia, at 2:30 p.m. before 35 men, women and children at the base of a silk cotton tree in the center of the village.

[2] In Wolof, *haj*, dog, and *golo*, monkey. The dog appears in Wolof narratives as a figure of consistency and trustworthiness. He often appears as the foil to contrasting character-types like the monkey. The monkey consistently appears as pretentious, having no justification for his boasting and ostentation. In this narrative he pretends to sophistication, taking tobacco like a gentleman of means and boasting of his physical strength. When his prospective bride tests his character, his dishonesty and weakness are revealed.

[3] Onomatopoetic expression recreating the sound of the oar being pulled through the water and the resulting glide between the strokes. Derived from the Wolof *jab*, to gallop, as of a horse running at great speed.

[4] Ideophonic expression creating the image of the monkey walking very erect and tall. He is extending himself to his fullest height. This is *not* a monkey's normal observed manner of walking.

[5] Onomatopoetic expression creating the sound of the monkey sitting down hard on a very soft cushion, a sinking into the cushion itself.

[6] Onomatopoetic expression recreating the hollow metalic sound of a tobacco tin being struck into the cupped palm of the monkey's hand.

[7] Ideophonic expression recreating the image of the monkey while picking up the tobacco from the tin and placing it under his upper lip.

[8] In Wolof, *jahatu*. Although this fruit resembles other tomatoes in color and relative size, its distinguishing characteristic is its deeply ridged bottom. When these fruits are red ripe they can be likened to the posterior of the *golo nar*, the red monkey.

[9] The repeated reference to excrement in numerous Wolof narratives (see "The Young Man and the Talking Skull") is a literary device employed to emphasize degredation and defeat. The presence of excrement is a strong image connoting weakness and fear. In the narrative it highlights the depths to which the monkey has fallen in the eyes of his betrothed and her family. He had pretended to strength and dignity but all that was spurious imitation. When called upon for active proof, his true character is revealed.

PART THREE
STORIES
Statement—Analogy—
Conclusion

THE YOUNG MAN AND
THE TALKING SKULL[1]

There was a story . . .
Our legs are crossed . . .
It happened here . . .
It was so . . .

There was once a young man. He traveled to a town which was called Njargen.[2] There he noticed a young woman who was extraordinarily beautiful. Immediately he fell in love with her and longed to make her his wife.

Later in the day when he returned to his own village, he approached his father and said to him, "Father, I have seen a young woman whom I want to marry." The father listened politely and then responded, "My son, we never go there to Njargen to negotiate our marriages. It has been so from the time of our grandfathers and even of their great-grandfathers. We do not intermarry with the people of that village. Why do you not seek a bride somewhere else?" "I must marry this woman from Njargen," he replied. His father looked at him gravely and said, "You are your own master!"

The following day the young man returned to the village of Njargen. There, he himself negotiated all the details of the future marriage. Her parents agreed to the engagement and soon the young man started to visit her town regularly. One day before leaving to visit her, he went to his father and said, "Father, I am going to visit my wife." "I am not going to your bride. I am not sending her anything; let no one involve me in this affair. You own yourself. You can do whatever you like," responded his father.[3]

So the young man left for the village alone. When he reached the middle of the forest he was startled to see a skull, a plain skull. It had no feet, no chest and no hands. It had nothing. This head sat in the middle of the road so that when the young man approached it, he tried to side-step it and move just a little bit faster than he had walked before. But the skull called out to him,

81

"Come here and carry me with you!" The young man replied, "I . . . I am going on my way . . . in a hurry. How can I stop to take you with me?" "Take me along with you!" ordered the skull. Now the skull was a devil[4] who carried along with him a blacksmith's hammer, but still the young man refused. The skull then sprung high up into the air and rapped the young man on the head with a resounding 'KOW.' The young man was dazed but he picked up the skull and placed it into his traveling bag. Then he continued on his journey.

He walked on for a long time until he felt tired. Sweat was running down his cheeks. "I am sweating and very tired," he said to himself. But the skull chided him, "Who do you think sweats more, me in the sack or you out in the open?" The young man understood what this meant so he continued to travel farther.

When he reached his destination the young man greeted the people of Njargen and they responded politely. He entered into his fiancée's room and hung the traveling bag on one of the bedposts. After a while, the skull ordered him to place it on the bed but the young man refused. Immediately the skull sprung into the air and knocked the young man to the ground 'KOW.' So he removed it from the bag and placed it where it desired.

The young man's new in-laws soon brought him four large bowls of rice with goat-meat sauce to eat. The young man said that he was going to call some of the inhabitants of the compound to share the meal with him. But the skull told him not to call them. When the young man began to argue with the skull, it gave him another knock on the top of his head with the hammer. With that the young man became subdued. After closing the door of the house they sat down together to eat. But the skull ate everything. He ate from bowl to bowl until all of them were empty.

After finishing, the skull ordered him to wash all the food bowls. Again the young man refused saying, "That is not my job. I will call the children to take them." But the skull once again sprang up into the air and struck him with his hammer. The young man then washed everything and took them outside where he handed them over to the people. When they saw him with the cleaned bowls they were surprised to see that the four large bowls of rice and meat were completely empty. They said among themselves, "We do not understand our guest at all. His customs are very strange."[5]

Again near suppertime, the people prepared four more large bowls and presented them to their guest. They set the food down before the young man and departed. He then said, "I must call the people to come and share this meal with us." But the skull refused to share it. Instead, it ate everything by itself. For five successive days it continued to behave in that manner.

Late one evening, after the last cock crowed, the skull ordered the young man to carry it to the mosque. This time the young man agreed. He carried it inside the mosque and set it down on the floor. At once the skull began to defecate profusely. It continued until all the feces were ankle deep throughout the mosque. "Now let us get back to the house," said the skull. "Carry me," it ordered.

Just before dawn, an old man arose and prepared to go to the mosque to pray. He walked very slowly and stiffly POROK—POROK—POROK—POROK[6] until he reached the entrance to the mosque. "Alahu-ak-bar! Alahu-ak-bar,"[7] he intoned, reciting all the necessary prayers before stepping inside it. First he placed his hand down to touch whatever it was that was covering his feet. He smelled it and said, "Humm! Humm! Who has done this dreadful deed?" Shocked, he left the mosque and hurried back to his own compound. He remained there until mid-morning.

When he finally left his home, he called all the people together and asked them who defecated in the mosque. They all answered that it was not them. The old man decided to arrange a time for the entire village to assemble and be interrogated.

When the appointed time arrived, everyone showed up except the young man. He refused to go. The skull then ordered him to carry it into the assembly. When the young man refused the skull landed a severe blow to his head with his hammer 'KOW.' Subdued, the young man picked up the skull and placed it under his arm and proceeded towards the village square.

When he arrived there, the people asked "Who defecated in the mosque?" Then the skull said to him, "Go ahead. Tell them it was you!" But the young man refused. The skull sprung up from under his arm and hit him on top of his head 'KOW.' The young man began to stammer. The people again asked, "Who defecated in the mosque?" The skull insisted, "Tell them it was you!" but he still refused saying, "I am ashamed to admit that in front of my brother-in-law, father-in-law, and the rest of the people." The skull then delivered still another crack to the middle of his head 'KOW.' Then the young man fell down on the ground and cried out, "It was me! It was me! I defecated in the mosque. I defecated in the mosque."

With that admission the crowd began to scatter, whispering to one another, "That is *her* husband. That is *her* husband."

That same day there was a divorce. The young man was humiliated. He could no longer remain in that village, so he decided to return to his home.

On the road where he first encountered the skull, he was ordered by it to set it down and leave it. From that point, the young man continued on his journey alone.[8]

[1]Recorded by Malik Boye, a griot, in Porli, The Gambia. This narrative was recorded on November 1, 1973, in the compound of Bessi Njay before 53 men, women and children at about 8:00 p.m.

[2]An imaginary town often referred to in fictional narratives. It is a town recognized for its adherence to traditional customs.

[3]According to tradition, the first marriage is arranged by the parents. The young man may go to his father and tell him that he has met a girl he loves and wishes to marry. Inquiries are then made by the father concerning the suitability of the girl and the integrity of her family. Griots are usually consulted regarding the ancestral lineage of the intended spouse. If he decides the marriage should take place, the father sends her father a gift (usually kola-nuts) with the request for his daughter in marriage. After receiving it, the father consults his daughter and her mother for their consent. On their agreement, he gives their consent and shares the gift among the people in his compound, his friends and neighbors. After this, the young man may begin formally visiting his beloved.

[4]The Wolof narrator used the term *seytane,* from the Arabic for Satan. Since the final confrontation between the young man and the skull occurs in the Islamic mosque, Malik Boye's choice of Arabic terminology over a more traditional Wolof word is appropriate.

[5]Sharing, especially food, is a mark of cultural and personal pride. To refuse another food is a social disgrace, a positive sign that one is uncivilized.

[6]In Wolof, the verb *porok* or *parah* means moving with great dignity and formality. The repetition of the word is a literary convention which both fixes the image of the elder's movements in one's mind while it connotes the necessary background associations required for the fullest assault of what he encounters in the mosque.

[7]Wolof expression of Arabic formula *Allah Akbar,* Allah is Good.

[8]The behavior of the skull in the mosque is an abomination. Not only does it dishonor the young man as an accomplice but it brings shame to the entire community whose life revolves around the mosque and the religious ideals of Islam. The act represents a total scorn for the community, its ideals and standards. As such, it is a metaphorical statement, reflecting, on another level, the young man's rejections of his father's advice. By refusing to follow the traditional marriage customs, the young man mocks their relevance for him. In this story, the skull is the symbol of the highly individualistic, self-centered young man who refuses to follow traditions.

THE KORANIC TEACHER[1]

There was a story . . .
Our legs are crossed . . .
It happened here . . .
It was so . . .

I met a man, you know, who used to teach Koranic students. But any student who was sent to him to be taught, would be murdered by him. He murdered three students.

One child heard about this Koranic teacher, went and said, "Father," and he replied, "Yes?" He said, "As for me, the Koranic teacher who teaches there, I want him to teach me!" He said, "Oh, son, have you not made a mistake. That man, whomever he teaches, he destroys him. You said that you want him to teach you." He replied, "Me, I am going to learn there." He said, "Ah, Praise be to Allah, if it please you."

The child packed up his things and went to the Muslim teacher.

The Muslim teacher began to teach him.

It happened that one day the Muslim teacher was going to negotiate for a new wife. On that day he said to his new student, "Come with me to negotiate for a new wife." They mounted and rode on their horses KORPAT-KORPAT-KORPAT.[2] They traveled a very great distance. When they stopped, the teacher dismounted and went into the bushes to urinate HO-RO-RO-RO-RO and then he farted BIPP.[3] The young student then began to laugh HE-HE-HE-HE-HE-HEI. He said, "Ah, what are you laughing at?" He said, "I am laughing at nothing except the horse who is trying to catch flies." He said, "Yes, that is very good!" He continued to urinate until he was finished. He did what he had to do and then he mounted his horse again.

They traveled and traveled and traveled until they reached the town. He greeted all the people of the girl's compound with a very religious greeting. They responded to him with a religious greeting. They entered the house and sat down. They remained there until the next morning.

In the morning the people killed a goat, pounded the *chere,* and cooked the meal. They cooked and cooked for a long time.

The young student got up and went and said, "The Koranic teacher said that you should give him some *chere.*" They gave him some *chere.* He returned to their room and after a short while he went back and said, "The Koranic teacher said that you were to give him some meat to eat." They took some of the meat and gave it to him. The child went and ate everything himself. He ate it until he was satisfied.

He remained there until he knew that they were coming to serve dinner. He went and said, "The Koranic teacher said that you should send him two bowls. One bowl is insufficient."

Now the Koranic teacher did not know anything about this. The girl's family served two bowls and then brought the food to them. The Koranic teacher questioned, "Ah, they have sent two bowls?" The student said, "Ah, I understand by this that I do not have to share the same bowl with you. That is why this bowl is for you and this one is for me." The teacher said, "Yes, Praise be to Allah." The child sat in a corner and ate from his bowl. The teacher sat with his bowl and ate. The child ate and ate and ate until the bowl was finished. Then he returned to the house to sleep. The teacher also left the house of the girl's parents to sleep.

The child slept until it was night time. His stomach churned HURR-HURR-GUK! His stomach churned HURR-HURR-HURR, he farted BIPP and defecated *PARACHE-CHA-CHAJ.*[4] He said, "Hey, I have shit myself." Then he got up and took a small calabash spoon and picked up some of the shit. He took it to the house of the Koranic teacher's wife. The woman was sleeping. He put it on her. He returned and picked up some more. He returned to the man and put it on the Koranic teacher as he was sleeping.

The woman slept until she had to get up and urinate. She got up and moved about *YANG-YANG-YANG.*[5] She cried, "Mother . . . Mother, I have done something awful, I have shit myself. I do not know how to explain it." She said, "Go and wake up your father, child. Go and wake up your father." Her father was sleeping. He said, "Who is that?" The mother said, "Please do not shout, Samba. The child wants to go to the toilet. She just got out of bed and wanted to go to the toilet when she shit herself. She wants you to help her." The father then got up. When he got up, he touched something and felt something wet. He brought it to his nose to smell it. "Humm . . . Humm. I have done something. He brought it to his nose to smell it. "Humm . . . Humm. I have done something." She said, "What? You have done that?" The woman got up and felt as she touched it. She brought it up to her nose and smelt it and said, "OH . . . Oh, I do not know what to say about this."

The young student went and washed himself. He returned and listened intently.

The Koranic teacher was still lying in bed sleeping. The shit was on him but he did not know it because he was still sleeping, *HURR-HURR-HURR-HURR.*[6] They said, "Speak quietly; otherwise, if he wakes up, there will be trouble. I do not know what to say about this. If he wakes up, there will be trouble." They kept quiet.

When the cock crowed, the student got up. When he got up, he went into the town and called all the people together saying, "The Koranic teacher said that you should go and greet him. The Koranic teacher said that you should go and eat breakfast with him! You should eat with him." The whole town came to his room.

They came and opened the door where the Koranic teacher was sleeping. He got up and touched something wet. He smelled it. It smelled like shit. He said, "HE-HE-HE-HEI. I do not know what to say about this." He walked out and went to the toilet.

When he entered the toilet he said, "AI . . . AI . . . AI . . . I am a Koranic teacher. I do not know what to say about this. I do not know what to do with myself. I do not know how to explain this. I do not know how to get out of here. I do not know where I should be. I do not know what happened. I never heard of this before. I never saw this before. I do not know what to say about this. I do not know what to do."

The people then went to the Koranic teacher. He came out of the toilet and packed his luggage.

He set out on the road and told the young student to go home with him. He rode on his horse, galloping out from the back of the girl's compound. The child said, "Ah, Koranic teacher." He said, "Yes?" He said, "Stop! You said last night when we ate dinner, you said that a stranger does not suck the bones. The bones that you packed away, I forgot to bring them. Let me go and get them so that you may suck them." The Koranic teacher became very embarrassed. He was very embarrassed and he stopped. The child went and collected the bones and brought them back.

When he returned, the Koranic teacher looked at him with hate in his eyes. He looked at him with very evil eyes but he could not say anything because all the people were there.

The people walked with them for a while and then said, "Yes. Give our regards to your family." He said, "Yes, they will hear of it." "Let me be free. Let me be safe."

The people left them. The Koranic teacher said to himself, "He-He-He-Hei. I do not know what to say about all this. But *this* child, I am going to kill. I will kill him in a way which I have not used before on earth. It will be a very bad murder. He will never do it again."

They traveled for a long time until they reached a very muddy spot. They stopped. There was a deep hole on the side of the road. The Koranic teacher said, "Yes, come here. The shame you put on me. By the name of Allah, of all the students that I had and killed, you are going to be the next. By the name of Allah, I will kill you in a way which I have never killed any of my other students." He asked, "Yes?" and he replied, "Yes!"

Then he rushed at him with his horse. But there was thick mud and he slipped on it. He had wanted to kill him with his horse. The child ran towards the hole. He ran around the hole and the teacher followed him on the horse. When the horse was near the edge, the child pushed them. The horse fell into the hole while the Koranic teacher grabbed some weeds on the edge and he was dangling into the hole. He called out, "Come here! Come here! Do not go. Come and help me. Come. Come. Do not go. Come and help me." He said, "Teacher, what is it?" He said, "Go and call the townspeople to come and help me. Go quickly before I die. Go and help me before I die."

The child said, "What will you pay me? You must pay me before I go." He said, "Go to my herd of cattle in the Eastern Region. If you go there, there is a stick stuck into the ground. I have buried some money there, a lot of money. You can take it." He said, "That is not enough. You must add something else to that." He said, "You can take my whole herd of cattle and the three milking cows. Come and help me."

The child then strutted away WAHANY-WAHANY[7] and arrived at the town. He went to the compound and began to cry, "Al . . . Al . . . Al . . . Al." He met a woman who asked him, "Hey, why are you crying?" "My teacher and I were traveling together. He asked me to dig some dirt for him but I have no digging tool." She said, "Is that why you are crying?" He said, "Yes!" She said, "Come." He followed her. She said, "Here, take this *daba*,[8] which Allah gives to you. If you go, use it." He took the *daba*.

He returned to the Koranic teacher. The teacher said, "Are the people coming?" He replied, "Yes, I have brought a *daba*." He asked, "What are you going to do with it?" He said, "I am helping you." Then he cut off the weeds HEHU-HEHU-HEHU-HEHU[9] until the weeds were completely cut off. The Koranic teacher fell into the hole MURU-MURU-MURU.[10]

The child then left there walking WAHANY-WAHANY-WAHANY and returned to the compound and cried, "Al . . . Al . . . Al . . . Al." He said, "I am worried." They said, "You, why are you crying?" "As for me, I went with my teacher. We came to a road and he fell down and died in the bushes. He said that he gave me the three cows in his herd. I came back so that they would give them to me."

One man said, "You are lying! That is not the usual habit of our Koranic teacher."

The child then left the people and traveled into the Eastern Region where the herd of cattle was pasturing. He went to the stick in the ground and picked out the money. He approached the cows and asked the herdsman for them but the elders there refused.

He took the money. He took the money and returned to his father's home. He said, "Father, I told you to send me to the Koranic teacher. He is the one who could teach me. He taught me. I killed him. Now I have money. The money is here."[11]

[1]Narrated by Momat Sise, age 38, in Maka Gui, Senegal, at 9:00 p.m. on November 18 before 75-90 men, women and children. Momat Sise is a member of the gewel caste whose relatives live in Njau, The Gambia. He is an extremely active performer, moving about before his audience mimicking the characters he creates. When someone in the back of the audience creates a disturbance, however, he does not hesitate to shout out, *nopil-len,* shut up, everyone! or *deglu-len,* listen, everyone. He stated that this was the largest audience to which he narrated stories. In such large groups, he had to employ less creative techniques to control his audience.

[2]Onomatopoetic expression recreating the sound of galloping horses.

[3]Onomatopoetic expression recreating the sound of explosive flatulence.

[4]The use of these expressions provides a source of great humor to the narratives. The violent outbursts of the child and the Koranic teacher enables Momat Sise to draw his audience into the creative process, expressing their disgust for the characters and their unsociable behavior. The audience's laughter is confirmation of an opposing social etiquette.

[5]Onomatopoetic expression recreating the reverberations from the jewelry around her waist. Some young Wolof women wear hollow beads or small bells around their waist.

[6]Onomatopoetic expression recreating the sound of heavy snoring.

[7]An expression used to indicate that the young boy walked with very hard and determined steps as an indication of his supposed unhappiness.

[8]An agricultural instrument designed to plant small millet seeds. It is a six-foot-long pole with an iron blade at its tip. The farmer punches a series of holes with the blade thrust into the ground. Millet seeds are then placed in these holes and covered with soil. The blade must be very sharp to pierce through the hard crusted soil.

[9]An onomatopoetic expression recreating the chopping sound of the *daba* cutting weeds and beating the ground. The expression is related to the Wolof verb *heh,* to battle or wage war with someone or something.

[10]Ideophonic expression from the verb *muru,* to be covered or hidden. As the teacher falls into the hole, the image provided here indicates that quantities of dirt fell down on top of him and covered him up. This accounts for the fact that the teacher died in the hole.

[11]There exists in the Wolof traditions a large number of tales which feature precocious children (see "The Mendacious Child"). These narratives demonstrate that young children can learn from and then out-perform adults. Their purpose is often to highlight the weakness (both moral and physical) of those who should be exemplary models of good character. The impact of this narrative depends upon its pervasive sense of irony. There is the religious teacher who is hypocritically immoral and uncivilized; there is the young child who is vicious and cynical. The boy here bests his superior in wickedness and cunning. The theme of the narrative emerges from the shocking effect; adults must provide positive models for children to emulate.

KUMBA THE ORPHAN GIRL[1]

There was a story . . .
Our legs are crossed . . .
It happened here . . .
It was so . . .

Once there was an old woman who had very many children. Her children were lions, hyenas, tigers, and all the other wild animals.[2] She lived at the Sea of Denyal[3] with her children.

There were two girls who were both named Kumba. One of the girls' mothers was still alive while the other girl's mother was dead.

One day both Kumbas were tending their rice fields when two strange men approached them. When they reached the rice fields, they passed by Kumba the orphan to ask the other Kumba for some water, "Girl, please give me some water to drink." But she replied very rudely, "Not from my hand and surely not from my mother's calabash. Use your own hands." "But I cannot use my hands," said the man. "Then go away," barked the girl. So the men left her and approached Kumba the orphan. They said, "Girl, please give us some water." She took her calabash and filled it with water. Then she politely handed it to the men. "Thank you," said the men, "and may a white chicken clap for you."[4] They drank and drank until they were very full. Then they left.

When the step-mother arrived, her daughter told her what Kumba the orphan had done. The step-mother was very angry. She did not approve of Kumba the orphan using her calabash to give water to strange men. She yelled at the girl, "Now, since you were so daring, giving strange men water to drink, you must go to the Sea of Denyal and wash my calabash." Kumba the orphan picked up the calabash and began to cry and cry. She suddenly remembered all of the evil things that she had heard about the Sea of Denyal.

The next morning Kumba the orphan began to walk. She walked a long time until she reached the Sea of Denyal. There she saw an old woman who had one hand, one leg, and one ear. She greeted her and the woman said, "May a white chicken clap for you." She passed on, until she saw a tree that was braiding itself, branch to branch. She greeted it and it said to her, "May a white chicken clap for you." Farther along on her journey she saw two coconuts. They were trying to crack each other open by knocking into one another. She greeted them as she had greeted the others. She got down on her knees and said, "Salaam Alekum."[5] They replied, "Alekum Salaam. May a white chicken clap for you." Even farther along the path, she saw a cloth laundering itself and then two cows attempting to carry each other. She greeted them and they replied in turn, "May a white chicken clap for you."

Soon she encountered an old woman. She genuflected and greeted her, "Salaam Alekum." The old woman replied, "My child, Alekum Salaam. What are you doing here?" The girl replied, "We were at our ricefield when a man approached and asked for some water to drink. After I gave him water in our calabash, my mother sent me down here to wash it." "That woman, is she your real mother?" asked the woman. "No," replied the girl. "Then what is she to you?" "She is my step-mother. She is my father's second wife; she takes care of me since my mother is dead." "Alright," said the old woman. "Then hide your calabash in the tree and come and cook my meals for me." Kumba the orphan agreed.

She gave Kumba a piece of wood and a match stick. Then she brought a cooking pot and handed her a cup of water to pour into the pot. After the water was boiling, she gave her a year-old bone and told her to place it in the pot. Then she gave her a grain of rice to add to the mixture. It cooked and cooked until it was ready.

Later Kumba the orphan returned and opened the pot. To her surprise, it was full of rice and meat.

When the old woman returned she said, "Let us eat now. I have very bad children and since the sun is setting, they should soon be on their way home." They sat down and ate and ate until they were full. Then they drank until they were satisfied.

As it was getting late, the old woman told Kumba the orphan that it was time to go to bed. She advised her, "Slightly stab my children with this pin through the mattress during the night. They will think that this bed is full of bugs. In that way they will rise up early in the morning and then you can safely return home." Soon after Kumba crawled under the bed, a hyena arrived and said, "Mother, I smell human meat. You must have been eating meat again." "I am the only one here, unless you want to eat me," said the woman. "Of course I would not eat you, Mother," replied the hyena. Then the lion entered the compound. He said, "Mother, I too smell something." The mother replied, "It is nothing. Just go to bed." Soon the tiger returned and asked the same question.

He got the same reply. "It is nothing. Now go to bed."

Soon they were all asleep in the same bed. Kumba the orphan was under it. She began to jab the lion with her pin. He yelled out, "Mother, there are too many bugs in this bed." He got out of bed and scratched himself. Then he got back into bed. Kumba then pricked the hyena with the pin. He cried and cried about the bugs in his bed. "Mother, these bed-bugs are terrible," he moaned. The tiger too complained about being bitten. He got out of bed and scratched himself, crying and complaining. All night long they kept getting out of bed and scratching and complaining. At hearing the first cock crow in the pre-dawn light, they all awoke. They gladly hurried out of their beds thinking that they were running away from the bugs.

When her children had gone far away, the old woman awoke Kumba. She told her to go and wash the calabash in the water. When the girl returned, the old woman gave her three eggs. As she handed them to her she said, "After you walk some distance, break this egg. But do not be scared. In this one egg there are many cows. There is an entire herd of cattle. After you go farther on your journey, you should break this second egg. This one contains a flock of goats. Later, you should break the last egg. In it there are numerous servants." With that the old woman released the girl.

Kumba the orphan began to walk back to her village. After a long distance she cracked open one of the eggs. She saw a herd of cattle following her. She walked farther and cracked the second egg. Out came a flock of goats. She walked farther and then broke the last egg. Immediately numerous servants appeared. So they all walked in procession back to the girl's village.

When they arrived at the village, all the people were very surprised. When her step-mother arrived she asked, "YOU, where did all this come from?" Kumba the orphan replied, "I brought it home from the Sea of Denyal." The step-mother was very jealous so she asked, "How did you get all these riches?" The girl explained, "When I went to the Sea of Denyal, I met an old woman whose children were lions, tigers, and hyenas. She allowed me to stay there at her home for the night because it was too late to return to my own village. She gave me some wood and a match to light a fire. Then she handed me a cup of water, an old bone and a grain of rice. When the water was boiling in the pot, I added the bone and the grain of rice to cook. After it was cooked I looked into the pot and saw that it was full of meat and rice. Then we ate. When it was time to go to sleep, the old woman gave me a sewing needle. She said that her children were lions, tigers, and hyenas. She ordered me to sleep under their bed and to prick them with the needle throughout the night. They complained about the bed-bugs so they rose early in the morning and left the house. She then gave me three eggs and told me to break them on my way home. When I broke the eggs a herd of cattle, a flock of goats and numerous servants began to follow me. That is how I got all these things from the Sea of Denyal."

Kumba's mother was so jealous that she beat her own daughter. Kumba cried and cried. Her mother ordered her, "Now you too will go to the Sea of Denyal and bring home all those riches. You will do all those things that she did." So Kumba ran around the village telling everyone that she was going to the Sea of Denyal. "I am going to the Sea of Denyal. Do you see all the riches that Kumba the mother-less got from there? I bet that I will have *more* things since I have a living mother."

Kumba began her journey to the Sea of Denyal. She walked and walked until she reached the tree braiding itself. "My, what is this? Where have you ever seen a tree braiding itself?" she exclaimed. The tree replied, "You are very different from your companion that was here before. But go on, life is ahead of you." She walked on, until she came across the woman with one leg, one hand and one ear. "Now look at this strange sight," said the girl. "I know that if Kumba the orphan saw this she would have died." She yelled to the woman, "Hey, One leg, one hand, one ear, how do you walk?" The old woman was too astonished to answer. Kumba then said, "Get out of my way. I must go to the water to wash and clean myself."

She walked closer to the water where she met the woman whose children were lions, tigers and hyenas. The old woman approached her and warned, "You, be careful. Your companion was here but she did not act this way." "I don't care about anybody here," screamed the girl. "That is the way I shall act," added Kumba rudely.

The old woman then asked, "Why do you not come and cook for me?" But the girl replied, "I am going to wash first before I cook for you." "Why do you not cook for me first? Do you not know that this sea belongs to me? That is why it is called the Sea of Denyal." "I don't care who owns this sea. I don't care about that," answered the girl. Then she went into the water and washed.

When she was finished, the old woman gave her a piece of firewood and a match to prepare the fire for cooking. "Is this all the wood you will give me?" questioned the girl. "How can I light a fire with only this one piece of wood?" When the fire was built the old lady gave Kumba a pot and a cup of water to put in it. When the water was boiling she gave her a year old bone and a grain of rice. "How can I cook a meal for you when you only give me this old bone and one grain of rice?" asked Kumba. The old woman said, "Just cook it, that is all." Kumba kept complaining like that till it was time for them to go to sleep.

The old woman handed Kumba a sewing needle and told her, "You must sleep under the bed because I have very bad children. If they discover you in their bed, they will kill you. When they go to sleep prick them through the mattress with the needle so that they will get up early and leave the house." The girl took the needle.

When the lion, tiger and hyena arrived home they said, "It smells like human meat in here." Their mother replied, "It is only me that you smell. Now go to bed." After they were asleep, Kumba stabbed the lion with the needle. He woke up and yelled, "Hey, these bugs are getting worse. They bite much harder than before." Their mother said, "Just endure it. It will soon be morning." Kumba then jabbed the hyena. He cried out, "Mother, these bed-bugs are terrible. I can't stand it." "Just shut up. You are always complaining. Go back to sleep," returned his mother. Kumba then stabbed the tiger likewise, and he complained, "These bed-bugs are too much. I just can't sleep here." Before the first cock crow all the woman's children were out of bed and running in the bush.

In the morning the old woman awoke Kumba and greeted her, "How is the morning?" Kumba replied, "Where are my eggs? You are supposed to give me some eggs." The old woman gave Kumba her three eggs. Then she told her, "After you walk a short distance you must break this egg. After a little farther distance break this other egg. Then later you should break the last egg." Without listening, Kumba grabbed the eggs and began to run off towards her village. When she was only a short distance away she broke all three eggs at one time. Immediately there emerged numerous lions, tigers, and hyenas. As soon as they saw her they attacked her, tore her up and ate her. The only thing that they left was her necklace. It lay on the ground.

A bird was flying by at that time and saw the necklace. It swooped down and picked it up. It then flew towards the village. There Kumba's mother was waiting for her daughter to return with all the riches as Kumba the orphan did. She sat in front of her compound preparing her evening meal of steamed millet. The bird soon arrived in the village and began to sing:

THE GIRL WHO WENT TO THE SEA OF DENYAL,
THIS IS HER NECKLACE!
THE GIRL WHO WENT TO THE SEA OF DENYAL,
THIS IS HER NECKLACE!

Then the bird dropped the necklace into the pot of millet. Kumba's mother picked up the necklace and immediately recognized that it belonged to her daughter. At that moment she knew that her own Kumba had died at the Sea of Denyal.[6]

---

[1] Narrated by Yasay Djak, age 43, in Banjul, The Gambia, in her own room before four men and one child at 8:00 p.m. Yasay Djak is a member of the caste of silversmiths, *tega*.

[2] This old woman has human features but is the mother of all wild animals. In this tale she functions as an omnipotent being who has the ability to reward good conduct and punish evil.

³From the verb *deny,* disappear. This is the only reference to the Sea of Denyal which was recorded. Although there are numerous stories which feature large bodies of water with mysterious beings living there (see "The Evil Co-Wife" and "Tumani and His Mother's Promise"), this name appears only in Yasay Djak's tale. It is used here to signify that the location is a dangerous place, and that those going there disappear.

⁴An expression of good luck. The prized white chicken flaps its wings and announces to all that Kumba's behavior merits reward and honor. In Wolof narratives the chicken functions as a character who cannot keep secrets, a tattle-tale, a gossip. Here the chicken will spread praise.

⁵This Arabic expression of greeting conveys the awareness that Kumba the orphan is both polite and religious. Had she spoken a more traditional Wolof greeting, the religious dimension of her character would not have been implied by the narrator.

⁶The parallel structural development of this narrative provides contrast between the respective behaviors of the girls named Kumba. The girls each confront identical events from the initial sequence of the strangers' request for water, through the bizarre scenes on the road to Denyal, to the interaction with the mother of all the wild animals. The theme of this narrative evolves out of the contrast between the two paths chosen by them. Kumba the orphan chooses to express herself according to the ideals established for young Wolof women. She is hospitable, respectful, obedient, religious, courageous, and exhibits self control in the most illogical of situations. She is the ideal model of young Wolof womanhood. Her counterpart, however, chooses to express an anti-social personality, diametrically opposed to that of her step-sister. The rewards presented to the orphaned Kumba represent society's acknowledgment of her positive behavior. The death of her sister underscores the negative response of the community to her behavior. Kumba the orphan, however, is described as motherless to strengthen the mother's role in the development of her children. The mother who finds her daughter's necklace in the pot, was herself depicted as selfish, inhospitable and greedy. The negative model she presented to her daughter is reflected in that daughter's behavior. Mothers who want good daughters must themselves be good. Kumba's punishment is thus shared with her mother. For an African/American analogue of this tale see Alcee Fortier's tale from New Orleans, Louisiana, in the Journal of American Folklore, July-September, 1888, entitled "The Talking Eggs."

THE BROTHERS SAMBA[1]

There was a story . . .
Our legs are crossed . . .
It happened here . . .
It was so . . .

There was a man who had two wives. Each of these wives had sons who were named Samba.

When one of the wives died, the other wife became responsible for both of the sons, Samba the orphan and the Samba who had a mother.

Their father had a large herd of cattle which these sons shepherded in the fields.

One day Samba who had a mother took the herd of cows out into the fields. When he returned his mother approached her husband and said to him, "Tomorrow I want you to send Samba the orphan out to guard the herd. If you don't sent him to the river, I will leave you." She wanted Samba to go to the stream because there he would surely be killed by the lions, leopards, or other wild animals who hunted there. It was the Jerijang[2] river. This river was called the Jerijang.

That night the father called Samba and said to him, "Tomorrow you must take the cattle to the Jerijang river." The son replied, "Yes."

The next morning Samba prepared to leave for the Jerijang river. As he left the compound he began to sing:

> TODAY I WILL TEND THE CATTLE AT JERIJANG.
> FATHER SAID TEND THE CATTLE AT JERIJANG.
> I SAY TEND THE CATTLE AT WALO.[3]
> FATHER SAID TEND THE CATTLE AT JERIJANG.
> I SAY TEND THE CATTLE AT FAJONG.[4]
> FATHER SAID TEND THE CATTLE AT JERIJANG.

Now there was one large bull in the herd who answered:

> I, WHO AM STRONG, I, WHO AM BRAVE[5]

TODAY I WILL PROTECT YOU AT JERIJANG.

When he returned home his father asked him, "You, where did you take the cattle?" He replied, "I took the herd to Walo." His father then became angry. He said, "I told you to go to Jerijang, but you went to Walo. Tomorrow you *must* go to Jerijang."

In the morning the young boy untied all the cows and departed for Jerijang. On his way he sang out:

> PEOPLE SAY TEND THE CATTLE AT JERIJANG.
> FATHER SAYS TEND THE CATTLE AT JERIJANG.
> I SAY TEND THE CATTLE AT WALO.
> FATHER SAYS TEND THE CATTLE AT JERIJANG.
> I SAY TEND THE CATTLE AT WALO.
> FATHER SAYS TEND THE CATTLE AT JERIJANG.

The bull answered:

> I, WHO AM STRONG, I, WHO AM BRAVE
> TODAY I WILL PROTECT YOU AT JERIJANG.

When they returned home in the evening his father asked him, "You, where did you go today?" The young man replied, "I went to Walo." The father said, "Didn't I tell you yesterday to go to Jerijang instead of going to Walo?" His wife heard what Samba the orphan had said. She arrived and said to the husband, "If Samba the orphan does not go to the Jerijang river, then I will leave you."

The father then went to the boy and beat him severely.

Samba went to the place where the bull was tethered and asked him, "What should I do? I do not know what to do!" The bull replied to him, "You must get ready to leave for the Jerijang river tomorrow morning." The boy returned to his father.

In the morning they woke up and the father told his son, "If you do not go to the Jerijang river today I will surely kill you." He replied, "Alright."

Samba prepared the herd for the journey. As he walked out of the village he sang:

> TODAY I WILL TEND THE CATTLE AT JERIJANG.
> FATHER SAYS TEND THE CATTLE AT JERIJANG.
> I SAY TEND THE CATTLE AT WALO.
> FATHER SAYS TEND THE CATTLE AT JERIJANG.
> I SAY TEND THE CATTLE AT WALO.
> FATHER SAYS TEND THE CATTLE AT JERIJANG.

The bull replied:

> I, WHO AM STRONG, I, WHO AM BRAVE
> TODAY I WILL PROTECT YOU AT JERIJANG.

When he began to tend the cattle at Jerijang, a lion attacked him. But before the lion could touch him, the bull gored it with his horns and it died. Then a leopard approached and attacked Samba. Before he could reach the boy, the bull killed the leopard with his horns. A snake then came out of the bush and attacked the boy. The bull killed him before he even got close to the boy. The boy then cut a piece of flesh off each one of the animals and placed it into his sack.

When he got ready to leave, the boy placed the sack over his shoulder and began to walk home. On the way home the boy stopped and sang again:

TODAY I TENDED CATTLE AT JERIJANG.
FATHER SAID TEND THE CATTLE AT JERIJANG.
I SAID TEND THE CATTLE AT WALO.
FATHER SAID TEND THE CATTLE AT JERIJANG.
I SAID TEND THE CATTLE AT WALO.
FATHER SAID TEND THE CATTLE AT JERIJANG.

The bull answered:

I, WHO AM STRONG, I, WHO AM BRAVE
TODAY I WILL PROTECT YOU AT JERIJANG.

They walked and walked until they reached the father's home. When they arrived, the father asked him, "Where did you take the cattle today?" The boy replied, "I took them to Jerijang." He said, "You, you went to Jerijang and returned?" He said, "Yes!" Then he called his wife and said to her, "Samba the orphan went to the Jerijang river today and has returned." She said, "Has he brought back any evidence?" The boy then opened up his sack and showed them the pieces that he cut off from all the animals they killed. The wife could not believe that Samba the orphan could have gone to Jerijang nor that he killed all those animals. As she left the father's house the boy sang:

TODAY I TENDED CATTLE AT JERIJANG.
FATHER SAID TEND THE CATTLE AT JERIJANG.
I SAID TEND THE CATTLE AT WALO.
FATHER SAID TEND THE CATTLE AT JERIJANG.

and the bull replied:

I, WHO AM STRONG, I, WHO AM BRAVE,
TODAY I WILL PROTECT YOU AT JERIJANG.

In the morning Samba who had a mother was to tend the cattle. His mother called him and he came. She said, "You will tend the cattle at Jerijang today." He said, "That is good!"

He prepared the cattle and left for Jerijang. When he arrived there, the lion, the leopard, and the snake all attacked him. They fought with him until he died. They killed him. Samba who had a mother died.

When the cows returned home without Samba who had a mother, Samba the orphan went to his father and said, "Samba has not returned with his cattle." It was then that the father knew that Samba who had a mother had died.[6]

[1] Narrated by Aliu Sise, age 18, in Ker Jargo, The Gambia, on November 28 at 9:15 in the compound of Alkali Ibrama Gasama before 75-80 people.

[2] Exact location unknown, said to be a branch of the Senegal River near Walo State.

[3] One of the original Wolof States south of the Senegal River and near the Atlantic coast.

[4] Exact location unknown, said to be a small town near Louga, Senegal.

[5] In Wolof, *bansar,* a strong and courageous man.

[6] This narrative is structurally similar to the narrative "Kumba." Samba the orphan, despised by his step-mother, and unloved by his father, overcomes the fear of the river Jerijang and becomes a hero in his village. At first afraid, he accepts the encouragement of his favorite bull and faces the danger. The character of the bull in Wolof narratives is a symbol of male strength and courage. For Samba the orphan he provides a courageous model for him to imitate. This contrasts sharply with his own father who does not have the courage to stand up to his domineering wife. His jealous step-mother wants her own son to be recognized as a hero. She sends him to Jerijang but he is unprepared to face the dangers there and is destroyed. He did not have a courageous model to follow. It is significant that the closing image is that of the father, a pitiable man who lost control of himself, his wife, and his son.

SIDI NGALI AND
HIS TRAVELING COMPANIONS[1]

There was a story . . .
Our legs are crossed . . .
It happened here . . .
It was so . . .

There was a man who had twelve sons. Among the twelve sons the one who was the most violent was named Sidi Ngali. Sidi Ngali was responsible for the murder of the other eleven children. If he went to the farm and any of the other children bothered him, he would beat them with the back of his hand until they fell down and died. In this way many of the children died.

One day the father told him, "Now I am driving you out of my compound, Sidi Ngali. No one can live with you. You are a monster. Come on, GO! Go out of my house." The father drove his son out of town.

Sidi Ngali traveled a great distance in the bush until he spotted a withered tree. They call that tree *jana*.[2] He went, cut it and used it as a walking stick. He walked farther on until he came up to a stream. There he found a man lying on its bank sleeping. His name was Samba Hurr. Samba Hurr lay by the stream sleeping. Sidi Ngali approached him and raised his stick high up in the air and struck him repeatedly. Samba Hurr turned over and muttered, "Oh, this stream is not very nice to sleep near. While you sleep a whirlwind throws leaves against you." Sidi Ngali looked at him and said, "Get up, my friend, I think we can travel together."

They walked on and on for a long time until they approached a hill where they met a man by the name of Samba Tongo. When they met him, he was sleeping. Sidi Ngali raised his club and began to strike him repeatedly. Samba Tongo said, "Oh, some little creature is stinging me." Sidi Ngali said to him, "Man, let us go! We can live together!" He too got up and joined the other two men. There were three men in the traveling company now.

100

They traveled together for a long time until they came to a baobab tree. This was a very large baobab tree. As they approached the tree they said to one another, "Does this tree have a door?" They searched and said, "Oh yes, it *must* have a door!" They began to walk around it; they circled it for one week until they found the door.

They went inside the tree. When they were inside the tree, they met a *konderong*. The *konderong* lived there with his dog. The *konderong* asked them, "What is your mission here?" They replied, "We are looking for someone to live with." He said, "Yes?" and they said, "Yes! Our partner should be able to hunt." The *konderong* said, "We can do that." They all agreed to live together. The *konderong* said, "Praise be to Allah! You can stay with me." So they all lived with him in the tree.

In the morning the *konderong* said, "I will be going to hunt today. The forest has many elephants." The *konderong* went into the bush in the morning, killed ten elephants and put them on his head. He killed another ten elephants and placed them under his right arm. Then he killed ten more and stuffed them under his other arm.

After accomplishing that, he returned home. They lit a fire and placed a large cooking pot on it. Then they put the elephants into the pot and cooked them. The elephants cooked and cooked until they were well done. Then the *konderong* said, "Let us taste them." The *konderong* took an elephant and tasted it. Sidi Ngali took one and tasted it. Samba Tongo picked one and tasted it. Samba Hurr chose one and ate it. The dog then took one and tasted it. Sidi Ngali said to them, "Is this the way we have to live with this dog? If we cook and taste our food, does he taste the food too?" The *konderong* said, "Oh yes, certainly." Sidi Ngali said, "Alright, but I know that on the day I hunt, if we cook our food until it's ready to taste, and I taste it, if your dog then tastes it, I will knock him on his back until he chokes and goes *NGEH.*"[3] The *konderong* replied, "Then you will learn that I can beat you. I will knock you till you choke *NGEH.*" Sidi Ngali answered, "Alright!"

On the next day Samba Hurr went to the bush and killed ten elephants and placed them on his head. He killed another ten and put them under one arm. He killed another ten and put them under his other arm. When he returned home they prepared a fire with a cooking pot on it. They dropped the animals in and cooked them until they were well cooked. They put salt in the pot. The *konderong* then said, "Let us taste it now." He took one and ate it. Sidi Ngali took one and ate it. Samba Hurr chose one and ate it. Then Samba Tongo picked one and tasted it. The dog took one and tasted it. Sidi Ngali said, "Man, the day I go hunting, if you taste my food I will beat you till you say *NGEH.*" The *konderong* said, "That day I too will knock *you* until *you* say *NGEH.*"

Thereafter there remained only two to go hunting. Samba Tongo said, "Then tomorrow I will go hunting." In the morning he went into the bush and killed ten elephants and put them on his head. He killed another ten and put them under one arm and then killed another ten and placed them under his other arm. His total count was thirty elephants.

He returned home and the fire was prepared with the cooking pot on it. They cooked the elephants. Then they put salt on them. The *konderong* said, "Praise be to Allah, let us taste." He took one and tasted it. Sidi Ngali then took one and tasted it. Samba Hurr grabbed one and ate it. Samba Tongo chose one and tasted it. The dog came and selected one and tasted it. Sidi Ngali said to the dog, "I know that you are a depraved dog. When anyone hunts and we cook it and it is ready to taste, you also taste it. If I go to hunt and you do it, I will beat you till you say *NGEH.*" The *konderong* said, "Then *you* will learn. I will beat *you* until you say *NGEH.*" He replied, "Yes, Alright! Praise be to Allah."

The next morning Sidi Ngali went into the bush to hunt. He killed ten elephants and put them on his head. He killed another ten and put them under his right arm. He killed another ten and put them under the other arm. He said to himself, "I don't want to just be equal to them." So he killed an extra ten to share with his hunting partners. His total count was forty elephants.

He carried all of them back home and they began to cook them in the pot. The pot boiled until all the elephants were well cooked. Then they said, "Praise be to Allah. Let us salt the elephants." They took the salt and added it to the pot. The *konderong* said, "Let us taste them." He took one and tasted it. Sidi Ngali took one and tasted it. Samba Tongo took one and tasted it. Samba Hurr chose one and ate it. The dog selected one and tasted it. Sidi Ngali then knocked the dog on its back. The *konderong* returned the knock. The other men then said to themselves, "Our friend is being beaten by the *konderong.* We must help him if the *konderong* is to be defeated." Samba Hurr grabbed the *konderong.* Samba Tongo also grabbed the *konderong.* They fought and fought until a week's time had passed.

The tree in which they lived ascended into the sky "FUR-R-R-R-R-R-R-R[4] and landed in a field of millet. In this field there was a blind man who was scaring away the weaver birds. When the stones he had been throwing were all used up, he searched for more stones with his hands, crawling on the ground. When he touched the tree with his hand he thought that it was a stone. He put it into his sling shot and hurled it a great distance.

At that time there was a Fula[5] walking in the distance. He had just stopped and set down his calabash of fresh milk. When he opened the top of it to look in, the tree fell directly into the milk. The Fula took it out with his little finger and flipped it away.

It landed in the eye of a young child whose mother had just set it down. The child cried out, "Mother, you have just put something into my eye." The mother questioned, "Where is it?" But the child quickly responded, "Oh it is alright now. It has disappeared."[6]

[1]Narrated by Lamin Jeng in Bati Hai on November 1 at 8:45 p.m. in his father's compound before 31 men, women and children.

[2]In Wolof, *jana,* a very tall, thin hardwood tree. When they are cut up they are often used as ridgepoles in constructing roofs on homes and grain storage bins.

[3]Onomatopoetic expression recreating the sound of a person choking.

[4]The Wolof adverb *fur,* very, is used here to emphasize the tremendous distance the tree traveled in the sky.

[5]In Wolof, *Tukulor.* This refers to the group of people whose ancestors resided in the Futa Toro region of Senegal in the ancient state of Tekrur. The Fula people who reside among the Wolof are today known as shepherds, caring for their own large herds of cattle or those that belong to wealthy Wolof farmers and traders.

[6]This narrative is intended to stress the general relativity of all things in the world. It achieves this by focusing on excessive, destructive behavior and its relative value to other human beings. The excessive fratricidal behavior of Sidi Ngali in the initial narrative sequence provides the model for the interpretation of his subsequent activities. Sidi is presented in exaggerated Bunyanesque strokes whose exploits overwhelm the natural and social order of things. The following acts of sadism, the massacre of the elephants and their gluttonous consumption are depicted in an equally excessive design. The four repetitions of the hunting sequence emphasize this wastefulness. The grotesque behavior of Sidi Ngali and his traveling companions, however, does not amount to anything valuable or praiseworthy. In relation to the life of the small child at the end of the narrative, this behavior has no impact. It is judged worthless and inconsequential. Although the traveling companions acted like they were especially gifted in strength and endurance, their efforts were not accounted for by the other human beings in the tale. The *konderong* observes that their behavior is animalistic and predatory. He punishes them for thinking that they were better than his lowly dog. He reduces them and, thus, the relative value of their behaviors, to insignificance. What at first appeared overwhelming has been washed away in the blinking of the child's eye.

SAMBA THE SATAN AND
OMADI THE RIGHTEOUS[1]

There was a story . . .
Our legs are crossed . . .
It happened here . . .
It was so . . .

There was a man. He had two sons. One of them was named Samba the
Satan. The other was named Omadi the Righteous.

Their father told them, "Now I am going on a journey. The horse is here.
Your mother is pregnant. Kill the sheep for your mother if she delivers a child.
Name the child. If the horse delivers, then give her the hay and tie her in the
stable. Give her the hay to eat. It is time for me to depart and I do not know
when I will return." After that he left.

Soon afterwards their mother delivered a child. Samba the Satan took the
mother and tied her in the stable.

Omadi the Righteous said, "Samba! My father did not say to do that. He
said that if our mother delivered a child we should kill the sheep for her, and, if
the horse delivered, we should give her the hay." He replied, "This is what I am
going to do anyway." He tied his mother up and gave her the hay to eat. His
mother said, "To tell you the truth, I cannot eat hay." Then he beat her and beat
her until she died.

Omadi the Righteous said, "Oh, what shall I do? I am confused. I do not
know what we should do." Samba said, "I do not care. This is what I am doing
and if you don't watch out, I will kill you too."

Then the horse delivered. He went and killed the sheep which was to be
killed for the mother. He gave it to the horse. The horse refused to eat it. He
then killed it and its young child.

Omadi the Righteous then said, "Now, Samba the Satan, we must run away
from here. This is too much. Truly, we *must* run away." "Let us go."

104

They went. They walked and walked and walked until they came to a village. A chief owned that village. When they arrived there they went to the chief. The chief gave them his stable to sleep in.

Samba the Satan said, "This chief, why should he keep us in this stable to sleep. I am going to cut off the testicles of his horse." In those days, chiefs rode on horses.[2]

Samba the Satan went and cut off the testicles of the horse.

Omadi the Righteous wanted nothing but peace. He wanted only peace. So he said, to him, "If the chief discovers what we have done, he will kill us. Let us run away in the night."

They got up in the night and ran away until the people woke up and discovered what had been done to the horse's testicles. They said, "Let us go and catch them so that we can kill them." Then they left so that the people could kill them.

It happened that Samba the Satan had a very sharp knife. Just as the people were about to capture them a huge hawk flew down, picked them up and flew away with them just to help them. He flew away with them. Both of them knew that they were safely away from their pursuers.

Samba the Satan looked up and saw the belly of the hawk and said, "I will cut open the belly of the hawk and we will have a lot of meat." So he grabbed his knife and stabbed the belly of the hawk, and they all fell out of the sky.

When they landed each of them died.

After they had died one *jinn*[3] came along. He whipped them with his whip of life. They all got up. After they were standing the *jinn* said to them, "Get up! You see this? There are two roads here. If you take one, you will fight and fight and fight. If you survive you will be king. The other road, if you pass by on it, you will meet all types of pleasant things, but when you reach its end, you will become blind."

Samba the Satan said, "I will take the road where they will fight." So he traveled that road.

Omadi the Righteous said, "Come on, let us take this road." He replied, "No, I will not go that way."

He traveled on the other road and fought and fought until, when he reached the end of it, he became a king.

Omadi the Righteous traveled on the road of pleasure until, when he reached the end of it, he became blind.

When he became blind, he had to beg and beg and beg. One day he arrived at the compound of Samba the Satan. When Samba the Satan recognized him, he said, "What is your name?" He replied, "I am called Omadi the Righteous." He asked, "Do you know a brother of yours called Samba the Satan? Do you know what compound you are in?" He answered, "I am in the compound of a king." He said to him, "Yes, *that* is me."

Then he picked up a needle and thread and said, "Thread this!" He said, "I cannot thread that." He beat him severely. Then he took the whip of sight and beat him with it until he could see. Then he told him, "Look at all of this. I am its owner. What gave it to me was desire and heroism."[4]

[1]Narrated by Babu Cebu Cham, age 36, a blacksmith, *tega*, in Banjul, The Gambia, in his own room before 5 men on November 25 at 8:15 p.m. Babu Cham speaks English and French, having spent five years living in Dakar, Senegal, acting at the Daniel Sorano Theatre. Although he is not a griot, he has a reputation for story-telling both at the shipyards where he is employed and in his home neighborhood.

[2]This statement of historical fact is intended to clarify Samba the Satan's motivation. He seeks revenge for what he sees was a gross injustice. He feels that his honor and caste membership do not warrant such poor living arrangements. He feels the chief is deliberately dishonoring him; thus, he strikes out at the traditional authority figure. But his method of seeking justice confirms his shameful character.

[3]In some narratives this character appears as *jine*. The use of the term bears witness to the strong Islamic influence on the Wolof. This being functions in narratives just as the indigenous character termed *konderong*.

[4]Babu Cebu Cham's narratives consistently reflect his individual philosophy of life. As this story illustrates, his philosophy conflicts with the more communally oriented value system. A man living alone, far from his place of birth, his family and relatives, Babu Cham's narratives emphasize individualistic values. The behavior of Samba the Satan strongly illustrates his anti-social behavior. The initial sequence sets up the behavioral model which is continued throughout the tale. In this matriarchial society, his act of matricide represents a complete rejection of the society. Yet, unlike more traditional narratives, his anti-social hero is rewarded for his behavior. He becomes an important, wealthy king, glorying in his own strength and power. In discussing the narrative afterwards, Babu Cham stated, "If you are in this world you must have desire and bravery. To remain cowardly will not bring you happiness. Desire and heroism can give you everything." Omadi the Righteous, thus, becomes the narrative model for cowardice. He fails to find happiness precisely because he has accepted society's moral codes. In the hands of a traditional griot, this narrative would have had diametrically opposite results.

TWO LOVERS PUNISHED[1]

There was a story . . .
Our legs are crossed . . .
It happened here . . .
It was so . . .

There was a woman who had a husband. She also had a young man as her lover. The husband owned a sheep which he cared for. He fed it so well that the sheep became very heavy.[2]

One day he told his wife, "I am going on a journey." His wife replied, "That would be good. Are you going to stay away for a long period of time?" He answered, "I may be gone from home for two or three days." The woman said to him, "Oh, but that is quite a long time to be away."

The next morning the husband left home. He traveled only a short distance until he was out of the direct sight of his compound. He went behind a *naf*[3] and hid there until it became very dark. After the sun had completely set, the husband secretly returned to his compound and hid there.

Later in the evening, the woman's young lover entered the compound and went directly to his lover's house.

Then it began to rain.[4]

It was then that the husband disguised himself as a Koranic student. He approached his wife's house and began to chant, *"Alara bi Laram. Alara bi Laram. Alara bi Laram!"*[5]

The wife heard this singing and called out, "Who is that?" He replied, "I am an Islamic student." The woman questioned him, "What are you doing outside on a terrible night like this?" "I am soliciting alms," he answered. The woman said, "Alright. Come here then." When he approached her she gave him his alms.

Then he asked her, "Since it is raining this night, might I spend the rest of the night here?" She replied brusquely, "You, I wonder why you are even outside begging on a night like this. Oh, alright, lay down over there and go to sleep."

The young lover and the woman returned to their bed. When they had stretched out, the woman asked, "Student, what is your name?" He replied, "My name is 'Tomorrow is Shit.' " At that the wife and her young lover began to laugh loudly, "HA-HA-HA-HA-HA-HA!" Then she repeated her question, "What is your name?" Again he replied, "My name is 'Tomorrow is Shit.' "

They all remained inside the wife's house that night. In the morning, when the first rooster crowed, the husband awakened his wife after he had stabbed her young lover. The woman did not at first realize this. When she got out of bed she lit her oil lamp. Then she noticed that there was blood all over the bed and the floor. She turned to the student and he said to her, "Did I not tell you that 'Tomorrow is Shit'? I have killed your young lover. I am your husband." Then he proceeded to kill her.[6]

[1]Narrated by Momadu Kane, age 52, in Kuntair, The Gambia, on November 27 in the compound of the village chief, Aba Kan, before 7 men and 3 women at 9:15 p.m.

[2]A literary convention used to indicate that the person is very wealthy and important in the community. A person who owns a fat, well cared-for sheep has the necessary large farm to produce its feed and the hired help to look after the animal.

[3]After ground nuts or millet are harvested, they are stacked on the farms in large, round mounds to dry. These are often encircled with makeshift fencing to discourage wild animals from eating the crops.

[4]A literary convention used to indicate a very dangerous situation. It is for this reason that the beggar is allowed to spend the night with the woman and her lover.

[5]Wolof version of Arabic plea for alms, *Aribi Karam,* Allah's gift.

[6]Although this narrative may have general applicability as a warning to potential adulterous couples, it also illustrates an immediate social adaptability. Immediately after this tale was related, the three women in the audience hurriedly left the compound. When asked the reason for their abruptness, Momadu Kane smiled and said that the women knew that the story was intended for them. It appears that they were angry with him for exposing their friend in public. The guilty woman was, like the woman in the story, married to a very wealthy man in the village. The comparison was immediately recognized as it was intended. Mamadu Kane stressed that he told this narrative to inform the woman that her affair was not as clandestine as she believed and that she should end it. The grim ending of the tale was presented as a warning of possible disastrous repercussions that might eventuate if she persisted in her illicit affair.

THE BAG OF MONEY[1]

There was a story . . .
Our legs are crossed . . .
It happened here . . .
It was so . . .

There was a man who courted a woman until she became his wife. He brought her into his compound and he became her husband. The day he took her home was the last day that he ever had any money.

Although he had only that one wife, she was very disrespectful to him. Sometimes she cooked but refused to give him any food. If the husband wanted to go and visit his companions he had to go and ask her permission. When his wife would say, "No, you won't go to that house," he would go into his room and sit down.

He lived with his wife like that until they had their first son. They had another son when the first stopped breast-feeding. In time they had another son.

The hardships this man lived with made him very bitter. The woman would often sit and scold the man. When she beat him, he would run inside his house and cry and cry until his heart would cool down enough for him to sleep. He lived like that until his three sons grew up. Each of them became strong and very healthy.

They worked, but, whenever they earned any money, they would give it to their mother. They too did not care about their father. Because he was ashamed of his life, the husband stayed in the compound. He rarely left it.

If the wife cooked, say if she cooked *bena chin*,[2] the aroma of the food would reach him. The smell of the food would reach him but he would not be able to taste it.

He was afraid to go to another compound. So he continued to live with his hardships. He stayed with them until these things overcame him.

When the three sons were grown up, they shared their money with their mother and not their father. In addition to that degradation, he was never given a piece of *guru*.[3] He never could give any *guru* to his wife because he never had any money since his marriage began. That was the last time he ever held a penny in his hand.

One night when these torments became too painful, when his hunger was ravaging, and the beatings were unbearable, he decided to leave home. All of these degradations were due to his wife.

He had one friend in the village. One day the husband sat at home until it was night time. He listened to his wife until he knew that she was asleep. Then he opened his door without any noise and went to his friend in the village. He said to him, "My friend, I am tired. I am going away. I cannot say where I am going, but I am tired. I am going to look for something better. If I find it, I will return here. But please do not tell my wife. Go there in the morning and ask for me. If they tell you that I am not there, then tell them that I have gone on a long journey. Do not tell them anything else!" So the husband left in the middle of the night.

His friend slept until dawn and then came to the compound and asked the wife, "Where is your husband?" She said, "I have not seen him." He said, "He told me that he was going on a long journey sometime." She said, "Let him die wherever he has gone." With that his friend left that compound and went back to his own.

When the husband left town, he went into the world to search for money. But he did not find any. One day he met up with a man who gave him a two-shilling coin.[4] You know, he spent a year in the world searching but he could not find anything. There was only that day when he was given the two-shilling coin. He looked at the two-shilling coin that he had in his hand. He thought about the year that he had spent in the wilderness and wondered how he could go home.

You know these things they use to make water jars?[5] He picked up some pieces from one of the broken ones. He picked them up and placed them in a large pile. His mind told him to pick up those broken pieces of water jars. He took them home.

He took the two-shilling piece and placed it on top of them, measured them and cut them to the same size. For about one month he measured and cut the water jar pieces into the size of the two-shilling coin. When he had a bag full, he got a piece of cloth and measured it with the bag. He sewed it and put the pieces of stone that he had measured with the two-shilling piece into the bag until it became full. You know, if it's a cloth bag, the pieces will mark the sides of the bag just like a two-shilling piece.

He then prepared to go home. He put the real two-shilling piece inside. When he arrived home it was in the middle of the night. He saw that the wife had gone to bed and was asleep. He moved quietly and opened the door and entered inside. Then he put down the sack of stones. He took the sack of stones and placed it beside his bed. Then he closed his door quietly and slept.

When it was dawn he opened his door. When he opened it, one of his sons woke up and came out and saw the open door. He said, "My mother, what has opened my father's door?" She said, "It is open?" He replied, "Yes, it is open." She said, "I don't know what opened it." He went and peeped in at the door and found his father squatting in the middle of the bed. He did not greet him, but went back to his mother and said, "My mother, father is back home." She said, "Back?" He replied, "Yes." She said, "Let him die where he sits. Who asked him to return?"

The man heard her but he remained still. They all ate their breakfast but he still remained sitting. The wife still did not go to greet him or see him. She did not know what he came home with.

He sat for a while and then called one of his sons from among the three sons. He called one of them. He said, "Come here," and he came. But before he came he got up and untied the cloth bag and put the real two-shilling coin inside with the rest of the sack of stones. When the son came into the house, he untied the sack and took out the two-shillings and said, "Go and buy me some *guru*." He asked, "How much?" He said, "A shilling's worth."

The child went and bought a shilling's worth and brought it. He broke off one piece and said, "Go and give this to your mother." The son asked, "What about the change?" He replied, "Keep it."

The child went and gave his mother the *guru*. She said, "I am very surprised. I have never received anything like this since I was married and brought here. This is the first time that I have this from him. This surprises me very much." He said, "In the name of Allah mother, this two-shilling coin which he gave me to buy a shilling's worth of *guru* was from a sack of money. A full sack of money which he placed by the side of his bed." She replied, "A full sack of money?" He said, "Yes! Yes . . . a sack of money! It was my present. He untied it and gave me a two-shilling piece." She said, "Ah! That's it."

This wife sat for a while and said, "Let me go and greet him." She approached the door and said, "Salaam Alekum." The husband replied, "Alekum Salaam. How are the people?" She said, "They are in here." "Are they in peace?" She replied, "They are in peace. Ah, you have been gone a long time!" and he replied, "OH, yes!"

Then she returned to her house. She said to her other son, "Come here. Where has your father been? Your father, since he was born, he never had a sixpence. Today he has a sack of money. I don't know where he got the money. Has he stolen it?" They said, "No, he was only in the brush for a year working. If he returns with a sack of money, that is only fair." She said, "Then take good care of your father."

This woman had a large herd of goats; they were extremely numerous. There were also very many sheep and chickens in the compound. In the past they had killed a chicken every day but the husband had never tasted them before. When she saw the sack of money that morning, she went and caught one chicken and prepared it with all the proper ingredients. She went and met him in his house and knelt down and placed it in front of him. She left and returned with water for washing his hands and for drinking. All these things the woman never did for him before.

The husband ate until he was satisfied. Then he called her and she came and removed the basin.

The husband sat in the bed and said:

> ALHAMDULILAI, RABIL HALAMINA.[6]
> OH ME, LA ILA HA ILAHA.
> SINCE I MARRIED THIS WOMAN, UNTIL TODAY,
> I HAVE NEVER GOT THIS FROM HER.
> TODAY I HAVE CHICKEN WELL PREPARED.
> ALHAMDULILAI, RABIL HALAMINA.

They remained sitting until it was lunch time. She went and caught another chicken. She killed it. She cooked it until it was perfectly seasoned with all the proper ingredients. She then took everything and brought it to him to eat lunch. He ate until he was satisfied.

When evening was approaching, she returned and killed another chicken for dinner. When it was prepared he ate all of this chicken.

When he knew that it was bedtime, he called the eldest son and he came. He said to him, "Before I left here, I saw you with a sack of cement. Is it still here? Is there a little bit of it left?" He replied, "Yes, I have a sack left." He said, "Go and bring it to me and also bring me a shovel." He went away and returned with a shovel and the sack of cement.

He said to him, "Move the bed aside and place it over there." In the past whatever he told them to do, they refused. Now they moved the bed aside. He said to them, "Dig a very deep hole here." He said, "Wet the cement and mix it with sand. Then plaster the inside." They plastered the inside of the hole. He said, "Now stop!" He did not allow them to touch it. He took the sack, pretending that it was heavy and put it in the hole and said, "Bury it." They covered it. He said, "Cement the top of it." They cemented the top. He said, "Now return the bed to its place." They returned the bed. He said to them, "Sit down," and they sat down.

He said, "You have seen what I have done. Do you know why?" They replied, "NO! NO!" He said, "Ever since I was born, I have had no money. I remained that way until Allah helped me to find a sack of money. You are my three sons. I used to think as I was living here that I might die without leaving anything at all for you. That used to be my dream at night. But Allah has removed those thoughts from me. Now the money is here. I will not eat even one *butut.*[7] You will not eat one *butut.* And I will not give your mother even a sixpence. I will not do anything with it. I will not buy even a shirt for myself. So when I die you will be able to take it as your inheritance. Take this sack of money and share it among yourselves, so that you may know that your father has left you with something. This is what I have called you for. Now go to bed."

They went away. Their mother asked them, "What did he call you for?" They replied, "In the name of Allah mother, he has a big sack of money. We dug a big hole and he put it under the middle of his bed. He cemented it and put the sack into the hole. Then he cemented the top of the hole. He said that he wants us to take the money if he dies, since we are his heirs. But he is not going to eat even one *butut* out of it." She said, "Ah, your father has been spoken to by Allah. Serve him well. What I used to do to him now will end. I will serve him until he dies."

Every day she would kill a chicken for him. On the day that they cemented the sack of money she even killed a fat sheep in the morning and served lamb for lunch and dinner and then again breakfast. Other days she would begin by killing a chicken; she would also kill sheep and goats. If she killed a goat in the morning for lunch she would also kill a chicken in the afternoon for supper.

They lived that way for a long time. The supply of chickens never diminished. Even the supply of goats was unending. Yet the husband had never tasted these things before. Now he sat and lived such a good life that he became very fat. If you saw him, he looked very fresh.

His sons worked. They made money and gave it to their mother. She kept this money. She bought some cloth for her husband to wear. The husband wore this cloth, ate all her meat and sat around the house. That is all he did until one day he became very sick. When he became ill his wife took good care of him, following him here and there, up and down, until finally, he died.

When he died, the eldest son went into town and told everyone, "My father is dead." He notified the whole town about it.

At the funeral all the people attended. The eldest son called his two brothers. They came and he said to them, "Our father is dead. We have no money now. What we had in money is what we have been using. Now it is finished. Since he has left us a big sack of money for his funeral, we should do all we can so that the people will know that he has left behind valuable sons.

114

Tomorrow, if we go and take the money, they will say, "Their father has left a lot of money, a whole sack of money. They will never be poor again."

The second eldest son said, "What are we to do now?" The eldest replied, "I will borrow a bull, a bull that is just three years old. Whatever they will charge me, I will pay for it. When we share our inheritance, I will take out the cost of the bull from it and pay for it." They replied, "That is good." The other sons said, "I, too, am going to borrow a bag of rice." The youngest said, "I will be responsible for the tomatoes, onions and oil. Let them be in my hands."

Then they all went and borrowed what they needed for the celebration and brought it home.

Soon all the people gathered in their compound. When the people arrived, they killed the bull and cooked it. The people ate until they were satisfied. After the funeral they left.

When the people had departed, the sons had to bury their father. The people had departed for their own compounds and villages. After they had waited until night time, the eldest son called the two younger brothers together and said, "Come now." They went inside their father's house and locked the door. They lit a lamp. The eldest said, "Now, since father is dead, I would like to see what he left for us, so that tomorrow I can go and pay for my bull, you can pay for the rice, and you too can pay for your oil, tomatoes, and onions." They said, "Praise be to Allah, that is good."

Then they picked up the shovels and started to dig. They dug and dug and dug until the uncovered the sack. Then they pulled it out and placed it in the middle of the house. They began to untie it. They held the sack by its sides and poured it down in disbelief. They said, *"LA ILAHA ILAHA.*[8] What is all this?" The second son said to the eldest, "My brother, what is this?" He said, "Praise be to Allah, have mercy on us. Look what our father has done to us." The eldest son said, "Yes, but what really worries me and what is on my mind is the bull which I borrowed from that nobleman.[9] I told him that I would pay him tomorrow morning." The second eldest said, "What about me and the rice I borrowed?" Their youngest brother said, "Me, I am only a child and I have nothing. I borrowed all the oil, tomatoes, and onions."

The eldest son then said accusingly to them, "What do both of you know about this? What do you know about what father has done to us?" They both answered, "Nothing." He said, "Then let us go and uncover his grave, take him out and beat him."

[1]Narrated by Keba Hadi Sise, age 44, in Njau, The Gambia, on October 17 at 10:00 p.m. before 10 men, 1 woman, and 1 child, in his own compound. Keba Hadi Sise is a well-known griot whose specialties are drumming, singing and story-telling. One week after harvesting his ground nuts and

millet, he departed for a tour of villages in Senegal where he would perform for dances, wrestling contests and engagement celebrations.

[2]Meal made from rice with a relish of fish or meat cooked in peanut oil with onions, tomatoes, pepper and spices. This meal can also be served with steamed millet, though rice is preferred.

[3]Wolof for Kola-nuts. Most are imported from Sierra Leone. Although used as a stimulant and as an aid in alleviating hunger, its principal importance is social. It is a goodwill offering, a sign of mutual respect and openness. The sharing of *guru* preceeds any formal occassion from welcoming a visitor, negotiating for the purchase of a goat or cow, seeking advice from a friend or elder, to distributing gifts at a funeral.

[4]In Wolof this is called *tulalibar* and reflects the French influence on the Wolof in The Gambia. The Wolof *libar,* pound, is derived from the French *livre.* Migrant farmers from Senegal have introduced many French-influenced words into Gambian Wolof.

[5]These are made with clay which has been drawn into a thin-walled vase with a narrow neck line. The clay pots are fired in an open air fire that is maintained with dry grass. Quality vases are extremely thin to minimize the total weight of one filled with water.

[6]Arabic expression for "Praise be to Allah. I have faith in the Lord."

[7]Current Gambian term for a penny. In the British colonial period, this term signified a half-penny.

[8]Wolof expression for the Arabic phrase *La illahi ila Allah,* There is no God but Allah.

[9]In Wolof, *jambur.* This term is used to refer to: members of the royal lineages, from which the rulers of the traditional Wolof states were chosen; members of the noble lineages, who had the right to select the rulers; and the common peasant farmers who were not born into any of the craft castes.

NGURMI THE LAZY HUSBAND, I[1]

There was a story . . .
Our legs are crossed . . .
It happened here . . .
It was so . . .

There was once a man who was very greedy in his eating habits. He woke up every morning and went to his farm. His wife stayed at home cooking for him. After he ate his lunch he was still hungry.

One day he devised a plan. His wife took food to him in the field and he ate it until it was finished. He devised a plan. He removed his ears and put them in a baobab tree. He hung them in the tree and walked back to his village. He thought, before my wife brings me my lunch, I will beg for more food. He went into the village and begged and begged until he felt that he was satisfied. He then returned to the field.

Soon after his wife brought him his lunch and he ate. After lunch he went into town and sang: "Ngurmi[2] is begging." He took all the food offerings of the people and ate them until he was full. Then he hid the bowl with which he used to beg. He returned to the tree, took back his ears and reattached them to his head.

Then his wife came and brought him dinner. "Thank you," he said to her. "Your work seems undone today," his wife noted. "My whole body is in pain. Today all my bones are aching." When his wife set his dinner down, again he ate it until he was satisfied.

The next day he again went out to his farm. He went to the farm and worked a little. Then, remembering his scheme to obtain food, he took off his ears, hung them on the tree and returned to the village. "Ngurmi is begging," he said at every compound he visited. When they gave him food, he ate it. After he was finished he went back to his farm.

Whenever he wanted to reaffix his ears he would say:

116

EARS, NOSE, CHIN, COME BACK TO ME!
COME, OBEY YOUR MASTER!

The ears would fly from the tree and take their rightful position on the man's head.

The next day he went back to the farm and did the same thing. He went to the village and begged and begged. Before he left, he put his ears in the tree and went to the village. All the people in the town gave him some food. Wherever he went he said, "Ngurmi is begging," and they gave him food.

Allah is so good, that one day his daughter looked at him for a long time and went and told her mother, "The beggar's eyes are just like my father's." "Allah forbid. Never say that! Do you think that your father would come here to beg and say 'Ngurmi is begging'?" The girl insisted, "But he *looks* like my father."

After that the woman became very troubled. She went to one of the elders and said to him, "My daughter says that the man without ears who comes to town to beg for food and says 'Ngurmi is begging' looks just like my husband. My daughter says she recognizes him. Is it her father?" The elder replied, "Yes, your husband always keeps his ears in a tree by his farm. I have seen him. He comes to town and says 'Ngurmi is begging.' After the people give him food, he eats it and returns to his farm. When he wants to take back his ears he says:

EARS, NOSE, CHIN, COME BACK TO ME!
COME BACK TO YOUR MASTER!

Then the ears go back to him. When you go and meet him at the farm, you do not know that he has eaten food from the whole town. You give him lunch and he eats that too." When she heard this, the woman only nodded her head affirmatively. "Do you know what to do?" asked the elder. "Tomorrow you should go to the tree before he arrives there. If you go just say:

EARS, NOSE, CHIN, COME BACK TO ME!
COME BACK TO YOUR MASTER!

Then you can take your husband's ears."

The woman went home and thought about the plan which the elder had told her. She cooked lunch until it was halfway prepared. Then she left it cooking and went to the farm. When she arrived there, she saw the ears hanging on the tree. She said:

EARS, NOSE, CHIN, COME TO ME!
COME BACK TO YOUR MASTER!

The ears flew towards her and she caught them. She folded them into her robes and brought them home.

The husband was all this time in the village saying, "Ngurmi is begging." The people there gave him food. After he ate all of their offerings and hid his bowl, he went back to the farm. When he approached the tree he said:

EARS, NOSE, CHIN, COME TO ME!
COME BACK TO YOUR MASTER!

But nothing happened. He repeated:

EARS, NOSE, CHIN, COME TO ME!
COME BACK TO YOUR MASTER!

Again there was no response. He said, "Oh, I don't know where my ears are, or who took them." He left and went to a thorn tree. This is a very dangerous tree. He scratched himself with its thorns until his blood spread all over his body. He then began to wander around in the bush. When his wife saw him she said, "I was just bringing lunch for you, but what has happened to you?" "Oh, what has happened to me I cannot say. I climbed a tree and fell down. Don't you see my body? Do you see how the blood runs all over me? Even my ears were caught there in that tree." "What?" she asked. "Yes! My ears were cut off by the sharp thorns."

"Oh, my husband, you do not know that I had been to the farm before you. I went to the tree where you hang your ears before you go to the village to beg for food while singing, 'Ngurmi is begging.' " He said, "Humm!" She said, "I went to that tree and said aloud:

EARS, NOSE, CHIN, COME TO ME!
COME BACK TO YOUR MASTER!

The ears flew to me. I caught them and kept them somewhere. But you know, Ngurmi, you are very shameless. Really, you and your insatiable hunger. We gave you everything we had and now that is finished. Still, you left your ears in the tree and came back and sang:

EARS, NOSE, CHIN, COME TO ME!
COME BACK TO YOUR MASTER!

I thought you would *never* do that!"

Ngurmi became very ashamed and regretful. His wife scolded him, "Ngurmi, if you are going to be this way, I will not remain with you!" With that Ngurmi became so ashamed that he turned into a monkey,[3] ran off, and lived in the wastelands.

[1]Narrated by Lamin Jeng in Bati Hai, The Gambia, in his father's compound on November 20 at 4:15 p.m. before 7 men.

[2]Literally, one without ears.

[3]In Wolof, *golo*. In the Wolof narrative tradition the monkey is a shameless character, regularly clowning about in distasteful situations. As a result it is viewed as shameful and weak (see "The Dog and the Monkey Court the Same Girl"). In this tale, Ngurmi realizes that he has acted shamefully, like a monkey, and so becomes one. November, being the normal month for the beginning of the millet and rice harvest, is an especially difficult month for subsistence farmers. With food supplies rapidly dwindling, hunger and excessive greed are common themes which appear in tales. After the harvest, when food reserves are again plentiful, these themes rarely appear. That they feature in tales at this particular time is indicative of their social utility. See the following two tales, "Ngurmi the Lazy Husband, II" and "The Greedy Father" for comparison.

NGURMI THE LAZY HUSBAND, II[1]

There was a story . . .
Our legs are crossed . . .
It happened here . . .
It was so . . .

Once there was a man who was extremely lazy. He decided to cultivate a farm. Every day he would go to the farm like all the other men. Everyone said that Ngurmi was a good man. Every day Ngurmi would pack up his tools and travel to his field. When the other farmers were out of sight Ngurmi would go and sit down underneath a *nger*[2] bush. He would then call out:

EARS, CHIN, EYES AND MOUTH,
COME, LEAVE YOUR MASTER!

After saying that his face would change its appearance; his ears, chin, eyes, and mouth would fall from his face and hide under the *nger* bush. No one could recognize him.

He went into the village and asked all the women if they would let him pound their millet. The women would say to him, "Come, follow me." He would enter into their compounds and tell the women that he only needed the powder from the pounded millet and the water from its rinsing. The women would sing:

NGURMI IS DEFORMED; NGURMI IS DEFORMED;

as they pounded their millet. Then they would sit down and winnow the pounded millet until it was clean. When they gave it to Ngurmi, he would eat all of the powder until he was satisfied. Then he would drink the rinse water until his stomach was full. Then he would get up and leave the village.

When he returned to the *nger* bush he would repeat:

EARS, CHIN, EYES AND MOUTH,
COME TO YOUR MASTER!

Then the parts of his face that had departed would return from under the bush. His face would return to normal.

He then went into the field and stood there. He saw his wife approaching the farm. She said to him, "It does not look like you have done any work today." But he replied, "I am only one man; I am only one man." The wife then began to prepare his lunch for him. He ate until it was finished and she returned to the village.

Ngurmi picked up his *iler*[3] and began to hoe and scrape the soil. He worked and worked until he realized that his wife was out of sight. He then threw his *iler* far into the bushes, and returned to the foot of the *nger* bush and said:

> EARS, CHIN, EYES AND MOUTH,
> LEAVE YOUR MASTER!

His eyes, chin, ears and mouth would then leave him and rest under the tree. His face would be deformed. He walked back into the village. He asked the women if he could help them pound their millet. The women would sing:

> NGURMI IS DEFORMED; NGURMI IS DEFORMED;

as they prepared their millet. They would winnow the millet until it was clean. Ngurmi would eat all of the powder until he was full. Then he would drink the rinse water until his stomach was bloated. When he could barely stand up, he left the village and went back to his fields. When he returned, all the other men were working in the hot sun. They said to each other, "What is happening at his farm? If we do not work, we will have nothing." Ngurmi saw that his wife was approaching in the distance. He raised up his arms, pretending to work, as he shouted out loud, "I am only one man, I am only one man."

His wife arrived and accused him, "You, your farm looks very different from all the other men's farms. As I was walking here, I saw one *iler* laying on the side of the path. If you do not watch what you are doing and work, you will not harvest anything." "Who told you that?" he countered. "I am the hardest worker here in the fields. You see that I get up at dawn every morning and never rest." The woman nodded her head and said, "Yes." She then prepared Ngurmi his meal. He ate it until it was finished.

When the woman returned home, Ngurmi again went back to the tree. Standing at the foot of the *nger* tree he said:

> EARS, CHIN, EYES AND MOUTH,
> LEAVE YOUR MASTER!

Immediately his ears, chin, eyes and mouth would fall off his face and drop to the foot of the tree. His face would be completely transformed. Then he would walk back to the village and beg some food from the women. He helped them pound their millet. The women would sing:

> NGURMI IS DEFORMED; NGURMI IS DEFORMED;

as they prepared their millet. They would winnow their millet until it was clean. When they gave it to Ngurmi, he would eat all of the powder until he was full. Then he would drink and drink the rinse water until his stomach was bloated.

When he was completely satisfied, he returned to his farm. He stood at the foot of the *nger* tree and said:

EARS, CHIN, EYES AND MOUTH,
COME BACK TO YOUR MASTER!

His ears, chin, eyes and mouth would leave their hiding place and reattach themselves in the proper places on his face.

He acted like that for a whole season until it was harvest time. One day when he went to the foot of the tree he said:

EARS, CHIN, EYES AND MOUTH,
LEAVE YOUR MASTER!

His wife was hiding nearby in the bushes. She saw how his ears, chin, eyes and mouth left him and hid at the foot of the *nger*. She saw how her husband changed his face. After Ngurmi left for the village, his wife approached the *nger* bush and said:

EARS, CHIN, EYES AND MOUTH,
COME TO YOUR MASTER!

When she said that, her husband's ears, chin, eyes and mouth flew out from under the tree and landed in her open calabash. She caught them there and held them inside the calabash. Then she went home.

When Ngurmi was finished begging food in the village, he returned to the fields. He stood under the *nger* bush and said:

EARS, CHIN, EYES AND MOUTH,
COME BACK TO YOUR MASTER!

But nothing happened. He said:

EARS, CHIN, EYES AND MOUTH,
COME BACK TO YOUR MASTER!

But again nothing happened. He waited for a while and then repeated:

EARS, CHIN, EYES AND MOUTH,
COME BACK TO YOUR MASTER!

But he saw nothing. He shouted, "MY ALLAH!" He frantically turned in every direction, looking for his facial parts, but he saw nothing. He fell to his knees and scampered and crawled to his village.

When he arrived in his compound, he called out, "KUMBA! KUMBA!" and she replied, "Yes." "Kumba, please help me. There has been an accident. Throw me my cutlass." Kumba immediately got her husband's cutlass and threw it to him. But the man screamed out so all the people in the neighboring compounds could hear, "Help me, please help me. Kumba cut off my head, she cut off my head." The people rushed into their compound and saw how deformed Ngurmi's face was. Then they asked where the parts of Ngurmi's face were. No one could find them.

They decided to call the chief. When he arrived he ordered Kumba to approach him. He asked her if she had killed her husband. She said, "Do you see any blood around here? How could I have killed him and there not be any blood remaining? He just asked me to throw him his cutlass, so I did." The people then began looking for blood on the ground, but they found none.

Kumba then said, "Go and look at his farm. He has no millet to harvest. He was *too* lazy to work like the other farmers. I used to go to his farm and cook for him; I have cooked everything I had for him. He used to stand before the *nger* bush and say, 'EARS, CHIN, EYES AND MOUTH, LEAVE YOUR MASTER.' After his ears, chin, eyes and mouth would fall from his face, he would walk to the village and help the women pound their millet. He would eat all the remaining millet powder and rinse water and then return to his field. One day I went to the tree and said, 'Ears, chin, eyes and mouth, come back to your master,' and took parts of his face away." Then she opened the calabash and showed all the people the facial parts. When she did that, her husband was so embarrassed that he died.

[1]Narrated by Yasay Djak, age 44, in Banjul, The Gambia, on November 8, at 8:30 p.m. in her own compound before 4 men and one child.

[2]A short squatty shrub covered with small, whitish-colored leaves.

[3]A half-moon shaped, bladed farming instrument on a short handle used to weed around groundnut plants. Its construction necessitates the assumption of a squatting position whereby the tool can cut through the dry soil in a scraping motion.

THE GREEDY FATHER¹

There was a story . . .
Our legs are crossed . . .
It happened here . . .
It was so . . .

During the hungry season, there was a very greedy man. Whatever his wife cooked for him was not enough to satisfy him.

He decided to transfer their food reserves to his hiding place in a hollowed out baobab tree. He removed the stored food reserves and put them in the baobab tree.

One day the child approached his father and said, "Father, I am worried about the stored food." His father replied quickly, "You know, every day we use the food from the food reserves and we do not add anything new." "But father, there is *too* much missing."

The father kept on transferring the food to the secret cache.

One day the father gathered his children and told them, "One day this sickness that I have will kill me. If I die, bury me in the hollowed out baobab tree. That will be my grave."²

Not long after that this man died. One of the children remembered what his father had said and told the family, "My father has left a message." So the people took the dead man and buried him in the baobab tree. He remained there for a long time.

One day a young boy went to a field near the baobab tree to scare away the birds from the family's millet crop.³ The child sang:

> THERE IS GREAT SUFFERING, GREAT SUFFERING,
> MY MOTHER HAS GOT A HEARTACHE,
> MY FATHER FARMED BUT WE DID NOT EAT.

A voice replied:

> YOUR FATHER IS DEAD BUT HE IS HAPPY;
> DEAD IN THE GRAVE, DEAD IN THE GRAVE;

ONLY SOME SALT HE HAS FORGOT;
SAMBA HAS GOTTEN USED TO THE SNAKES.

The child stood motionless for a long time staring at the tree. Then he went home.

At home he told his mother, "Mother, there is something in that tree." "You are just afraid to be near that tree where we buried your father; you are only scared. It is nothing." The mother then cooked their meal and they ate it.

The following day the young child returned to his post in the field of millet and sang:

THERE IS GREAT SUFFERING, GREAT SUFFERING;
MY MOTHER'S HEART IS BROKEN;
MY FATHER FARMED BUT WE DID NOT EAT.

A voice replied:

YOUR FATHER IS DEAD BUT HE IS HAPPY;
ONLY SOME SALT HE HAS FORGOT;
DEAD IN THE GRAVE, DEAD IN THE GRAVE;
SAMBA HAS GOTTEN USED TO THE SNAKES.

The child said, "Oh, Allah! I will tell no one of this except my mother."

He ran back to the village and said, "Mother, honestly mother, there is something talking in that tree." His mother replied, "It is nothing, my child; it is nothing. Your father has been buried there. We will transfer you to another lookout post." But the boy persisted, "Honestly mother, just come with me when I am scaring away the birds." The woman relented and agreed to go with him the next morning.

In the morning the woman and her child went to the millet fields. The boy climbed up into his raised lookout post while the mother sat under it. The boy sang:

THERE IS GREAT SUFFERING, GREAT SUFFERING;
MY MOTHER'S HEART IS BROKEN;
MY FATHER FARMED BUT WE DID NOT EAT.

A voice replied:

YOUR FATHER IS DEAD BUT HE IS HAPPY;
DEAD IN THE GRAVE, DEAD IN THE GRAVE;
SAMBA HAS GOTTEN USED TO THE SNAKES;
ONLY THE SALT HE HAS FORGOT.

The child stared and said, "Hai! Hai! I think Samba[4] is talking; he is inside this thing." The child repeated his song and the voice repeated the reply.

The woman and her child then returned to their compound and called the father's eldest son. They said to him, "Come and listen; someone is talking in the tree." He replied, "You are both scared. My father has been buried there. Just keep quiet. He has been buried there." The woman persisted, "Honestly, just come and listen; there is someone in there." The eldest son agreed to accompany them the next morning.

When they all arrived there the next morning the child stood up on the platform and sang:

THERE IS GREAT SUFFERING, GREAT SUFFERING;
MY MOTHER'S HEART IS BROKEN;
MY FATHER FARMED BUT WE DID NOT EAT.

A voice replied:

YOUR FATHER IS DEAD BUT HE IS HAPPY;
DEAD IN THE GRAVE, DEAD IN THE GRAVE;
SAMBA HAS GOTTEN USED TO THE SNAKES;
ONLY THE SALT HE HAS FORGOT.

They went to the tree and parted the reed mat over the entrance of the hollowed out tree. They peered into the tree and saw the man. "This is Samba!" the eldest boy called out. "My father is here," cried the young boy. "What are you doing here?" asked the child. The father replied, "I am doing nothing." "Are you pounding and cooking for yourself in here? Father, if you have a family, you must know for yourself that greed forced you to transfer all the food reserves here. Now you are pounding and cooking for yourself." The man became so ashamed that he changed into a climbing vine.[5] He looked just like the climbing plants which you see on the trees.[6]

[1]Narrated by Yamangu Mbou, female griot, age 48, in Bati Hai, The Gambia, on November 1 at 9:45 p.m. before 53 men, women and children.

[2]There is some evidence to support this custom of burying griots in hollowed out baobab trees. (See, for example, R. Mauny, "Baobabs-cimetieres a griots," *Notes Africaines* I.F.A.W. juill., 72-76.) It was believed that griots would pollute the earth if they were buried in the ground with members of the other castes. This is indicative of the social stigma which has been directed at the griots.

[3]Young boys assume this role of their maturing process. Each day during the growing season, they guard their family crops from birds, antelope and other wild game. They sit on top of a specially constructed wooded-pole platform about 5-7 feet off the ground. From this position they are able to see and throw stones at the animals.

[4]The father.

[5]In Wolof, *roy*, plant used to make straps and ropes to tie wooden pole structures together.

[6]The contrast between the lament of the child and the chorus of the father underscores his complete self-centeredness. His response to the child does not acknowledge the pain and suffering which his feigned death has caused his family. His loss has brought both loneliness and starvation. The father, however, is only concerned with himself and his own satisfaction. This psychological revelation builds on the narrator's initial projection. The gravity of the husband's deed is accentuated by the time reference for his behavior. The hungry season is a period when last year's food supplies are noticeably dwindling before next year's harvest can replenish them. At this time everyone feels the gnaw of hunger. It is the father who should, ideally, set the example of strength and courage for his family. The father, however, abdicates his role as a positive model and falls victim to the demands of self-satisfaction. His transformation into the climbing vine results from the social condemnation he feels directed at him at his exposure. The words of this child express the moral truths of the community.

THE MAURITANIAN
AND HIS WEALTH[1]

There was a story . . .
Our legs are crossed . . .
It happened here . . .
It was so . . .

There was once a Mauritanian who lived in a Wolof village. He left his own village in Mauritania and came to this town to work at selling food and other small goods. He sold his wares and earned a large sum of money. He earned so much money that he could go home, build himself a house and marry a wife.

One day he decided that he was going to return to his homeland. You know that Mauritanians are the world's greediest people. He decided that he was not going to buy a car; he was not going to ride a horse or a camel. He was not going to use any type of transportation; he was going to walk all the way to Mauritania. Because he was afraid of thieves, he gathered all of his money and put it into one large sack which he hung on his back. He did not tell anyone in the town that he was leaving, although everyone in the town knew him. Because of his greed, he left without anyone noticing.

He walked and walked and walked until he reached the desert. He continued on until he became very tired. He decided to rest under a date palm tree. When he reached that place he put his sack down by his side. But all the time he did not want to sleep because he was afraid to sleep. He had not slept since he left the town. He leaned up against the tree and began to feel his exhaustion. He was just beginning to fall asleep when a deer came and KOF snatched up his sack in his mouth.

The Mauritanian jumped up and said, "La ilaha ilaha. Oh deer! Are you just teasing father Mauritanian?" He stood up straight. As he was getting up, the deer became frightened, hopped CHIRIP-CHIRIP[2] and ran away. The Mauritanian stood still and said, "Wala ila![3] Deer, you are still teasing father

126

Mauritanian!''

You know, the deer ran a little and the Mauritanian followed. He folded up his gown as he ran. The deer stopped and just looked at him. The Mauritanian stretched out his hand to touch the deer but the deer moved away just a little bit.

He said, "HUMM! You deer, I beg you, please don't play with father Mauritanian." But the deer just ignored him. As he raised his foot, the deer jumped away and ran. The Mauritanian could not bear his greed any longer and ran quickly after the deer. He ran *DAG-DAG-DAG.* [4] But the deer was also moving swiftly *CHIRIP-CHIRIP* for short distances and then stopping. The Mauritanian stopped too and said to it, "*Wala ila!* Deer, please forgive father Mauritanian. I have worked for ten years for this. I am begging you, please, stop! Put down my sack!"

The deer only continued moving away. When the deer moved, the Mauritanian tried to catch him. They continued like that until the Mauritanian became very tired. The deer still held the sack in his mouth. Time after time, the Mauritanian cried, "Oh, you are just teasing father Mauritanian. Oh deer, please stop! Here, TCH-TCH-TCH,[5] take this." But the deer did not even seem to hear him.

That is the way they continued until the Mauritanian died. Chasing after his wealth.[6]

[1] Recorded by Momadu Djak, age 22, in Njau, The Gambia, on November 14 at 9:45 p.m. before four adult men and three women. This narrative captures the primary reasons underlying the traditional animosity Wolof people have for the Mauritanians.

[2] Onomatopoetic phrase which conveys the light, high-leaping, easy movements of the deer. Derived from the verb *chirip*, to lob something into the water with a high arc.

[3] Wolof expression of the Arabic phrase *Wallahi*, By Allah.

[4] Ideophonic expression used to convey the frantic, shaking movement of the Mauritanian after the deer. It is derived from the verb *dagdagi*, to lunge forward to obtain a desired object or goal.

[5] The sound used in calling a domesticated animal.

[6] In the Wolof tradition, the deer is the symbol of unexpectedly changing circumstances. It appears as a narrative device to convey a sense of non-causality; something just happens which cannot be logically explained. The results of the deer's action must be accepted as one of the vicissitudes of life. The use of the deer in *this* narrative provides direct contrast to the lifestyle exhibited by the Mauritanian. His is cold and calculating; it is focused on the acquisition of money. That he is willing to live without friends or family while among the Wolof, highlights his deliberate scheme. The arrival of the deer, as the unexpected, unplanned, and unforeseeable twist, thwarts his carefully laid plans and precipitates his early destruction. The greed he exhibits undermines all his plans and dreams. He thus becomes a negative model; his behavior exemplifies anti-social practices. Given the accepted animosity for Mauritanians among the Wolof, his choice as model welds that antagonism to socially destructive behaviors.

THE HYENA WRESTLES
THE KONDERONG, I[1]

There was a story . . .
Our legs are crossed . . .
It happened here . . .
It was so . . .

A *konderong*[2] went into the bush to gather some honey. He collected a calabash full and decided to return home. On his journey home he met the hyena behind some compounds on the edge of the village. It was about twilight time.

The hyena called out to him, "Oh, *konderong,* where are you coming from with such haste on those skinny legs of yours?" The *konderong* replied, "Hey, do not make fun of me. I am just going about my own business. I do not want to have anything to do with you." But the hyena continued, "Yes. What do you have?" "I have some honey," replied the *konderong.* "Then give[3] me some of the honey," ordered the hyena. The *konderong* answered, "Give you what?" He said, "You know, if I say give me some, I just meant as payment for some work that I will do for you." But the *konderong* replied, "Me, I am not looking to make a farm nor trying to find someone to work it for me." The hyena countered, "Hey, if I say work, I do not mean just work in the fields, but wrestling. That is what I mean." The *konderong* questioned, "Yes?" So the hyena said, "Yes!" Now you know, a *konderong* does not really care about wrestling, yet he gave some of the honey to the hyena.

Afterwards, the hyena left for his home. He said to himself, "Now I have really placed myself in a difficult position. I do not know how or where it is going to end. But I know that I *will* win in the end. The *konderong* has set himself up for a defeat. I know that he is like a small child who has no strength; to throw him down will be very easy."

The hyena then bathed and ate his supper. When the *konderong* arrived at his compound, he said to him, "Uncle Hyena?" and he replied, "Yes?" He said, "I have come to take care of our business!" Now the *konderong* was quite small. If you would see him you would think that he was just a child. But the *konderong*, with all of his magic power, is not like that at all. But the hyena boasted, "You, if I squeeze you today, you will certainly die."

Thereafter, as they were wrestling, the *konderong* gripped the hyena, picked him up and threw him down *FUR-TAKA-TAKA-WACHI-MOLBIDAK-KUNKUNG!* [4] He threw him down thirty times. Then he said to him, "Let us postpone this match until tomorrow." The hyena agreed, saying "Allah protect me from the devil. This small thing has done this to me through trickery. I do not think I will venture to risk waiting for him tomorrow." So the two wrestlers separated until the next day.

The *konderong* arrived the next day. When he came he was just a little bit bigger this time than he was the day before. When they began wrestling, he threw him down *FUR-TAKA-TAKA-WACHI-MOLBIDAK-KUNKUNG-KUN-KUNG!* He threw him down forty-eight times and then said, "Let us postpone this match till tomorrow." The hyena said, "Before this thing ends, I hope I will not die."

The hyena then went to his wives and said to them, "Now we should do something about this, for if we do not, then I will die." They said to him, "What plan should we use?" He replied, "Now I will get into the cooking pot and you will close the lid. Then put a little fire under it. If he comes and asks for your Uncle, you tell him that I went on a journey. I will be safe inside the pot." You know, his plan amazes me because no one hides from a *konderong.* The hyena then got into the pot and his wives lit the fire under it.

The *konderong* soon came and greeted them, "Salaam Alekum," and they replied, "Alekum Salaam." He asked, "Where is your Uncle?" They replied, "Ah . . . our Uncle has gone on a trip." "What are you doing?" asked the *konderong.* "We are just boiling some milk," replied the wives. "Then let me help you," offered the *konderong.* So he took two pieces of firewood and added them to the small fire. Soon the cooking pot began to be very hot. The hyena jumped out of the pot BRANG[5] and said, "You bastard. Are you trying to kill me? Did we agree to *this?* We said wrestling only. That is what we agreed to and now you want to kill me." The *konderong* then said, "Hey, is that you?" the hyena replied, "Yes." "Then let us proceed," suggested the *konderong.*

They went again to wrestle. The *konderong* threw him down *FUR-TAKA-TAKA-WACHI-MOLBIDAK-KUNKUNG-KUNKUNG!* He threw him down forty-nine times and then said to him, "Let us postpone this match until tomorrow. Tomorrow I will continue it." The hyena said, "Hey, you and I . . . where will I end up with you?"

The hyena then went to his wives and said, "Now you hide me under the bed. If he comes, tell him that I have gone to the other bank of the river." Afterwards he came and greeted them, "Salaam Alekum," and they replied, "Alekum Salaam." He asked, "Where is your Uncle?" "He has gone to the other bank of the river. He went a long time ago." The *konderong* said, "Where did he go? What we agreed to do is not yet completed. He went on a journey? No man can hide from a *konderong*." Then he jumped up and landed on the bed. The bed broke and fell to the floor. The hyena stuck out his head and said, "You son of a bitch. Do you want to kill me?" "Ah, is that you?" asked the *konderong*. He replied, "Yes." "Then let us continue," ordered the *konderong*.

They proceeded to the red ant hill[6] and there the *konderong* pinned the hyena down again, *FUR-TAKA-TAKA-WACHI-MOLDBIDAK-KUNKUNG-KUN-KUNG!* He threw him down sixty-five times. Then he said, "Let us postpone this match until tomorrow." "Oh my," cried the hyena. "I do not know what to do."

As he was approaching his wives, an elderly woman called out to him. She said, "Do you know what to do? You must go to the Koranic school. Since you have never been to school, if you go, just murmur and harmonize with the other children's voices. No one will recognize your voice as being different from the other children's." The hyena replied, "Yes, I will do that." After he reached home, he stayed there for a while before going to the school.

When he arrived there, he sat down with the pupils and murmured with them. He mumbled, "What you are saying, I am saying. What you are saying, I am saying."

The *konderong* searched and searched for the hyena but he could not recognize his voice. So he walked to the back of the school and said in a very loud voice, "Who owns this dead donkey? Who owns this dead donkey?" At that, the hyena rushed out and said, "It is me. It is me." The *konderong* said, "Ah, is that you, Uncle Hyena?" He replied, "Yes." "Come on then. We must continue with our business agreement." The hyena moaned, "Hoo . . . You and I . . . I do not know what to do."

They returned to the anthill. The *konderong* pinned him down again, *FUR-TAKA-TAKA-WACHI-MOLBIDAK-KUNKUNG-KUNKUNG!* He threw him down seventy-eight times and then he said to him, "Go home now." He had broken his left foot and his right hand. He said, "I will let the rest of you go." The hyena replied, "Hey, shit, our wrestling match is indeed finished."[7]

[1]Narrated by Bessi Njay in Porli, The Gambia, on October 18 at 2:30 p.m. in the center of the village before 32 men, women and children. This was the first time Bessi Njay related this tale (see following story).

[2]See "The Handsome Suitor, II," note number 3.

[3]In Wolof, *may.* This word implies a gratuitous exchange in contrast to *joh,* give what is owed. The hyena is attempting to appeal to a mutual friendship which has never existed.

[4]Ideophonic expression recreating the sound-image of the *konderong* violently grabbing the hyena, *taka,* throwing him to the ground, *wachio,* and slapping him with the back of his hand, *kunkung.*

[5]Onomatopoetic expression recreating the sound of the hyena's head crashing into the lid of the cooking pot as he tries to escape from the excessive heat inside of it.

[6]In Wolof, *wan.* These tall castle-like mud structures are believed to be one of the homes of the *konderong.* Numerous tales relate how people who are wandering around in the wilderness are sometimes caught by the *konderong* and taken to live in these anthills.

[7]This narrative illustrates the attendant consequences of uncontrolled speech. The opening image depicts the excessively talkative hyena becoming entangled in his own verbal trap. The initial greeting shows the abusive way he uses language and his inability to control his tongue before he thinks. With each subsequent sentence he is dangerously involved with the *konderong.* His request for a taste of honey becomes a contract for work, which becomes the prize for winning a wrestling contest. The episodic presentation of the wrestling match emphasizes the interminable consequences of such garrulousness.

THE HYENA WRESTLES
THE KONDERONG, II[1]

There is a story . . .
Our legs are crossed . . .
It happened here . . .
It was so . . .

A *konderong* is a *jine*[2] to us. *Jine* went to collect honey in the bush. When he was returning, he met the hyena. The hyena said to him, *"Jine,* give me some of your honey." "It is not to be given away," replied the *jine.* But the hyena continued, "Then sell some of it." But the *jine* replied, "It is not for sale." "Then hire me to care for your farm," urged the hyena. But the *jine* said that he was not preparing a farm, so he did not need a strange-farmer. But still the hyena persisted, "If I tell you to hire me, I don't mean for work, but rather, to wrestle. That is why I told you that." So the *jine* said, "Yes." Thereafter, the *jine* took out some honey from his calabash and gave it to the hyena. Then he told him, "Tomorrow I will come."

In the morning, the *jine* arrived. He was only the size of a small child. They began to wrestle. He grabbed the hyena and threw him down *FUR-TAKA-TAKA-OLBIT!* He threw him thirty times.

On the following day he returned. This time the *jine* was the size of an adolescent. He came to the compound and said, "Where is the hyena?" The hyena said, "I am here." "Then let us go to the match," said the *jine.* He threw him down *FUR-TAKA-TAKA-OLBIT,* twelve times and then went home.

On the following day the *jine* returned and now he was the size of a fully grown man. The hyena said, "That is not you, is it, *jine?"* "It is me," replied the *jine.* They went to the wrestling area.

The *jine* threw him down *FUR-TAKA-TAKA-OLBIT,* forty-five times and then said, "Let us go till tomorrow."

The next day the hyena crawled underneath his bed. A person cannot hide himself away from a *jine*. So when he arrived at the hyena's compound, he asked the wives, "Where is the hyena?" They said, "He is gone." Then the *jine* sat very heavily on the bed. The hyena screamed, "You son of a bitch. Are you killing me?" They went again to wrestle. The *jine* threw him twenty times. Then he left.

On the following day the *jine* returned. He acted like that for a long time until one day the *jine* nearly killed the hyena. So the hyena went to study in the Koranic school so that the *jine* would not be able to recognize him when he was with the other students. The hyena kept on repeating, "WHAT YOU ARE SAYING, I AM SAYING IT. I WILL READ THE BOOK AND THEN GO."

Thereafter the *jine* came and looked and looked and looked but he did not see him or recognize his voice. He then went behind the compound and said, "Who owns this dead donkey?" Then the hyena ran out and came and said, "It is me. It is me." So the *jine* said, "Come on, let us go to our match."

They went again and the *jine* threw him down *FUR-TAKA-TAKA-OLBIT*, forty times. He broke his right foot and his left hand. Then he said, "I now forgive you the rest." The hyena cursed and said, "Shit. It's finished."

Since then, the hyena has never gone into business with the *jine*.

---

[1]Narrated by Bessi Njay in Porli, The Gambia, on November 1, at 9:15 p.m. in his own compound before 38 men, women and children. This version of the tale is considerably shorter than the previous version. The sequence of episodes follows the same pattern; the differences relate to allied details and character development. This appears to be a skeleton version of Bessi Njay's "The Hyena Wrestles the Konderong, I."

[2]From the Islamic term for *jinn*. As this narrator states, the *jine* have assumed the role of the traditional *konderong* in many oral narratives.

THE HYENA EATS
THE OSTRICH'S EGGS[1]

There was a story . . .
Our legs are crossed . . .
It happened here . . .
It was so . . .

The hyena and the hare were traveling together. They walked a short distance until they approached a divided road. There was a small path and a wide road. There the hyena said to the hare, "You dead dog, do you think that if you walk with your father, you can ask him to take the small path? I will take the wide road this time." So the hare turned onto the small path and said aloud, "Small path, Allah gave you to me. Small path, Allah gave you to me. Every step I take, let it be a step of peace."

The hare walked a long time until he met up with an ostrich that was preparing to go and fetch some water from the river to drink. The ostrich said, "Hare, where are you going?" He replied, "Me, I was walking with the hyena. I at first took the wide road and he called me a bastard, saying that if I was traveling with my father, I would not take the wide road. So I walked on the small path." Then the ostrich said, "Well, since that is all, kindly wait for me here. Sit on my eggs while I go to the river. If you want to leave the inside of this tree and go somewhere, just say 'tree open' and the tree will open up for your business. When you return, you just say 'tree close' when you get inside. It will close." So the hare did as the ostrich instructed.

The hyena, meanwhile, followed the wide road far into the wilderness. The only animals that he caught there were yellow and red spotted lizards and gechos.[2] He was continually licking the sand. Since they were the only things he caught, he soon became very thin.

One day he again met up with the hare and said to him, "Hare, you bastard. You are so fat. Before we parted you were not this fat." The hare replied,

"Uncle Hyena, I am in a place where, you know, if I say 'tree open' then I can go out and do my business. When I re-enter the tree and say 'tree close' the tree closes. Then I can eat what is inside. The ostrich was going to fetch water so she left me to guard her eggs." The hyena said, "Let us go there so you can show me where this tree is located."

They traveled together until they approached the tree. The hare said, "Uncle Hyena, we are almost near to the tree. When you arrive there say 'tree open' and the tree will open up. Eat what you find there until you are satisfied and then say 'tree close' and leave." The hyena agreed to do that.

When he reached the tree he said, "Tree open!" and the tree opened up and he went inside it. When he saw all of the eggs there, he ran back to his own compound and called Toj Geda, Wida Nyamul Saket and Njonkon Cheli.[3] He told his wives, "Come with me, for I have seen an extraordinary gift." So they followed him back to the tree. There each of them stole a bag of eggs and returned two or three more times. Then the hyena got inside the tree and said, "When you go home, use those for *your* food. I will stay here for there are many more eggs. Besides, if the eggs are this good, I think the layer will be even better. I will wait for her." So he said, "Tree open," and when it opened, he entered inside. Then he said, "Tree close," and it closed. He stayed inside there.

The ostrich stayed away from her eggs until she was satisfied drinking. When she was returning, the hare, who was nearby, called out, "Uncle Hyena, say 'tree open' because the ostrich is returning from the river. Say 'tree open' for she is a dark cloud in the middle of the day. Say 'tree open!' "

The hyena replied, "Tree close. Oh sweet tree; FOYOX-MOYOX."[4] The hare repeated his warning, "Uncle Hyena, say 'tree open' for the ostrich is coming from the river. Say 'tree open' for she darkens the sky. Say 'tree open' for she is a dark cloud on a shining day. Say 'tree open!' " But the hyena only said, "Tree close. Oh sweet tree, FOYOX-MOYOX."

So the hyena stayed within the tree until the ostrich approached to within the distance of, say, between here[5] and Njau. The hare then said, "Uncle Hyena, say 'tree open' for the ostrich is coming from the river. Say 'tree open' for she darkens the sky. Say 'tree open' for she is a dark cloud on a shining day. Say 'tree open!' " But the hyena again said, "Tree close. Oh, sweet tree, FOYOX-MOYOX."

The hare said, "He will not say 'tree open' because he will miss eating a few eggs." He stayed there until the ostrich arrived. She said to the hare, "You, why are you outside the tree and not inside of it?" He replied, "Uncle Hyena came here and took me out and got inside it himself."

So the ostrich said, "Tree open" and the tree opened up. She caught the hyena and jabbed a horn up his ass and turned it around until the hyena's ass became very wide. She then set him down and took some mud and stuffed it in his ass until it was full. Then she took two fish from her fishing net and used them as a stopper.

Afterwards, she sent the hyena home. When he arrived there he said to his wives, "My wives, let us pray! I will lead you in prayer. Come and pray." Thereafter he went to pray. He bent down and intoned, *"Cho no noli, cho leet. Cho no noli, cho leet."* [6]

When he bent down to pray, they all saw the two fish stuffed up his ass. One of his children got up from praying and pulled one of the fish out. The co-wife then said to her child, "You bastard. You saw the fish in your father's ass but you let him take it out. Now I won't have anything to cook today." So her child went and pulled on the second fish sticking in his father's ass. When this child pulled it out, all of the mud shot out and splattered into his eyes.[7]

[1] Narrated by Bessi Njay in Porli, The Gambia, at 1:30 p.m. in the center of the village under a large shade tree before 38 men, women and children. Bessi Njay demonstrates a fine control of his voice. He gives life to his narratives through the modulation of his voice, reproducing the intonations and tensions of the changing circumstances. Fear, surprise, hatred, love, skepticism, disgust, and many other emotions are incorporated in his narrative through his voice.

[2] In Wolof, *yal* and *sindah.*

[3] The names of the hyena's wives vary with the storyteller but they are all indicative of the worst type of wife a hyena could have. These names indicate their peculiarly repugnant characteristics: "one who breaks things and grumbles"; "one who refused to eat maggots" (since hyenas are scavengers, this wife desires to put extra burdens on him since he must bring fresh meat home to her); and "one who waits by the crossroads" (the crossroads are locations where secret lovers are believed to meet; this wife's name hints at her unfaithfulness).

[4] Onomatopoetic expression recreating the sound of the hyena crunching greedily into the shells of the ostrich's eggs.

[5] Porli.

[6] This is the hyena's version of the Islamic call to prayer.

[7] All the derogatory associations of excrement are called upon in this image to effect an awareness of total humiliation. The hyena's father can give nothing else to his children; his act is the final insult and punishment for his previous uncontrolled, greedy behavior.

THE BEARDED ROCK[1]

There was a story . . .
Our legs are crossed . . .
It happened here . . .
It was so . . .

There was a rock which had a beard. It stood in the middle of the road and said, "He who says 'Rock that has a beard' will die."

The hare approached there but he knew about it.[2] He sat down right beside it.

An elephant approached and the hare asked him, "Elephant, do you know this rock?" He said, "No." The hare pointed and said, "This *here* rock." He said, "I know it! It is a rock with a beard." He immediately fell down and died.

A lion passed by that place. He said, "Lion, do you know this?" He replied, "Yes! It is a rock with a beard." Then he fell down and died. The hare took the lion away.

He cooked and cooked the lion until the hyena arrived there. He asked, "Where did you get this meat?" He replied, "Go straight ahead. You will see a rock with a beard. Stay there. Any animal that approaches it, ask him to say, 'Rock with a beard.' "

The hyena then went away.

Any animal that passed by him he would say, "Come here. Do you know this rock?" They would answer, "No." He would say, "This rock!" They would say, "No." The hyena would say, "Go away, you don't know anything."

Then a leopard passed by there. The hyena said, "Come here, leopard. Do you know this rock?" He said, "No." He said, "It is a rock with a beard." Then the hyena fell down and died.[3]

---

[1] Narrated by Serin Sise, age 8, in Porli, The Gambia, on November 20, at 8:30 p.m. before 39 men, women and children in the compound of his uncle Bessi Njay.

137

138

²The rock.

³This simple narrative told by this young griot illustrates the structural importance of repetition. The questioning episode is established as the model or pattern: the hare successfully obtaining food by manipulating the magical words "Rock that has a beard." When the hyena attempts to follow the pattern he not only fails but he becomes a victim of his own lack of verbal facility. The plan worked twice for the hare while it failed twice for the hyena. This type of modeling is one of the structural devices that can be employed by Wolof narrators regardless of age. The value of this narrative emerges from the change in the pattern, and the distortion of the original plan.

THE DOG CAPTURES THE HYENA[1]

There was a story . . .
Our legs are crossed . . .
It happened here . . .
It was so . . .

Dog and goat. Dog went to engage the goat for marriage. He took her and made a home for her in the middle of the bush.

A hippopotamus[2] saw them. He walked and walked and walked until he reached their home. He said to them, "I am going to tell the hyena."

He went to the hyena and said, "Have you not seen the home of the goat and the dog?" He replied, "No." He said, "Then follow this path."

The hyena took that path and came to their new home. He found the goat there cooking dinner. He said, "Goat, where is the dog?" She replied, "He has gone to the farm." He said, "Yes!" and then went home.

When the dog returned he asked, "Has the hyena been here?" His wife answered, "Yes."

The dog then dug a deep hole.

After dinner was finished, they both went and hid in the hole by the side of their fence.

The hyena, in the middle of the night, came. He looked and looked and looked for the goat and the dog but he did not see them. So he went back home.

He returned the next day and asked the goat, "Where did you hide last night?" She said, "We hid by the fence." When the dog came home, the hyena asked him, "Where were you?" The dog said, "We hid at the fence." Then the hyena left.

They went and dug a hole in the middle of the road, right where the hyena would pass. The dog said to the goat, "Go in front of me." The goat said, "You know I will not let you be in front of me with your very smelly ass." The dog then got into the hole first and the goat followed on top of him.

The hyena came along and caught hold of the goat's horns and said, "So this was the stone I kicked and tripped over. Let me go and get an axe and take it out." He went to the dog's compound and brought back an axe. He hit her horns KENG . . . KENG![3] The goat cried out MBEEEEE!

The hyena took her to the bush and told her, "Wait for me." He went to get a cooking pot. He left. The goat moved. When the hyena returned he said, "You have moved from where I left you." The goat replied, "Look at the moon and then look at me. You will see that I did not move."[4]

The hyena left again to get a knife. He told her, "Don't move from here." She said, "Yes."

When the hyena left, the goat moved up to the gate of their compound.

When the hyena returned he asked, "What is this?" She told him, "This is my father's ground in the middle of the bush. Why do you not go back and get the dog too, for we were in the hole together?"

When the hyena left, the goat moved away and went into her house. When the hyena returned he could not find the goat. He only found the dog waiting to attack him.

[1] Narrated by Serin Sise, age 8, in Porli, The Gambia, in his uncle's compound on November 20 at 8:30 p.m. before 27 men, women and children.

[2] In Wolof, *leber*.

[3] Onomatopoetic expression recreating the sound of a metal axe clanging against the goat's horns.

[4] This is a familiar escape motif used to avoid the hyena (see "The Pilgrimage to Mecca"), although presented here in skeletal form.

THE DOG AND MONKEY BUILD A TOWN[1]

There was a story . . .
Our legs are crossed . . .
It happened here . . .
It was so . . .

A dog and a monkey agreed that they would build a town in which to live together. But afterwards the monkey changed his mind and said to him, "I will not join in this endeavor with you."

The dog insisted and said, "Hey, let us join our towns together. If we do that, we will be able to drink, our children will be able to drink, and your children will be able to drink. That would be much better." The monkey replied, "I will not do that. If you want, you can build your own town. That is none of my business."

So the dog went and constructed his own town. He dug a well between his town and the temporary settlement of the monkey. He dug the well between his town and the monkey's. That is where he built it.

One day the monkeys secretly left their village and went to the well. They wanted to do their washing in the well. They washed their clothes until they were clean. They drew some water and began to wash. They sang:

SLOSH THEM IN THE WATER, SLOSH THEM IN THE WATER,
RAISE THE CLOTHES HIGH AND DUNK THEM AGAIN.
WRING OUT THE WATER; TWIST IT OUT.
LET THE SUN DRY THEM.

Thereafter a small dog came and saw them as they were going home. He quickly left and returned to his father. He told him, "Father, I think . . . what I have seen by the well . . . I think . . . they were the monkeys."[2]

Together they went to the well and saw the splattered water-marks in the mud and the traces of soap lying about. The father said, "Yes. It is alright."

The monkeys stayed away from the well until their clothes began to become dirty again. Then they went to the well and began to wash and wash and wash until you know they were almost finished. At that time they saw some dogs coming to get them. The smallest monkey, the one that first sighted them, said:

SLOSH THEM IN THE WATER, SLOSH THEM IN THE WATER.
RAISE THE CLOTHES HIGH AND DUNK THEM AGAIN.
WRING OUT THE WATER: TWIST IT OUT.
LET THE SUN DRY THEM AT HOME.

The other monkeys said, "Oh, he doesn't know what he is talking about. Dry them at home? Let us wash here. Any dog that comes here, we will beat him to death until his ass looks like a bitter tomato."[3]

But when the dogs sprang on the monkeys, they dropped their clothes in the mud. The dogs chased after them.

They followed one monkey and ran after him. That one was yelling, "The tree at Walo[4] is where I will be safe. The tree at Walo is where I will be safe." But when he met up with an old person he was told, "Some people have cut that tree down."

But the monkey continued, "The tree at Walo, that is where I will be safe."

He reached the tree and climbed up into it and rested there. He remained there for three months and ten days until the red ants began to walk on the dog who was still waiting for the monkey to descend the tree. He said, "That dog *must* be dead by now, I see that the red ants are even on him."[5]

So the monkey descended the tree. When he stood by the dog, he began to count its teeth singing:

THIS ONE HAS KILLED MY MOTHER;
THIS ONE HAS KILLED MY FATHER;
THIS ONE HAS KILLED MY GRANDFATHER;
THIS ONE HAS KILLED MY GREAT GRANDFATHER;
THIS ONE HAS KILLED MY WIFE;
THIS ONE WANTED TO KILL ME . . .

Then the dog snapped at his fingers. The monkey closed his eyes and said, "Oh my, I didn't know I too was going to end up in the dog's mouth."[6]

[1] Narrated by Bessi Njay in Porli, The Gambia, on October 18 at 2:40 p.m. in the center of the village before 38 men, women and children.

[2] The young dog in very excited about what he has seen. His stammering reflects his anxiety.

[3] See note no. 8 in "The Monkey and the Dog Court the Same Girl."

[4] The ancient town of the Wolof in central Senegal.

[5] The dog is very persistent and patient. He has waited so long for the monkey to descend the tree that the red ants have assumed he was dead and have climbed over him as if he were a rock.

[6] The monkey has failed to abide by his oral contractual agreement with the dog. His refusal to join in constructing the well is also a demonstration of his anti-social attitudes: he does not want to participate in any cooperative work project. This initial negative behavior pattern is illustrated further in the narrative with the clothes-washing episodes. The monkey was not content to refuse

help digging the well but he insists on ruining it for everyone else. The monkeys misuse the well as their washing basin, stirring up the silt and polluting the water with their soap-suds. Although this behavior is contrary to acceptable social etiquette, its deeper significance reflects an anti-social attitude, a disregard for other members of the community. The dog's patience at the foot of the tree is indicative of the importance of the resulting punishment. The monkey's anti-community attitude, as illustrated through his behavior, cannot be permitted to find expression. His death in the final episode confirms the value of social cooperation and mutual respect.

THE COURTSHIP OF YASIN[1]

There was a story . . .
Our legs are crossed . . .
It happened here . . .
It was so . . .

There was a very beautiful woman called YASIN-POINTED-BREASTS.[2] One day all the animals gathered together and said that they would compete for YASIN-POINTED-BREASTS. Each one wanted to marry her. The *Yirra*[3] flew to the gathering. The *Ndobin*[4] assembled; the *Gutut*[5] gathered there; the *Peget*[6] and the *Lichen*[7] went there; the *Jamba*[8] also flew to the competition.

When the day of the contest arrived, they all brought home some kola nuts[9] and carried them to the town where YASIN-POINTED-BREASTS lived. When they arrived there, they looked for a guest house to stay in. When each had found a host for the duration of the competition, each said to their host, "There is a beautiful woman here whom we have heard about; she is the reason we have come." The hosts answered, "Yes, the woman is in the compound of such and such owner. But you can still go there today."

Each of the birds walked there. As they walked, they began adjusting and preening their feathers.[10] When they arrived, they said to this beauty, "YASIN-POINTED-BREASTS! You made us come here." She said, "Yes. Since I made you come here, you must return to your host and talk with him. Since it is for my sake that you come." "Yes . . . yes," they answered.

They returned to their host who told them, "You must prepare a present to offer the woman."

After they prepared their presents, they said, "*Yirra*, you must go first, for you are the youngest." So *Yirra* got up and proceeded to the woman's compound. When he arrived there he sang:

DESCENDENT OF JAMBA;
CHILD OF THE JAMBA LINEAGE,
YASIN-POINTED-BREASTS,

144

```
YOU ARE MAGNIFICENT!
```
She replied, "Who are you? Who are you?"
```
IT IS I, YIRRA, WITH MY BLACK SKIN,
MY RED EYES AND MY SKINNY LEGS.
```
She responded:
```
YIRRA, SAMBA[11] HAS NOBILITY.
GO AWAY, FAR AWAY.
```
That one ran and said to his friends, "My friends, I have been driven away." Now that one is out of the competition.

Thereafter *Gutet* said, "Then I will go." He picked up his present and asked his host to accompany him to Yasin's compound. When they arrived there, *Gutut* sang:
```
DESCENDENT OF JAMBA;
CHILD OF THE JAMBA LINEAGE;
YASIN-POINTED-BREASTS,
YOU ARE MAGNIFICENT!
```
She replied, "Who are you? Who are you?"
```
IT IS I, GUTUT, WITH MY BLACK HEAD,
MY BROAD SHOULDERS, MY LONG TAIL AND MY SHORT FEET.
```
She responded:
```
GUTUT, SAMBA HAS NOBILITY!
START WALKING.
GO AWAY, FAR AWAY.
```
He left there and went to his friends and said, "Ah, friends, I *too* have been driven away." They said, "She has driven *Gutut* away too. Now let us try the other birds that are remaining. Alright, *Ndobin,* you go this time." *Ndobin* got up and shook himself, GIFF-GIFF,[12] and stretched RA-KA-KAT[13] his shoulders. They all said, *"Ndobin* is on his way." When he arose they gave him the gift he was to present. He took it and went with his host to the woman's compound.

When he approached the gate of the compound he began to sing:
```
DESCENDENT OF JAMBA;
CHILD OF THE JAMBA LINEAGE;
YASIN-POINTED-BREASTS,
YOU ARE MAGNIFICENT!
```
She replied, "Who are you? Who are you?"
```
IT IS I, NDOBIN, WITH MY WELL-SHAPED SHOULDERS,
MY BIG WINGS AND MY FINE STRUTTING.
```
She responded:
```
OH, NDOBIN, SAMBA HAS NOBILITY;
GO STRUTTING AWAY;
GO AWAY, FAR AWAY.
```

He returned to his friends and said, "Man, I *too* have been driven away." They replied, "Yes . . . Yes, they have driven *Ndobin* away too." So they all returned to their compounds. After a while they said, "Let us send *Lichen*." They called *Lichen* and told him to go and try his luck. He took his present and went with his host.

When they approached the gate of the compound he began to sing:

DESCENDENT OF JAMBA;
CHILD OF THE JAMBA LINEAGE;
YASIN-POINTED-BREASTS,
YOU ARE MAGNIFICENT!

She replied, "Who are you? Who are you?"

IT IS I, *LICHEN*, WITH MY CORRECT SHOULDERS,
AND MY SHARP BEAK.

She responded:

LICHEN, SAMBA HAS NOBILITY.
GO AWAY, FAR AWAY.

Lichen left her compound and met his friends and said, "Man, I too have been driven away." They said, "Yes, now let us try *Peget*." *Peget* got up and stretched. They gave him the present and he walked with the host to the girl's compound. He walked until he arrived at her gate. He began to sing:

DESCENDENT OF JAMBA;
CHILD OF THE JAMBA LINEAGE;
YASIN-POINTED-BREASTS,
YOU ARE MAGNIFICENT!

She replied, "Who are you? Who are you?"

IT IS I, *PEGET*, WITH MY QUICK MOVEMENTS
AND MY NARROW SHOULDERS.

She responded:

PEGET, SAMBA HAS NOBILITY.
GO STRUTTING AWAY;
GO AWAY, FAR AWAY.

Thereafter, the other birds said to themselves, *"Jamba* is the only one left now."

Jamba then got up. He stood before the gate of the girl's compound and announced, NGAH-NGAH-NGAH.[14] The girls outside the compound applauded him. They wanted him to win the competition. The *Jamba* stood before the gate of the girl's compound and sang:

DESCENDENT OF JAMBA,
CHILD OF THE JAMBA LINEAGE;
YASIN-POINTED-BREASTS,
YOU ARE MAGNIFICENT!

She replied, "Who are you? Who are you?"

IT IS I, *JAMBA JOBE,* WITH MY SHARP EYES,
MY YELLOW CRESTED CROWN AND MY BEAUTIFUL BODY.

She responded:

HE WHO IS NOT KING JAMBA, MAY HE DIE.
COME IN! COME IN!
KING JAMBA, COME IN, COME IN.
KING JAMBA, COME IN, COME IN.[15]

[1]Narrated by Lamin Jeng in Bati Hai, The Gambia, on November 2 at 9:15 p.m. in his father's compound before 32 men, women, and children.

[2]Yasin is a very common Wolof female name. The praise of her physical attributes reflects the Wolof conception of the ideal Wolof woman. The term *jongoma,* beautiful woman, refers to perfect beauty, that without blemish. Yasin-Pointed-Breasts thus becomes beauty personified.

[3]Black feathered birds.

[4]Large, wild turkies with long necks.

[5]Large, long-necked birds.

[6]Turtle doves.

[7]Vultures and other birds of prey.

[8]Trumpet birds distinguished by their yellow crested heads.

[9]In Wolof, *guru.* Imported from Sierra Leone, these nuts have a caffeine-like stimulating effect. They are more important as social lubricants, easing tensions and initial awkwardness before significant interpersonal meetings. It is customary for prospective suitors to offer the girl's family kola nuts as a mark of sincerity and respect for their position.

[10]They are preparing their external appearance so as to look their best when they meet Yasin.

[11]The potential husband of Yasin. She does not know who it will be, so she calls him by the "everyman" term conventionally used in the narratives.

[12]Onomatopoetic sound of the rustling of the bird's large feathers.

[13]Ideophonic expression creating the image of the vulture stretching and cracking his neck. From the Wolof, *rakakaki,* grind one's teeth; the noise of grinding teeth.

[14]Onomatopoetic expression for the cawing or crowing of birds.

[15]This narrative highlights the Wolof practice of intra-caste marriage. Although some inter-caste marriages occur, they are the exceptions to the ideal. The structure of the tale itself reveals this thematic interpretation. Each of the six birds professes his love for Yasin, using the same song of praise. The subsequent five rejections stress the moral requirements of her potential husband: he must have nobility. Although the five suitors all think of themselves as beautiful, they do not argue about their lack of nobility. Yasin is described as a descendent of the Jamba lineage and one who has great beauty. As a *jamba,* she seeks to marry a man who has honor and respect as great as the other members of her group. She seeks to marry another *jamba.* Only the sixth suitor fulfills her expectations because only the sixth is a member of her group. The unsuccessful birds suffer rejection because they sought the ideal beauty outside their own affiliation. The social significance of this metaphor between birds and Wolof marriage customs extends deeper into the realm of inter-caste social attitudes. It is striking that the choice for the ideal beautiful woman would come from the *jamba* family of birds. These are birds whose physical appearance, with the crown of yellow feathers on the heads, makes for their easy association with royalty. But the word itself is also markedly similar to the Wolof term for royalty, *jambur.* Only members of this *jambur* caste can assume traditional governing positions. The association of ideal beauty with the upper noble castes in the narrative reflects actual Wolof concepts of beauty and nobility. (see Judith Irvine,

"Caste and Communication in a Wolof Village," Univ. of Pennsylvania, 1973.) This narrative thus reinforces intra-caste marriage practices and confirms inter-caste perceptions of the hierarchical rankings of honor and beauty.

**PART FOUR
STORIES**
Statement—Refutation—
Conclusion

THE ETERNAL LOVERS[1]

There was a story . . .
Our legs are crossed . . .
It happened here . . .
It was so . . .

A ewe and a ram were strolling about the fields together. They walked and walked until they were very far from their home. In the field ahead they spied some stacks of millet[2] and remembered that those belonged to the king. The ram crossed to the grain and stood before the mounds. The ewe called out to him, "Let us be on our way!" But the ram urged her to him, saying "Come, let us eat until we are satisfied."

They ate and ate for a long time until they were both becoming full. At that time the king passed by them on an inspection tour of his harvest in the fields. When he came to the stacks of grain, he observed the ram eating it. He took out his gun and shot the ram. Then he carried its body back to his own town.

The ewe then began to sing aloud:

MY DEAREST RAM, MBELELAM;[3] MY DEAREST MBELELAM.
I SAID 'LET US BE ON OUR WAY'
BUT YOU SAID 'TO THE KING'S MILLET.'

The ram, which was shot, sang out to her:

EWE, MBALO,[4] DO NOT CRY WHILE I AM LIVING!

You understand, they were people. The king called his servants to him and told them to skin the ram. They took it and skinned it, cut it into small pieces and returned it to the king's compound.

The ewe approached the king's gate and began to cry:

MY DEAREST RAM, MBELELAM; MY DEAREST RAM, MBELELAM.
I SAID 'LET US BE ON OUR WAY'
BUT YOU SAID 'TO THE KING'S MILLET.'

The ram that was cut up into small pieces and placed in the king's bowls replied:

151

EWE, MBALO, DO NOT CRY FOR ME WHILE I AM LIVING!

The king's servants then took the meat, mixed it with oil and spices and poured it into the cooking pots.[5] When the oil was hot they placed the meat in the pot and stirred it until it was tender. When it was prepared they ate it.

The ewe entered just inside the compound gate and sang:

MY DEAREST RAM, MBELELAM; MY DEAREST RAM, MBELELAM.
I SAID 'LET US BE ON OUR WAY'
BUT YOU SAID 'TO THE KING'S MILLET.'

The ram which was being eaten by the people sang out:

EWE, MBALO, DO NOT CRY WHILE I AM LIVING!

After eating, all the people rested. Then the king himself arrived at the village resting area[6] and said, "Yes! I do not know who owned that ram but I am quite satisfied now." The people likewise replied, "Yes, yes! We are also satisfied."

The ewe approached the village resting area and sang:

MY DEAREST RAM, MBELELAM; MY DEAREST RAM, MBELELAM.
I SAID 'LET US BE ON OUR WAY'
BUT YOU SAID 'TO THE KING'S MILLET.'

The ram which had been eaten and was inside the king's stomach replied to her:

EWE, MBALO, DO NOT CRY WHILE I AM LIVING!

When the people heard this singing they said, "Listen! There is something in the king's stomach!" The king replied, "It is nothing really except satisfaction. I am just satisfied."[7]

The ewe sang out again:

MY DEAREST RAM, MBELELAM; MY DEAREST RAM, MBELELAM.
I SAID 'LET US BE ON OUR WAY'
BUT YOU SAID 'TO THE KING'S MILLET.'

The ram replied:

EWE, MBALO, DO NOT CRY WHILE I AM LIVING!

The people said, "King, there is something inside your stomach." He replied, "Cut it open and see what it is." But they protested, saying "But king, that is not safe; if we cut open your stomach you will die." "Just cut it open and you will see only meat there," he insisted.

So the people unsheathed a knife and incised the king's abdomen until there was a gaping hole. It was then that the ram jumped out past them and trotted away with the ewe.[8]

---

[1]Narrated on October 17 at 11:30 p.m. before 15 men and women in the compound of Keba Hadi Sise, by Kebba Cham, age 24, a blacksmith living in Njau, The Gambia. Two weeks before

recording this story, Kebba had become engaged to a beautiful girl whom he loved very much. Hearing this narrative, the other young men in the audience began to tease and chide him for his open admission of love.

[2] After cutting, the grain is stacked in the open fields and left to dry in the sun until its moisture content is low enough to insure proper storage in grain bins.

[3] Mbelelam, onomatopoetic sound of the bleating ewe. Its repetition fills the chorus with feelings of loss and sorrow.

[4] Mbalo, onomatopoetic sound of the calling of the ram to his loved one. Composed of deeper and stronger tones, it reflects the strength and courage normally associated with maleness.

[5] Less than choice meat cuts are usually marinated before cooking.

[6] Every village has a public area where the townspeople gather to socialize. This is often under a silk cotton or baobab tree. The people sit on a raised wooden platform with open sides and a palm, leaf-covered roof. A good community member visits this gathering area daily to learn about the important events in the lives of his neighbors.

[7] Social etiquette imposes strict sanctions against such outbursts caused by intestinal disturbances. To be afflicted by such internal rumblings and/or flatulence is a cause of great humiliation and loss of prestige.

[8] The release of the ram from the belly of the king illustrates two essential points: first, that the love which exists beween the ram and the ewe is eternal and will endure through the greatest of hardships; second, the action of the king in shooting the ram was totally unjustified. The extreme nature of the punishment did not fit the seriousness of the crime. Stealing is never condoned by the society, but the king, traditionally a wealthy and prosperous member of the community, would not have suffered in the least from the action of the ram. Having eaten the ram, the food did not agree with him, causing him intestinal unrest. As a result, the king is humiliated. The uncontrollable disturbance blemishes the honor and prestige of one of the nobles of the society, one of those people who are supposed to embody all the behavioral ideals of the culture. The king dies as a result of his inability to control his anger and follow the socially approved methods for reparation.

THE DONKEYS OF JOLOF[1]

There was a story . . .
Our legs are crossed . . .
It happened here . . .
It was so . . .

Those donkeys in the land of Jolof[2] long ago crowned a king called *Fari-Mbam.*[3] One day *Fari-Mbam* turned into a human being and came into the territory of Salum. He walked until he reached a village like Bati Hai.[4] No one knew him there. He stayed there a long time. He got married and fathered five children.

His people in Jolof said among themselves, "We miss our *Fari-Mbam.* We have not seen him for a long time. We must go now and search for him. A King should not leave his country like that."

So the king's relatives gathered together and changed themselves into human beings. They collected many types of drums, and departed the town of Masalaam[5] in Jolof. When they arrived in the center of Kaolack[6] they gathered into a circle in the middle of the marketplace and sang:

> *FARI-MBAM,* THE LOST DONKEY. KING OF THE DONKEYS.
> THE LOST DONKEY, *FARI,* KING OF DONKEYS. WHERE IS HE?
> WHERE IS HE? NAXE-NAXE,[7] THE GOOD DONKEY IS LOST.
> *FARI,* THE DONKEY. THE LOST DONKEY. *FARI,* KING OF DONKEYS!

Then they began to drum and sing:

> *FARI-MBAM,* THE LOST DONKEY. KING OF THE DONKEYS.
> THE LOST DONKEY, *FARI,* KING OF DONKEYS. WHERE IS HE?
> WHERE IS HE? NAXE-NAXE, THE GOOD DONKEY IS LOST.
> *FARI,* THE DONKEY. THE LOST DONKEY, *FARI,* KING OF DONKEYS!

They beat their drums and danced for a long time until one man approached them and said, "Your relative that you are seeking, I heard that he is living in a village called Bati Hai. They call him *Fari-Mbam.*" The people said, "Thanks and Peace be to you."

154

They packed up their belongings and left Kaolack. They soon arrived at Ndofan.[8] In the market of Ndofan they said, "We are looking for our relative." They began to drum and sing:

FARI-MBAM, THE LOST DONKEY, KING OF THE DONKEYS.
THE LOST DONKEY, FARI, KING OF THE DONKEYS, WHERE IS HE?
WHERE IS HE? NAXE-NAXE, THE GOOD DONKEY IS LOST.
FARI, THE DONKEY, THE LOST DONKEY, FARI, KING OF DONKEYS.

They continued to drum and dance for a long time. A man approached them and said, "The relative that you are looking for, we heard of him in a place called Bati Hai." So the people gathered their traveling bags and walked to Nyoro.[9] In the middle of the market there they began to drum and sing aloud:

FARI-MBAM, THE LOST DONKEY, FARI, KING OF DONKEYS.
FARI, WHERE IS HE? WHERE IS HE? NAXE-NAXE THE GOOD DONKEY IS
   LOST.
FARI, THE DONKEY, THE LOST DONKEY, FARI, KING OF DONKEYS.

A man came near to them and asked, "What are you doing here?" "We are looking for our relative who is called *Fari-Mbam.*" "Yes, we heard of him. He is living in the land of the English." So the people packed up their things again and went to Farafeni[10] at night. They began to sing:

FARI-MBAM, THE BIG DONKEY IS LOST, FARI, KING OF DONKEYS.
FARI, WHERE IS HE? WHERE IS HE? NAXE-NAXE, KING OF DONKEYS.

A man came out of his compound and asked them what they were doing. They replied, "We are looking for our relative. He was a king in Jolof but he became lost. We are looking for him throughout the country." Allah is so good. This man knew about him. He told them, "Go to a place called Kaur! There ask for a place called Bati Hai. That is where *Fari-Mbam* is living. He is a rich man now." So all the people collected their belongings and traveled to the marketplace in Kaur. They began to drum and sing:

FARI-MBAM, THE LOST DONKEY.
FARI, WHERE IS HE? WHERE IS HE? NAXE-NAXE, THE GOOD DONKEY IS
   LOST.
FARI, KING OF DONKEYS.

They drummed like that in the marketplace. Everybody around came to hear them and said, "These people are really good with that song. Where are they going?" One man from outside the crowd came and asked, "Who are you looking for?" "We are looking for our lost relative who is called *Fari-Mbam.* He is our king in Jolof. He changed into a man and came into this country. We are looking for him." The people of Kaur said, "Then go to Bati Hai."

They took their drums and went up to a village called Bantuk. They formed a circle and one of them got in the middle and sang:

FARI-MBAM, THE LOST DONKEY, FARI, KING OF DONKEYS.
FARI, WHERE IS HE? WHERE IS HE? NAXE-NAXE.

FARI, KING OF DONKEYS.

Then they all sang. Some people arrived and asked, "Who are you looking for?" "We are looking for our relative, whom we have lost. He is called *Fari-Mbam. Fari-Mbam* is the king of all donkeys." "We know a *Fari-Mbam* but he is a man. He lives in Bati Hai." So they all left.

When they arrived in Bati Hai[11] they went right to the middle of the village square. The gate of *Fari-Mbam's* compound was directly opposite to the meeting place. They began to drum and sing:

FARI, WHERE IS HE? WHERE IS HE? NAXE-NAXE, THE GOOD DONKEY IS
  LOST.
FARI-MBAM, THE LOST DONKEY, *FARI-MBAM.*

One section called:

FARI-MBAM, THE LOST DONKEY, KING OF DONKEYS.

while another part replied:

FARI-MBAM, THE LOST DONKEY, KING OF DONKEYS.
FARI, WHERE IS HE? WHERE IS HE? NAXE-NAXE.
FARI, THE KING OF DONKEYS.

After that *Fari* got up. He went to the center of his compound, then walked to his gate. He said to his wife, "I heard something very confusing. Those are my relatives. When I hear their singing, my hair tingles from my head to my feet. But I won't go to see them yet." He went back to the compound. Soon the people began to sing:

FARI, WHERE IS HE? WHERE IS HE? NAXE-NAXE?
FARI, KING OF DONKEYS.

Another section chorused:

FARI, WHERE IS HE? WHERE IS HE? NAXE-NAXE, THE LOST DONKEY.
FARI, THE KING OF DONKEYS.

After he heard that, *Fari* went into the house of his wife and said, "It's alright, I'm going in Peace."

He went and stood by the side of the ring and began to stamp his foot REK-REK-REK[12] and a donkey's foot appeared. Then the crowd sang:

FARI, WHERE IS HE? WHERE IS HE? NAXE-NAXE, THE DONKEY IS FOUND.
FARI, WHERE IS HE? WHERE IS HE? THE DONKEY IS FOUND.
FARI, THE DONKEY IS FOUND, *FARI,* KING OF DONKEYS.

Then the children heard the drums calling. The eldest son said, "My father has turned into a donkey. Is he going away with his relatives?" The mother answered, "Yes, but if you go too, I will be very lonely in this empty house." But the eldest sang:

FARI, WHERE IS HE? WHERE IS HE? NAXE-NAXE, *FARI,* THE DONKEY IS
  FOUND.
FARI, KING OF DONKEYS.

He then changed into a donkey. He stamped his foot REK-REK-REK and a donkey's leg appeared, an ear and he too became a donkey.

After that, the next eldest child came and said, "Mother, father is going and leaving us." "I sympathize with you," she said, "but if you go, I will be lonely. I have nobody but you." He too went to the middle of the ring and sang:

> *FARI,* WHERE IS HE? WHERE IS HE? NAXE-NAXE, THE KING OF DONKEYS
>   IS FOUND.
> *FARI,* KING OF DONKEYS IS FOUND.

In that manner two sons, you know, had gone over to *Fari.* The third one went to the mother and said, "My mother! Father cannot go and leave me here." "Alright," answered his mother. He went to the middle of the ring and stamped his foot. A donkey's leg appeared. He sang:

> *FARI,* WHERE IS HE? WHERE IS HE? NAXE-NAXE, *FARI,* KING OF DONKEYS.
> *FARI-MBAM,* THE DONKEY IS FOUND, *FARI,* KING OF DONKEYS.

He stamped his foot REK-REK-REK and a donkey's foot and ears appeared. He became a donkey. That was the third child.

The fourth one bid his mother farewell. She moaned, "I will be *very* lonely." But he walked away and went to the middle of the ring and sang:

> *FARI,* WHERE IS HE? WHERE IS HE? NAXE-NAXE, THE DONKEY IS FOUND!
> *FARI,* THE DONKEY IS FOUND! *FARI,* KING OF DONKEYS!

A donkey's ears and tail came out and he too became a donkey.

All the rest of the people from Jolof began to beat their drums. They were extremely happy. They said, "This town, Bati Hai, is a very good place to live. Our relative has been treated very well here. He even has a family! Thank you! But we will take our relative home with us."

They remained in Bati Hai for a short time. Then they began to sing as they headed back towards Jolof:

> *FARI,* WHERE IS HE? WHERE IS HE? NAXE-NAXE, THE DONKEY IS FOUND!
> *FARI,* THE KING OF THE DONKEYS!

They all went home together.[13]

---

[1] Recorded in Bati Hai, The Gambia, by Lamin Jeng, age 31, on November 20 in the home of his father Madoun Jeng, in the presence of 17 adult men and women, at 3:00 p.m. Lamin Jeng is noted as a griot because of his excellent singing voice. This narrative, with its repeated chorus, provides a proper context to demonstrate his talents. Another griot, with less vocal ability, would not repeat the chorus as frequently as occurs here.

[2] One of the major states in the ancient kingdom of the Wolof, located in Senegal. The other states of Kayor, Baol, Walo, Sine and Saloum owed allegiance to its ruler who resided in Jolof and was called *Bur ba Jolof.*

[3] *Fari-Mbam* is translated into English as King Donkey. *Fari* is another term for *Bur,* king, but it specifies that the ruler is a descendant of paternal *and* maternal royalty.

[4] Located on the North Bank of the Gambia River, McCarthy Island District. The 28 inhabitants

all belong to the *gewel* or griot class.

[5] Masalaam is situated in the center of the state of Jolof, Senegal. The name of the town bears witness to a strong Islamic influence.

[6] Kaolack is located about twenty-five miles north of the Gambia-Senegal border on the main road between Dakar, Senegal, and Banjul, The Gambia.

[7] Onomatopoetic sound imitating the braying of a donkey. In performance, this is a remarkably accurate reproduction which captures the sorrowful calling attributed to domesticated donkeys.

[8] A small town outside Kaolack, Senegal.

[9] An extremely small Senegalese village near the border between Senegal and The Gambia.

[10] A large border town in The Gambia where the Senegal-Gambia Highway passes. It is also the location of the up-river ferry crossing where vehicles can move from the North Bank to the South Bank of The Gambia. Its strategic position accounts for its unusually large and busy marketplace.

[11] This is another large market town where numerous foreign peanut exporters warehouse their produce before shipment to the capital, Banjul. The movement from Masalaam to Bati Hai has been southerly and is a route well known to the members of the audience, either through personal experiences or through other traditional, historical materials.

[12] From the verb *rekes,* to tamp or force down. The repetition stimulates the envisioning process and is characteristic of well-known narratives.

[13] Sorrow is the emotional thread binding the narrative elements in this tale. The stitching begins with the sorrow of the donkeys of Jolof over their king, who has deserted his realm. The tortured song encapsulates the pain caused by his loss. Each repetition of the song in a new geographical location increases their burden. When they locate their king, the weight of their sorrow is shifted. The emotional impact of the chorus dramatically shifts and takes on new perspective. The climactic joy of the donkeys at the end of their search does not lead to a cathartic sense of satisfaction. Their happiness only initiates the sorrow of *Fari's* wife, his children and the people of the village. The structure directs the impact of the narrative to the human characters. Their grief has no end. The initial focus on the sorrow of the donkeys of Jolof establishes the **essential emotional network for the appreciation for this dimension of sorrow.** *Fari's* **wife loses** her husband, her family and her future. In discussing the reasons for this thematic focus with Lamin Jeng, he stated, "Every woman should only marry someone she knows very well. If you marry someone you do not know, you may fall on Fari-Mbam's wife's problem: you will become lonely." With November being in the traditional time for negotiating marriages, the prospective young women of Bati Hai were subtly being advised.

SAMBA'S WIFE[1]

There was a story . . .
Our legs are crossed . . .
It happened here . . .
It was so . . .

Once there was a man named Samba who had a hyena for a wife. This hyena lived with him for a long time until one day the woman had a child. After it was born she nursed it.

One day this wife called her husband, "My Uncle,"[2] and he replied, "Yes?" She said, "I am going to have my hair braided at Bati Ndar."[3] Then she traveled to Bati Ndar. After she had her hair braided there, she left. She traveled on the road between Bati Ndar and Bati Hai until she reached the well. She stopped at the well and glanced up to the sun. She realized that the sun would soon be setting. She said to herself, "Oh, I am late, very late." Immediately when she said this, her leg changed into the leg of a hyena; her arm also changed into that of a hyena. She began to sing:

TREMBLING, TREMBLING, TODAY SHE WILL DIE;
I AM RETURNING HOME TO POUND IN THE MORNING,
AND TO COOK AT NIGHT.
TREMBLING, TREMBLING, TODAY SHE WILL DIE;
I AM RETURNING HOME TO POUND IN THE MORNING,
AND TO COOK AT NIGHT.

Then she changed herself back into a complete woman and returned home. At home she prepared supper for her family that night.

In the morning she pounded enough millet for the daily meals. She then went to her husband and called him, "My Uncle," and he replied, "Yes?" She said, "I am going to Bati Ndar to have my braids finished." "Alright," he answered.

The woman walked to Bati Ndar and had her braids completed. When she was returning to her village she stopped by the well. She looked up at the sun

159

and said, "Oh, I am late." Again when she had said this, one leg and one arm of a hyena appeared. As this happened she sang:

> TREMBLING, TREMBLING, TODAY SHE WILL DIE;
> I AM RETURNING HOME TO POUND THE MILLET IN THE MORNING,
> AND TO COOK AT NIGHT.
> TREMBLING, TREMBLING, TODAY SHE WILL DIE;
> ·I AM RETURNING HOME TO POUND IN THE MORNING,
> AND TO COOK AT NIGHT.

As she was singing this song, a hunter[4] came near to the well, climbed a tree and secretly observed her activities from the top of it.

When the woman had finished, the hunter quickly descended the tree and went to Samba's compound. There he said to him, "Samba, your wife is a hyena!" "A hyena?" gasped Samba. "Yes," assured the hunter. Samba said, "I do not believe you." But the hunter insisted, "Honestly, I saw her today. If you wait here until the sun is ready to set and then go and stand next to the tree by the well, she will meet you there." "I will do it," replied Samba.

Later that day, the wife came to Samba and addressed him, "My Uncle!" and he replied, "Yes?" "I am going to Bati Ndar to pay for the braiding of my hair." He replied, "Alright."

After paying her hairdresser, she left Bati Ndar and soon approached the well. She quickly brought forth a hyena's leg and arm as she continued to sing this song:

> TREMBLING, TREMBLING, TODAY SHE WILL DIE;
> I AM GOING HOME TO POUND IN THE MORNING,
> AND TO COOK AT NIGHT.
> TREMBLING, TREMBLING, TODAY SHE WILL DIE;
> I AM GOING HOME TO POUND IN THE MORNING,
> AND TO COOK AT NIGHT.

As Samba watched from behind the tree, he exclaimed to himself, "My Allah, so my wife *is* a hyena!"

This wife soon returned home and began to prepare her family's supper.

After eating, Samba rested for a short while and then called out to his wife, "Kumba?" and she replied, "Yes?" He said, "Bring me the child. I want to see the child." As she approached her husband she said to him, "Oh Samba, what is the matter? Why are you asking to see my child?" Kumba then gave the child to Samba. He kept silent for a long while and then he began to sing:

> TREMBLING, TREMBLING, TODAY SHE WILL DIE;
> I AM RETURNING HOME TO POUND IN THE MORNING,
> AND TO COOK AT NIGHT.
> TREMBLING, TREMBLING, TODAY SHE WILL DIE;
> I AM RETURNING HOME TO POUND IN THE MORNING,
> AND TO COOK AT NIGHT.

With this, his wife was astonished. She asked, "Samba, where did you hear this song?" "This song?" he replied. "It is just one of our circumcision songs,"[5] he tentatively suggested. "Samba, stop that song," she begged. "I will give you one of my cows in the herd if you stop singing that song." He replied, "I cannot stop this song. It is one of our circumcision songs." He held the child more firmly and sang:

> TREMBLING, TREMBLING, TODAY SHE WILL DIE;
> I AM RETURNING HOME TO POUND IN THE MORNING,
> AND TO COOK AT NIGHT.
> TREMBLING, TREMBLING, TODAY SHE WILL DIE;
> I AM RETURNING HOME TO POUND IN THE MORNING,
> AND TO COOK AT NIGHT.

Then the child began to repeat the song:

> TREMBLING, TREMBLING, TODAY SHE WILL DIE;
> I AM RETURNING HOME TO POUND IN THE MORNING,
> AND TO COOK AT NIGHT.
> TREMBLING, TREMBLING, TODAY SHE WILL DIE;
> I AM RETURNING HOME TO POUND IN THE MORNING,
> AND TO COOK AT NIGHT.

Kumba rushed from the kitchen area and said, "I can sing this song better than that." She sang:

> TREMBLING, TREMBLING, TODAY SHE WILL DIE;
> I AM RETURNING HOME TO POUND IN THE MORNING,
> AND TO COOK AT NIGHT.
> TREMBLING, TREMBLING, TODAY SHE WILL DIE;
> I AM RETURNING HOME TO POUND IN THE MORNING,
> AND TO COOK AT NIGHT.

As Kumba sang the song, she was immediately transformed into a hyena. The children in the compound changed into hyenas. Even the little child in its father's arms was transformed into a hyena.

After that, they ran from the village and returned to the wilderness.[6]

---

[1] Narrated by Awa Jeng, age 42, in Bati Hai, The Gambia, on October 29 at 2:15 before 12 men, 17 women and 18 children. All the people of this village are griots. Awa Jeng is the wife of Lamin Jeng, who is also an accomplished storyteller.

[2] In Wolof, *suma nijay*. Wolof women use this term for one's mother's brother as a sign of deep respect for their husbands. Awa Jeng emphasizes that the wife is a very good wife, devoted to her husband and respectful of his position in the family. This is in deference to the Wolof rules of succession and inheritance among low caste groups. Although Islam has forced attention to patrilineal descent, it is to his mother's relatives that he seeks assistance in the difficult time of his life.

[3] Although all women know how to braid hair, it is to the professional hairdressers that women go for elaborate patterning and designs. These hairdressers are usually griot women.

[4] In Wolof, *rabkat*.

[5]In Wolof, *lel*. These songs would not be known to the wife, for women are prohibited from attending circumcision rituals. Young boys are usually circumcised between 8 and 12 years old out in the bush in a specially constructed house, *mbar*. Those who are circumcised together form a special group who remain close for the rest of their lives.

[6]The wife's four-fold repetition of the chorus focuses attention on the inherent non-human characteristics of Samba's wife. Her frustration at returning home late for dinner leads her to temporarily lose control of the human disguise and reveal her true nature. She has been pretending to be something that she cannot, by nature, claim. The chorus reflects the unstable, emotional tension and fear that she feels as a result. In spite of her desires to be a good wife and mother (see note no. 2), she cannot overcome her in-born characteristics. These are revealed at this time of stress. With each repetition of the chorus, her true nature is revealed. She exhibits irrationality when she offers her husband an exhorbitant gift for simply ceasing to sing. Her lack of discipline is demonstrated when her child sings the chorus. She cannot bear to hear it repeated poorly. As revealed in other Wolof narratives featuring hyenas, she functions as a symbol of shame and dishonor, exhibiting characteristics which are antithetical to the Wolof ideals of honor. Her non-human characteristics have, however, been transformed to her offspring. She has contaminated the lineage of Samba. The effect of this highlights the intent of the narrative itself. Samba, unaware of his wife's identity, suffers for his ignorance. What is implied here is that Samba has obviously not followed the normal procedures regarding the selection of mates among the Wolof. (See David Ames, "The Selection of Mates, Courtship, and Marriage among the Wolof," *Bulletin I.F.A.W.*, 18, 1956.) Before a marriage, the parents of the prospective couple seek information regarding the hereditary background of the prospective spouse from the local griots. Samba, obviously, did not follow this practice, and consequently is left alone at the end of the narrative with neither wife nor children.

THE MARRIAGE OF TWO MASTERS OF THE WOLOF LANGUAGE, I[1]

There was a story . . .
Our legs are crossed . . .
It happened here . . .
It was so . . .

There was a young girl. This girl knew the Wolof language so well that she thought that she knew it better than anyone else in the whole world. Whenever a man came to court her for marriage she would only have to say two words to him and he would become confused. Then she would tell him that he was not suitable for marriage and drive him away from the village. She lived like that for a long time until one day a young man from the East heard about her. He said to himself, "I must see this lady."

What is the name of the lady? Jor Khan is her name. So the young man prepared himself and told his family that he was going to meet this girl.

The night before this young man left for the girl's village, the father of Jor Khan had, by chance, spent the night in the same village. In the morning, the father mounted his horse and set out on the road home. The young man also began his journey. He soon met up with the old man and so they traveled together. They walked and walked for a long time until the sun became very hot. At that time the sand was burning the young man's feet so he said to the old man, "Papa?" The old man replied, "Yes?" "I would like you to lend me one of your horses to ride," asked the youth. "There is only one horse, my son, and I believe I am more suitable to ride than you," replied the old man. "You are right," conceded the young man.

They walked on and on and on until they saw a small cotton field which was fenced in entirely. The youth said, "Oh Papa, look how beautifully this cotton field is fenced." The old man replied, "Yes! Yes, the fencing is quite nice; nothing can damage it for a year or more." They continued to walk for a long

163

time until they saw another cotton field. This one was so large that it spread all over the bush, but there was no fence surrounding it. He said to the old man, "Papa, look how *big* this field is!" "Yes, this cotton field is as large as the wilderness itself." "Father, concerning this field and the field before, if they were to give you one of them, which one would you take?" asked the man. "You certainly ask strange questions. Do you realize that this small field would produce only two *tengteng?*[2] I would take this *big* field," replied the old man. "You are right," accepted the young man.

They traveled on and on and on until they saw a herd of cattle, about fifty in number and all females. The boy said, "Look how beautiful those cows are." "Yes, they are so beautiful," replied the old man. They continued farther until they met up with another herd of cattle with about one hundred animals, all males. "Papa, look at those animals." "Yes, son, these are really beautiful and there are so many of them." "Oh Father, if you were to be given one of the herds, either this one or the one seen before, which one would you take?" "Son, if you are a fool, I certainly am not. The cattle we passed before are fewer than the ones here. There are about 100 head here compared to only fifty back there. I would take these cattle here." "Papa, you are right."

They walked on and on for a long time. The young man then turned to the old man and asked, "My Father, tell me, where are you going?" "To my home," was his reply. "Where is your home?" asked the boy. "Chon,"[3] replied the old man. "Do you live in Chon?" pressed the boy. "Yes." The young man was surprised because he said that he too was going to Chon. "Do you you know a girl by the name of Jor Khan?" asked the boy. "Jor Khan?" "Yes, Jor Khan! I heard of a Jor Khan who lives in Chon," added the young man. "Yes, there is a Jor Khan in Chon. She is my daughter," replied the old man. "Oh Papa, you are the father of Jor Khan?" The old man replied, "Yes . . . Yes." "That is good," replied the young man.

Now they both arrived in the town of Chon. The young man wanted to go to the other side of town, so he said to the old man, "If you go home, tell Jor Khan that I greet her." "Yes, I will," replied the old man. They separated but the youth called back to the old man and asked, "If you go, what will you tell her?" He said, "That someone is greeting you." "But what if she asks you who? Should you not ask me my name?" questioned the youth. "Yes . . . Yes, I forgot. What is your name?" asked the old man. The young man replied, "My name is 'Three days of Gamo laying down,' and my surname is 'Khan, bird's nest up, gourd down.' " "Yes, that is good," added the old man as he hurried to his home.

Jor Khan met her father at the gate of their compound, took the horse and tied it to a pole. Then her father said, "Jor, fetch me some water and I will tell you of my travels." The girl went and drew some water and took it to him. He drank it, then he said, "I met up with a man, but I think that he must be crazy." "Mmmmm," responded the girl. "Yes, because we traveled together for some time until he asked me to lend him my horse. I told him that I had only one horse and that I was more suitable to ride than he," continued the old man. Jor said, "Yes, Father. Do you know that while you were riding on your horse you had shoes on your feet?" He said, "Yes, and the sand was extremely hot." "Father, he was just asking to borrow your shoes. You know he had no shoes." "Yes, he had no shoes," said the father. His daughter said, "Yes, he was ashamed to ask you directly, that is why he asked you in that manner. It was the shoes he was after and not your horse."

The father continued, "We also came to a location where we saw a cotton field so small while farther on we saw a larger one. He asked me, between the two, which one I would choose if I were given one of them." "Father! Which one did you choose?" "What could I answer other than take the larger field because I could not even compare the larger one with the small one. I would take the big cotton field." The girl said, "Do you know why he asked you that? It is because the small field had been fenced in so that no one could spoil it, while the larger field was open. Anyone could steal from it or damage it." "You are right," conceded the old man.

The old man narrated some more details about his trip. "We saw a herd of cattle numbering about fifty cows. Farther along the road we saw another herd of about one hundred bulls. He asked me if I were to be given one of the herds, which one I would take." "Father, what was your response?" "I told him that I would not take the small herd; I would take the hundred." She said to him, "Father, do you know why he asked you that question? The large herd is composed of males only and males do not multiply." He said, "Oh . . . yes. You are right."

"Where is that man now?" asked the girl. "That man said that he greets you. He has gone to stay with some people on the other side of town," answered the father. She asked, "What is his name?" " 'Three days of Gamo' is his name, surname 'Khan, bird's nest up, gourd down,' " answered the old man. The girl replied, "Aha, that is Gamo Khan of Tagen.[4] Father, he is coming for me in marriage. When he comes, give me to him. *He* is the one I want to marry."

Jor Khan went and caught two chickens and cooked them very carefully and sent them with a young girl to Gamo Khan. She cut a pumpkin leaf, a red thorn and a piece of cloth and put them on the bowl's cover. The young girl then took the food to Gamo in the distant compound. When it arrived, Gamo looked at the cover and said, "Yes, Jor Khan says that is her compound, her house has pumpkins on the roof and that she is menstruating." Then he ate her food. He relaxed till evening and then went to Jor Khan's compound. When he entered, he greeted her people. Then he moved directly to Jor Khan's house. The people were astonished to see him walk straight to her house. They did not know who told him about the house.

Afterwards, they were married. After the marriage ceremony he told Jor that since Tagen was so far away, he would like to spend the rainy season at her village. Jor Khan became pregnant and in time delivered a child.

Gamo stayed with her until one day he went out to the bush to fetch firewood. He met up there with three Mauritanians. They began to argue. The three attacked Gamo, overcame him and threw him into a hole. Gamo told them, "You have done well, I praise you, because I thought that no man could beat me and overpower me as you have done. I am happy to meet up with you. Since my birth, I have never met up with a man who equals me. Now I am happy to meet you. I would like to send you to my wife." The Mauritanians said, "Yes . . . Yes!" So he said to them, "Do you see that village just ahead? If you go there you will see my wife. Ask for Jor Khan. But if you go, do not tell her that you beat me. Just tell her that you have met up with her husband in the bush and that he has asked you to come to her so that the two black sheep which are in the yard may be killed for you. The other sheep should be tied up until I return." When the Mauritanians arrived, they came to the compound and asked for Jor Khan, and related the message to her. Jor nodded her head and said, "Aha!" She brought them some tea, cups and a pot and gave it to them. They drank the tea.

Jor then went to the village square and told the people, "My husband has been beaten up by the Mauritanians. He said that we should kill two of them and tie the third one up until he returns." So the people went to her compound and they killed the two black Mauritanians and tied up the last one.

Jor then said to the people, "Now help me follow their footsteps so that we may find my husband." They followed her. Jor led the way following the footsteps until they came to the place where they had been fighting. Then they saw the hole where Gamo was thrown. The people began rushing about trying to retrieve Gamo by lowering ropes into the hole. "Do not be in such a hurry," Jor told them. "Listen to me. Let me speak with my husband. We do not know what condition my husband is in. I must ask him what state he is in." "You are right," they said. She turned around and picked up a branch from a tree. She cut it and threw it into the hole. The man in the hole, her husband, split the bark and threw out the white pith that was remaining. She told them, "What did I tell you? He said that he is naked down there." So she threw one of her own cloths into the hole and her husband wrapped it around himself. Then a few men descended into the hole and lifted him out. Afterwards they all returned home together.

When they reached their compound, Gamo proceeded to cut off one hand and one ear of the last Mauritanian. Then they sent him away.

This Mauritanian returned home and reported everything that had happened to him to his king. The Mauritanian king then sent his best soldiers, riding twelve camels[5] out on the road on look for Gamo Khan.

When they arrived, it was very hot in the afternoon. Gamo was bathing in the open washroom. Gamo looked over the fence and saw the Mauritanians approaching. It was too late for him to run back to his house because the Mauritanians would see him. They were quite near and Gamo did not know what to do. He called out, "Jor Khan . . . Jor Khan!" "Yes?" she replied. "Quickly now, run to my bed, under the pillow there is a pipe. Fill it with tobacco and bring it to me. I am about to vomit." The wife ran to the house. Under the pillow she found a pistol. She loaded it with twelve bullets and brought it to her husband. He parted the fence. When the Mauritanians were in front of him he began to shoot them one by one until there were only three left. When they realized what was happening, they turned around and fled.[6]

[1] Narrated by Momadu Njay, age 42, griot in the village of Ker Mu Ali in Senegal, on November 16 before 15 men, 8 women and 20 children at 9:50 p.m. Momadu Njay is recognized as the best griot in the village. Like most griots in Saloun, he also farms groundnuts and millet.

[2] A large winnowing basket used to clean the husks from pounded rice or millet. When used as a container it would hold approximately one-half bushel of cotton.

[3] Exact location of the town could not be secured. It is believed to be somewhere in the state of Jolof in Senegal.

[4] The only reference provided to the location of the town indicates that it is east of Senegal.

[5] In Wolof, *gelem.*

[6] This narrative provides a backdrop for the expression of the popular belief that Wolof is a most beautiful language. Mastery of its subtleties and nuances provides one with the facility to speak indirectly. This is considered a highly desirable ability, where control of one's physical and emotional faculties is a requirement for social recognition. Jor and Gamo Khan are presented as models of the ideal Wolof speakers. This item is expressly manifest in their reserved speech. Garrulousness is avoided because the tongue is believed to be like a lion, dangerous and difficult to master. The Wolof proverb *wah ju bare du wone nhel,* loquaciousness does not demonstrate intelligence, indicates where the true value of speaking is found. Speech is associated with action; just as the person never travels needlessly, so too he never speaks without having good reason to do so. Jor and Gamo Khan speak with clear and well enunciated voices. Speech with loud, high-pitched, or nasalized sounds in considered improper and shameful, associated with low caste speech patterns. For a detailed examination of this, see Judith Irvine's "Caste and Communication in a Wolof Village."

THE MARRIAGE OF TWO MASTERS
OF THE WOLOF LANGUAGE, II[1]

There was a story . . .
Our legs are crossed . . .
It happened here . . .
It was so . . .

There was a young man. In another town there lived a young woman. This woman was so beautiful that she surpassed all the other girls in her area. But all the young men who came to court her had a very difficult time talking to her. She only had to utter a few words to them and they would go away very confused.

One young man heard about her. He left his village and decided to see this extraordinary girl for himself. He started out on his journey.

At that same time, the beautiful girl's father was just returning home from a very long journey on his camel. At the crossroads outside of his town he met the young man. The young man called out to the elder, "Where are you going?" The man replied, "I am going on towards Panchang.[2] Then from Panchang I am going to Porli." You know, that is where the young girl lived. The young man said, "Stop. Either you take me along with you on your camel or I will carry you along." The old man said, "Ah, what are you talking about? Can you not see that I only have one saddle on my camel? How can you carry me, since you are only walking?" The young man replied, "Yes."

They began their journey together. The younger man was leading the way in front of the camel and the elder man followed, still riding his camel. As they headed towards the town they continued to converse with each other but the elder thought that the young man was crazy.

As they approached one village, they passed by the side of the 'great house.'[3] The young man pointed at the 'great house' and asked, "Father," and he replied, "Yes?" He said, "Wait, tell me who owns the 'great house' and is the

168

owner himself dead?" The old man said, "HUNNH? Do not bother me with such stupid questions. I do not want to be disturbed any more by you. Such a stupid question, TCH-TCH-TCH."

They continued on their way. They walked and walked until they neared another village. There they passed by a very large cassava field. The young man asked, "Father, whom does that cassava field belong to?" The old man replied, "That belongs to so and so."[4] He asked again, "Father, but that man does not have much cassava at all." He replied, "Hey, you child, you must be out of your mind. This field is full of cassava and you say that it has no cassava at all. Ah . . . Do not bother me any more, TCH-TCH-TCH."

They continued farther on their journey. They passed by another field of cassava. This field had only a few cassava plants and was surrounded by a fence. The young man asked, "Father," and he replied, "Yes?" He said, "Father, who owns the cassava field?" The old man replied, "That field is owned by so and so." The young man said, "That man certainly has plenty of cassava." The old man looked at him and said, "Do not be silly, my little child. There are only seven cassava plants here and you say that the owner has a lot of cassava? Ah, get out of my sight. Leave me alone."

They continued on their journey until they reached the town. When they arrived, the young man stayed in the compound of the head of the village.

The young girl slaughtered a fat sheep for her father's return and cooked it in a large bowl of *benechin*.[5] All the young men were invited to her compound for supper.

After cooking the sheep, she placed all of the meat into the bottom of the bowl and then covered it with rice.

All the young men arrived. The young visitor was also invited to eat supper there. When they arrived, they all began to eat. The young visitor refused to eat. They said, "Come on and eat with us." He said, "No, I do not want to eat now." They all ate and ate until they were satisfied. He waited until they were all finished eating and then had washed their hands. The young man washed his hands and then sat down in front of the half-empty bowl. The other men said among themselves, "Ah, he said he was full but now look at him, now he is ready to eat. What is the matter with him?" They spoke in a very low voice, you understand!

The young man thought to himself, "It is not normal practice of cooking *benachin* without including a single piece of meat in the bowl. Therefore there must be some trick behind this action." Then he picked up the big bowl and began to shake it around until the meat that was on the bottom showed up on top of the rice. When he saw the meat he took one piece of it and ate it. He called a child to take the remainder of the supper back to the young girl.

When the young girl saw the bowl with all the meat still inside she was convinced, since the meat was so abundant, that only one person had eaten some of it. She said that she was going to discover who that person was before anyone could tell her. She decided that since he was so intelligent, she could call him to come to her father's house without even telling him to come.

The young girl then took the sheep's skin and wrapped the sheep's head and legs up into it. Then she told her sister, "Take this inside the house where all the young men are sitting." She replied, "Yes." She took it there.

When she arrived, all the young men said, "Hey, why did you bring us this hide with the head and legs wrapped up inside? And why did you send us a supper of *benachin* without any meat in it? What kind of a trick was that?" Then they all left the house in disgust. But the visitor stayed there.

When they had gone, he picked up the hide with the head and legs inside and walked over to the girl's father's house. When he entered into the compound the people there asked him, "You, what are you doing in here with that sheep's skin, with the head and the legs wrapped up inside?" He replied, "I have been called here by someone!" Then the young girl appeared and asked, "Who called you?" He replied, "You, girl, you called me when you told me to come with my hands, you told me to come with my mouth, you told me to come with my eyes, you told me to come with my nose, you told me to come with my ears. You talk and I listen; then I will respond to you." He said to her, "When you talk, my ears hear it, my brain grips it and my tongue replies to you. My eyes see you and they see your mother."

After that the young girl stretched out her hand and shook the young man's hand. Then she went to prepare her father's supper.

When she arrived there her father said to her, "My child," and she replied, "Yes?" He said to her, "My child, that young man, he nearly burst my mind today." She said, "How did he almost split open your head?" He said, "That one is crazy." She said, "No!" He said, "Oh, yes! When he first saw me he said, 'Let me carry you or else you carry me.' If I would have asked him to carry me, how could he have done it, since I was riding a camel?" She said, "Father?" and he replied, "Yes?" She said, "Father, when he said, 'Take me or I will take you,' he meant that he would lead the way for you and you should follow. He knows two cannot ride on one camel."

He said, "No wait. That is not all. I am not finished yet." He said to her, "We passed by a village and approached a great house. He asked me, 'who owns this "great house"?' I told him that he was crazy because no one owns the great house. Then he asked me, 'Is the owner dead or alive?' Now is that not a stupid question. He is certainly crazy." The young girl said, "That is not crazy. When you heard him talk that way he was really asking if the owner left children to continue his name or not. That is why he asked if he was dead or alive."

The old man said to her, "I am still not finished yet. After that, we passed by a very big field full of cassava plants. Then he asked, 'Who owns this field?' I told him it belongs to Mr. so and so. Then he said, 'The owner only has a few plants.' I told him that he must be crazy because the whole field was full."

The young girl said to him, "Father," and he replied, "Yes?" She said to him, "Father, when he said that, he really meant to tell you that in the field the donkeys can go and dig up the plants and eat them; the monkeys can go and dig up his plants and eat them."

Then he said, "I am still not finished." She said, "And what else did you see?" He said, "We then passed by another field of cassava. It was much smaller than the other one and it had a fence around it. He asked me, 'Who is the owner of this field?' I told him Mr. so and so owns it. Then he said, 'He owns a great amount of cassava.' I told him he was crazy because there were only seven plants of cassava in the field."

The young girl said, "Father, when he said that, he really meant to tell you that whoever wanted to dig up and eat some of that owner's cassava, first had to go and ask the owner for the key to the fence gate. No one can dig there without a key. That is why he said that there was a huge amount of cassava there."

Then she said to her father, "Father, *this* is the man that I want to marry." So the father engaged her to him and they remained in Porli for a long time.

[1]Narrated by Malik Boye in Porli, The Gambia, on November 20 in the compound of Bessi Njay before 38 men, women and children. This evening's story-telling session developed into a contest between the excellent griots Alison Jalo, Bessi Njay and Malik Boye. They were competing against one another for the distinction of 'best story teller.' Although all were acknowledged as good story tellers, the audience did not lift any one griot above the other two. They were each praised for their own distinct narrative specialty.

[2]Located about 10 miles up the Gambia river from Njau and 3 miles from Porli where the beautiful girl lives.

[3]In Wolof, *Ker gu rey.* The Wolof refer to a cemetery, *robukay,* as the 'great house.' To speak openly of the cemetery would invite a visitation by death itself to one's own compound.

[4]In Wolof narratives, the hypothetical individual is usually referred to as *diu,* an indeterminate someone.

[5]A meal consisting of steamed rice and fish or meat, fried in peanut oil, with a sauce composed of onions, tomatoes, peppers and spices.

THE MENDACIOUS CHILD[1]

There was a story . . .
Our legs are crossed . . .
It happened here . . .
It was so . . .

There was a man who was trying to give a cow away. He said that he would give it to the person who could lie better than he.

It happened that he walked and searched, walked and searched a very long time. Whomever he met, he discovered that he, himself, could lie better than he. Whomever he met could not lie as well as he, himself, could.

He came upon a town. He met a child there. He met a child sitting by the gate of the compound. He said, "Child, where is your mother?" He answered, "My mother has gone to separate last year's water from this year's." He said, "Where is your father?" He replied, "My father has gone to help lift up Allah who fell down on his farm." He said, "He-He-He-He-He-He! Give me some water." The child ran after the cock. The man said to him, "Give me some water." He replied, "Yes, my mother keeps the water jar in the eye of the cock, that is why I am chasing it." He said, "Then leave it alone. Go and get some hot ashes from the fire so that I might light up my tobacco." He began to count the hot ashes. The man said, "What is that?" He replied, "My mother counted the ashes before she left." He replied, "He-He-He-He. Take the cow! You are the owner." He gave him the cow and left there.

After this man left, he met a hyena and told him, "Hyena, there is a small boy who, you know, took my cow. Let us go and you can take it from him. If you can take it, it is yours." He replied, "Yes!"

The hyena said, "Let us go. Get a whip and ride on me. Whip me." The man climbed up on the hyena. The hyena began to run. Now and then the hyena said, "Whip me!" The man would beat him on the neck, VIPP.[2] He said, "Yes, a cow is certainly worth it." He ran and ran and ran. Now and then he would say, "Whip me!" The man would beat him on the buttocks, VIPP. He said, "Yes,

172

come on, a cow is certainly worth it." He ran and ran for a while and then he said, "Whip me!" He then whipped him on his testicles, VIPP. He said, "Yes, come on, a cow is certainly worth it."[3]

They soon came to the town and arrived DIRR,[4] at the gate of the compound. The man got down. The child said, "Heeee father! Heeee father! Come quickly and see the man. See what he brought to you to repay you for the big cow that he owes you. Come quickly and see this small calf which he brought to you to repay you. This small calf could not even feed the people of this compound and this man thinks he can bring it to repay his debt to you."

The hyena heard this and he said that he would not be used to pay for anyone's debt. He said he did not know anything about the payment. The hyena began to run away. After he was a short distance away, the child then said to the man, "If the hyena gets very far ahead of you, he will tie the road up into knots and leave you here. You will not know which way to return to your home. If I were you, I would follow him quickly. If he goes, he will tie the road into a knot and leave you here."

When the man heard this, he chased after the hyena, TARBA-TARBA-TARBA.[5]

The hyena kept crying out, "You won't catch me! You won't catch me! You won't catch me!"

The child just sat there.[6]

[1] Narrated by Momat Mbay, age 28, outside the compound of Momat Sise in Maka Gui, Senegal, on November 18 at 9:20 p.m. before 75 men, women and children. Momat Mbay belongs to the *gewel* caste.

[2] Onomatopoetic sound recreating the crack of the whip on the body of the hyena.

[3] This motif is employed in numerous Wolof tales (see "The Hare Makes the Hyena His Riding Horse").

[4] Ideophonic sound representing the idea that the man and the hyena took aim at the compound with their eyes in order not to lose sight of any details before they attacked it. This is derived from the verb *dir,* to aim with a gun.

[5] Onomatopoetic expression recreating the sound of a man stumbling and falling down as he is running away.

[6] This narrative underscores the Wolof esteem for truth and honesty by conversely illustrating the ridiculousness of lying. The initial episodes indicate that the adult protagonist has a distorted sense of ideals; lying is so important to him that he would give a cow to anyone who could lie better than he. This is contrary to Wolof concepts of honorable behavior. Momat Mbay has insured that his behavior will be viewed in negative terms by his audience by intertwining his fate with that of the hyena, the traditional symbol of shame. The hyena will do anything for meat as evidenced by his willingness to become the man's riding horse and permit himself to be painfully whipped on the journey. The man follows after the hyena in a similarly ridiculous manner. His attempt to prevent the hyena from tying up the road into knots discloses his total lack of common sense. He becomes the fool, the object of ridicule. Yet, on a metaphysical level, the narrator is

commenting on the man's conduct. Like the hyena, his idealization of lying is shameful and contrary to that deemed honorable by the society. The man will never find his way home, for the path that he has chosen to follow is that charted for him by the hyena.

THE SEARCH FOR A FRIEND[1]

There was a story . . .
Our legs are crossed . . .
It happened here . . .
It was so . . .

There was a king in the land of Jolof[2] who had a son. When this son became a young man, he realized that he had never been anywhere; he did not know anyone outside his village nor did he have any friends.

One day this young man told his father that he was going to search for a true friend. His father said, "Yes?" and he answered "Yes!"

In the morning the youth walked and walked and walked until he reached another country. He stopped at its chief's home where he met someone his own age.

Now this chief had three wives. After exchanging greetings with him, they asked him, "Why are you traveling around the country?" He said, "I am the son of my village's chief. I am looking for a friend and I have heard about your chief's son. I liked the sound of his name very much and wanted a chance to meet him in person." So the women introduced him to the chief's son.

Now this young man had also never been anywhere; he did not know anyone nor did he have any friends. Since both of these young men's fathers were the traditional rulers of their respective countries, they soon became friends and lived very close to each other.

The host's father had three wives and the newest wife was very pretty. She was even prettier than Allah's wife. When the young man first noticed this woman, he liked her very much. When they were alone, he asked his friend, "Who is that woman and where does she live?" His host replied, "She is my father's wife and she lives at my compound." The guest then confessed that he loved her very much. "Is that really how you feel?" asked the host, and he replied, "Yes!" He said, "I will give her to you if you truly love her."

So the host arranged everything with his father's wife without much difficulty. The woman said to him that she also really loved him and would do anything he wanted, but that her husband was the chief. As such, whoever he wanted dead, would die; and whoever he caught with his possessions would certainly die. "Although the risks are great," she added, "we could still be together." She devised a plan for their rendevous and then called her step-son. She said to him, "I will put a calabash in front of my door at night. If the calabash contains two kola-nuts, that means that your father is sleeping with me. But if it contains only one kola-nut, that means that I am sleeping alone. Go now and tell your guest what I have told you." He replied, "Yes!"

The host then told his guest what the woman had told him. That night when he went to the calabash he saw that there was only one kola-nut inside. So the young man entered her house and lay down with the woman. He slept there. The next morning when they brought him some water, he bathed and then dressed himself.

After two or three days he returned to look at the calabash to see if he could spend some more time with the woman. That morning the woman brought two kola-nuts to be placed inside the calabash. But as she threw them into the calabash, one missed while the other kola-nut landed inside the calabash. She did not realize this and she went inside her house. The chief was laying there inside on the bed waiting for his wife. When the young man saw the one kola-nut in the calabash, he entered the house. After he got in bed he placed his hand on the old man's chest. The chief immediately grabbed the young man's hand. During those old days the chief's son was easily distinguished from common people. He would wear gold or silver bracelets on his wrists. When the old man grabbed his hand, the young man struggled to set himself free, but he left one of his bracelets behind.

Since he was the son of a warrior,[3] if anyone would ask, he would say that the bracelet belonged to him. In that way the chief would be able to identify him to be killed. The young man fled to his friend's compound and told him exactly what he did. "If that is all that happened, then you should not worry because my father will not kill you." He asked, "Are you certain?" The host replied, "I also am the son of a warrior like you are. I will not let him kill you." He said, "Yes," and he replied, "Yes."

It happened that the host had recently seen a lioness with her cubs in the middle of the bush. So this friend killed some of his mother's sheep and took the meat towards the king of the beasts. When the lioness spotted the host with meat, she advanced towards him. As she did, the host began throwing some of the pieces of meat towards her. The lioness devoured the meat greedily. As she was so occupied, he picked up one of the offspring and took it to his home. He placed it under his bed and remained silent about what he had done.

The next morning the chief awoke very early. This chief owned a very large ceremonial knife. Whenever this knife was picked up, a head surely would be severed.

The chief ordered the drums beaten and the whole town assembled.

The women were also called to this meeting. The chief's youngest wife was so beautiful that all the eyes of the people would turn towards her wherever she went. She was so beautiful that she lit up the whole area.

When the chief came towards the assemblage, he announced that someone had entered into his wife's house the previous night and he fought with him. Though the man escaped, he said, he left behind a golden bracelet. The chief wanted to know who owned the bracelet. Everyone interrogated replied that he did not own the bracelet.

When the host urged his guest to say that the bracelet belonged to him, he called out to the chief and said, "That bracelet belongs to me. It is my bracelet." After he said that, the chief ordered the knife to arise. As the servant raised the hand that was gripping the knife, the host intervened and caught the servant's hand as it was descending. He advised his father not to act too hastily. He told him that he should ask the accused what he had done before he had him killed.

Accepting this advice, the chief asked, "Why did you come to my house?" But before the guest could answer, the host himself answered for his friend. He said, "Father, this man did not come here out of disrespect for you. Neither did he want to destroy you. We were laying down in bed in the middle of the night, when everything, even the animals, were quite still. I asked him if he thought he was brave and he said, 'Yes.' I told him that I was much braver than he but he disagreed. So I asked him if he was brave enough to walk out to my father's wife's house and put his hand on your chest. He replied that he was. I said that if he could do that, then I would go out into the bush and capture a lioness' cub. That is why he came into your house while you were sleeping with my step-mother. That is why he put his hand on your chest. So when you grabbed his hand, he shook his hand and left his bracelet behind. Since he had done that, I too went into the bush, and tricked a lioness so that I could capture one of her cubs." He told them that the cub was still under his bed.

The chief then called a servant and ordered him to go and get the lion cub. When he returned with the lion cub, the chief was so satisfied with the explanation, that he praised both of them for their bravery.

[1] Narrated by Malik Boye in Porli, The Gambia, on November 20 at 10:45 p.m. in the compound of Bessi Njay before 14 men and women.

[2] Ancient kingdom of the Wolof in Senegal.

[3] In Wolof, *saltige.* These were respected both for their physical and moral strength. As such, they embody the ideals and values of Wolof society.

[4]Friendship is the focus of this tale. The initial episodes present images of two young men whose lives are incomplete because they do not have a friend. Once they discover each other, their behavior illustrates the essential criteria on which friendship is based. In the narrative it is revealed that the new friends belong to the same royal, warrior caste; they are approximately the same age; they have similar world perspectives; and they have mutually recognized needs. Their friendship is exercised according to the established social ideals. First, friends are entrusted with contributing to the happiness of the other. In this tale the host-friend arranges for the sexual liason between his guest-friend and his father's youngest wife. Second, friends are committed to protecting the other's life. Here the host-friend employs all of his intellectual and creative abilities to devise a plan that prevents his father from beheading his friend. Third, friends are obliged to sacrifice for the other. In this narrative the host-friend risks his own life in capturing the lion cub from its mother. This exercise of friendship is accomplished within the norms of honorable behavior. Their actions are perceived in the same light as that of the father himself. His pronouncement of their honor and courage in the final episode confirms social approval. One important issue in the tale centers on the protective scheme devised. Although the host-friend does not relate to his father the entire circumstances of the affair, at no time does he actually lie to him. This would run counter to the honorable model. Rather, he chose to highlight the secondary motivations for his friend's exploits and omits mention of his primary reasons. Since the father does not directly ask about sexual motives or activities, they do not inform him of them. However, if he would have asked, they would have been obliged to admit the truth. This is in fact stressed by the narrator himself. When he states, "Since he was the son of a warrior, if anyone would ask, he would say that the bracelet belonged to him." The father is impressed with his son's explanation of the entire episode and the dispute is settled. The issue of bravery being an important dimension of the concept of honor provides a means whereby the host-friend can save his friend's life without destroying his own, his friend's, nor his father's honor.

THE HARE SEEKS ENDOWMENTS
FROM ALLAH[1]

There was a story . . .
Our legs are crossed . . .
It happened here . . .
It was so . . .

The hare so underestimated his own intelligence that he went to Allah and said to him: "I want you to increase my intelligence." Allah asked, "Really?" and the hare quickly replied, "Yes!" Allah said to him, "You know hare, I never actually counted you among the fools." The hare replied, "Allah, my intelligence is really very slight. I would like you to add some more." Allah asked, "Are you sure?" and he again replied, "Yes!" So Allah said to him, "Now before I increase your intelligence, you must go and bring me a sack filled with black birds, the tusk of an elephant,[2] and the milk of a lioness. If you bring me these things, I will increase your intelligence." Eagerly the hare replied, "Yes! I am going."

After he ran a short distance, he stopped at the base of a big cottonwood tree. There he met some blackbirds who were singing this song:

THE SELF-SOWN MILLET . . . MILLET . . . MILLET . . . MILLET!
WHICH YOU PICK . . . PICK . . . PICK . . . PICK!
HAVE VERY LARGE GRAINS . . . GRAINS . . . GRAINS . . . GRAINS!

The hare called out to them, "Hey blackbirds!" They chirped, "Yes!" He challenged them, "You all cannot possibly fill up my bag." The eldest blackbird scolded him, "Don't you know that I am the leader here?" The hare replied, "Yes! I did not know that you were the leader, that is the reason I asked. Now we are arguing at our compound about my bag here. My friends said that this bag could not possibly hold all of the blackbirds." The blackbirds accepted the challenge and jumped into the bag, one after another until it was completely full. With that, the hare left the tree and went back to Allah.

He called him, "Allah?" and he replied, "Yes?" "You said that I should bring you a bag of blackbirds. Here is the bag." Allah replied, "Go! There still remains the milk of the lioness."

After leaving Allah the hare soon met a lioness who was nursing her cubs at the base of a tall ant hill. It happened that he brought a little calabash along with him. The lioness nursed her cubs for a long time until they were satisfied. Then the hare greeted her, "Aunt lion, peace be with you!" "Peace be with you also! Who are you?" she asked. "Me? I am a hare." She asked, "Hare, what are you looking for here at this ant hill?" He replied, "We were arguing at the village square where I had this little calabash. They said that your breasts could not fill it with milk. I told them that your breasts could even fill three calabashes." The lioness said to him, "You know I have only just delivered my babies the day before yesterday! So now just one of them could fill it. Come and try." So the hare squatted down and drew out milk from her breast until the calabash was completely full. Then he said to her, "Aunt lion, now what can I do with the breast milk?" She told him, "Ah, you know, since you were arguing, you should take it to the village square and show them that it is filled." He questioned her, "Yes? Are you giving it to me?" She replied, "Yes. Take it from me. I will give it to you."

The hare left the ant hill. When he reached Allah he bowed before him and said, "Our Master!" and he replied, "Yes!" He said, "The milk is here." Allah then reminded him, "There still remains the elephant's tusk."

The next morning the hare rested until he knew that it was mid-day. Then he traveled along the forest path until he met a bull elephant. He said to him, "Uncle elephant, do you want to play hide and seek with me?" In disbelief the elephant repeated, "Hide and seek?" and he replied, "Yes!" He said "OH . . . Oh hare, you are just a little child and I am much too big a man to be playing hide and seek with you." But the hare insisted, "Please just play! Last night I dreamed of playing hide and seek with you." The elephant sighed, "Praise to Allah! Whatever *is* the value you see in this." Quickly the hare poured water all around the area, making it very slippery and difficult to walk on. "Now we will hide from each other," he directed, "but let us not completely disappear from each other." So the hare stood near one ant hill and the elephant stood by another. They began chasing each other in circles until the bull elephant suddenly rushed the hare. The hare smoothly evaded the elephant with one quick leap. With that, the elephant slipped and fell, tusk-first, onto the ground. His left tusk snapped off completely, and he cried out, "Aiii! Hare, now you have really angered me. You broke my tusk." The hare begged him, "Uncle elephant, please forgive me, UK-UK-UK[3] and he went and bowed down, crying and crying. Surprised, the elephant asked him, "Why are you crying?" He replied, "If I broke your tusk, then I have to cry." So the elephant said to him, "I forgive you for it. Go away from me now!" Without another sob the hare said, "If you give me the broken tusk, I will take it." The elephant moaned, "Take it!" So he picked up the tusk and took it with him.

As soon as he arrived in heaven, the hare gave it to Our Master and said to him, "Now, I want you to give me more intelligence." But Allah scolded him, "If I give you any more intelligence, you will entangle the world and destroy it. What you have is sufficient."[4]

[1]Narrated by Ganga Jeng, age 47, in Bati Hai on November 1 at 9:30 p.m. before 53 men, women and children in the compound of his father Madoun Jeng.

[2]The presence of the elephant in many Wolof stories attests to its former existence in the Senegambian savannah regions. In the early years of European trade with the Senegambian people, ivory was an important cash crop. Today, Wolof people know about elephants only through oral narratives.

[3]Recreation of the hard sobbing sounds expressed by the hare, produced by the gasping for air which follows an extended crying period.

[4]For further discussion of other African and African-American analogues of this tale-type, see William Bascom, "African Folktales in America: II. Trickster Seeks Endowments, III. Measuring the Snake, IV. Challenging the Birds (Insects) to Fill a Container, V. Milking a Cow (Deer) Stuck in a Tree," *Research in African Literatures;* and Emil Magel, "The Source of Bascom's Wolof Analogue 'Trickster Seeks Endowments,' " *Research in African Literature,* Spring, 1980. The first Wolof version of this tale was published in 1858 in Paris by Abbeé Boilat in *Grammaire de la lanque Wolloffe* under the title "Le Lievre et les Moineaux." Three other Wolof narratives, "Le Loup et Abdou Dhiabare," "Le Loup, le Boeuf et l'Elephant," and "La Chenille et le Papillon," were also included in this language manual.

THE HARE SAVES
THE HIPPOPOTAMUS[1]

There was a story . . .
Our legs are crossed . . .
It happened here . . .
It was so . . .

The hare, the hyena, the donkey, the spider, the *jine* and all the other animals organized a wrestling contest to be held on the other side of the river. They said, "At the wrestling contest, everything will be supplied in abundance. There will be meat and rice and all other types of foods." At that time, the spider was as large as our donkey.

All the animals crossed the river. When they had all crossed the river, the spider came to the river and saw the hyena crying and crying and crying. He called to him, "Ah, Hyena!" He replied, "Yes!" He said, "Why are you crying?" He said, "All the other animals are crossing the river, going to the wrestling contest. I am not able to swim. The lion came by and I asked him to take me but he refused. The leopard came by and I asked him to take me but he refused. The *jine* came by and I asked him to take me across but he, too, refused. No one will take me across the river." The spider said, "Ah, hyena, that is because you never keep things to yourself. You are always revealing secrets."

The hyena said, "Honestly, if you carry me across the river, I will not tell anyone about it." The spider said, "Hyena, you are just lying." He said, "No!" The hyena said, "I promise I won't tell." He said, "That is good, but if I take you across and you tell someone then I will not bring you back." He said, "That is good."

The spider then prepared to take him across. He pulled a cord out of his sack and tied the hyena with it. The hyena clung to it as the spider crossed the river JEEFI-JAAFA-JEM . . . JEEFI-JAAFA-JEM . . . JEEFI-JAAFA-JEM[2] until they crossed the river. Then they went to the wrestling match together.

182

As soon as they reached the other side, the drums began to play and everyone there began to sing:

SAMBA, WHO HELPED YOU OVER?
SAMBA, WHAT BROUGHT YOU OVER?
SAMBA, WHAT BROUGHT YOU OVER?

He said, "It was . . ."

Then the drummers began playing:

SAMBA, WHAT BROUGHT YOU OVER?
SAMBA, WHAT BROUGHT YOU OVER?
SAMBA, WHAT BROUGHT YOU OVER?

He said, "It was . . . the spider. He pulled a cord out of his sack and pulled me JEEFI-JAAFA-JEM."

When he had said that, the wrestling match was declared over and all the animals began to leave. The lion returned home. The leopard returned home. The tiger returned. The *jine* returned. All the animals left. Only the hyena remained.

He sat near the edge of the river and cried and cried. Soon a hippopotamus arrived and called him, "Hyena?" and he said, "Yes?" She asked, "Why are you crying?" He said, "I can't get to the other side of the river." The hippopotamus replied, "Yes!" He asked, "Can you carry me across the river?" The hippopotamus replied, "You, you are too ungrateful. Whatever brought you here could have taken you back. I have just given birth yesterday and I am in a hurry to return to my little children. So let me be on my way."

The hyena said, "Ah, please carry me over. If you leave me here I will die because I cannot swim." The hippopotamus said, "I will not take you over because I do not trust you." He said, "Please take me across. I promise I will not harm you." The hippopotamus said, "You, you never keep your word. I will not take you over." The hyena again asked, "Please take me across with you. I will not harm you." The hippopotamus said, "Alright, but remember your promise."

The hyena climbed up on top of the hippopotamus' back. The hippopotamus crossed the river. She swam and swam until they reached the other shore. When they arrived there, the hippopotamus said, "Now you must let me return to my children." The hyena did not let her go. The hippopotamus said, "Let me go home to my children. This is what I feared from the beginning." The hyena said, "You must wait until my leg relaxes before you can go. When my leg is relaxed, you can go to your home." When the hyena's leg had relaxed, the hippopotamus said, "Now hyena, let me go home. I smelled that you would do a thing like this." The hyena said, "You must wait until my waist is relaxed." The hippopotamus waited until the hyena's waist was relaxed. Then she said, "Now, hyena, let me go home." The hyena replied, "Ah, what's the hurry? You just wait until my tongue is relaxed." The hippopotamus waited there like that for a very long time.

It happened that the hare passed by the river POROK-POROK-POROK-POROK-POROK.[3] He asked the hippopotamus, "Ah, why are you sitting here?" She replied, "I was just doing the hyena a favor. I brought him across the river from the wrestling match. Now he will not let me go home." The hare said, "You, hippopotamus, cannot carry the hyena across the river. There is *no* way that you could have brought him across." The hyena said, "PPPPPPPP!"[4] She brought me across, she brought me across, she brought me across." The hare said, "Ah, then go back into the water and show me." The hyena told the hippopotamus, "Yes, go back into the water and prove it to him."

They went back into the water, farther and farther out into the river. When they were in very deep water, the hare called out to the hippopotamus, "Dive under the water! Dive under the water!" The hippopotamus dove under the water with the hyena clinging to her tail. The hippopotamus remained under the water until the hare told her to come out. When she came out of the water, the hyena had already drowned. Then the hippopotamus returned home.[5]

[1] Narrated by Bessi Njay in Porli, The Gambia, in his own compound before 43 men, women and children at 8:40 p.m. on November 1.

[2] Ideophonic expression creating the image of the strenuous effort exerted by the spider in pulling the hyena through the water. From the Wolof *jef,* work; *jafa,* difficult; and *jem,* movement towards.

[3] See note no. 6, "The Young Man and the Talking Skull." The hare is walking with great dignity and composure.

[4] Onomatopoetic expression recreating the exclamation of disbelief. This bursts forth from the hyena's lips without forethought.

[5] This narrative clearly illustrates one of the hyena's characteristic anti-social behaviors: his failure to keep verbal agreements. In an oral society, there is high value placed on a person's verbal commitments. All important negotiations, transactions and contracts are formalized through the oral medium. One's word becomes sacred because it is a basis for the smooth functioning of the society. The hyena exhibits a total lack of appreciation for this social requirement. In this narrative he reneges on two solemn promises: one to the spider and the other to the hippopotamus. Such untrustworthiness is dangerous and, therefore, punishable. This is significantly accomplished by the hare, who uses his own verbal facility and intellectual acumen to save the hippopotamus from the hyena's death grasp. In contrast to the hyena, his use of language is trustworthy and reliable.

THE HARE AND HYENA
IN THE WELL[1]

There was a story . . .
Our legs are crossed . . .
It happened here . . .
It was so . . .

The hyena and the hare banded together in setting some traps. They joined up and set traps together. They went away and left the traps. The hyena and the hare went together.

When they returned, they looked at the traps, but the traps only caught a few animals. The hare said to him, "Uncle Hyena, we have only caught a little. What has been caught, is much too meager. In my compound there are only me and my wife. So you should give me this and tomorrow there will be much more. When we have more, you will take it for yourself. You know that your compound is very large." The hyena said to him, "Yes, alright, we will do what you say." Ah, the hare then took the things. When they went home, his people ate them.

The next day they again went trapping. When they checked, they again had only half a sack of game. When they collected a half-full sack, the hare turned and said to him again, "Uncle Hyena, this amount is much too small. Let me take it because tomorrow there will be much more. If you do this for me, then tomorrow, whatever we catch, I will give it all to you. You know that your house is big." He replied, "Alright, let us do what you say." So the hare took the things home.

The hare acted like that, he acted like that, he acted like that until you know, the hyena became very weak. He said, "Now, I believe that the hare wants to kill me. In my household they say that they want whatever it is that we catch there. Yes! He will not take and eat what we catch today because I have made myself a plan to get it.

He called the hare until the hare finally came. He attacked the hare and beat him. But he was not dead. He took him to a dried out well and threw him into it. He said, "Ha! He is the one, I killed him. He is dead."

Later he told his household, "Now we are the only ones left around here."

Now the hare was lying in the middle of the dried out well. Soon a sheep passed nearby there. He called out to him, "Uncle Sheep. Oh, Uncle Sheep! You are very bad." He replied, "Ah?" He said, "You, since I have been sick, until today, you have not visited me." He said, "Uncle Hare, how can I come and visit you?" He replied, "If you go this way and then that way, you will arrive here." So the sheep went here and went there and entered into the dried out well. As soon as he did, the hare caught him and killed him.

Soon a goat came. He said to him, "Uncle Goat." He said, "Yes?" He said to him, "You, Uncle Goat, since I have been sick until today, you have not even visited me." He asked, "Me? How can I enter your place?" "You pass this way and then that way until you are in here and you see me. Afterwards you can go home." The goat also passed here and there until he reached the well and fell into it. The hare grabbed him and ate him.

Then a cow passed by the side of it and he said, "Uncle Bull?" and he replied, "Yes?" He said, "You, since I have been sick until today you have not visited me." He said, "How can I visit you?" He said, "If you just pass here, then pass there, you will see me. Then you can go." This one also passed here and passed there until he fell down the opening of the well. Then the hare devoured him.

The hare acted like that until he became very healthy. He was strong and had grown bigger than a cow. When he was bigger than a cow, the hyena came and saw him. He said to him, "Is this you? You are again big and fat. I thought that you died there." He replied, "Ah, Uncle Hyena, when you threw me into this well I had one plan. It was the one method I had so that I could catch enough meat to be satisfied." He said, "Yes? Alright, now tell it to me." He said, "Yes, get out or I will beat you if you don't tell me. You know that I will enter into the well. Tell me the plan."

He said, "You see, if you go into the well, a sheep will soon pass by here. Just say to it, 'Uncle Sheep, you are very bad.' Then he will say, 'Ah, why?' You then tell him, 'Since I have been sick, until today, you have not visited me.' Then you say to him, 'Just pass by this way and you will pass by here and fall into the well.' Then you can devour him. Whatever passes by you, if you only do what I told you, you will be able to eat until you are satisfied." He said, "Alright. Get away!"

The hare was helped out of the well. He went, picked up a club and beat the hyena. He knocked him into the well. The hyena began to cry and cry. Then the hare left.

Afterwards a sheep passed nearby there. He said to him, "Uncle Sheep, you are very bad." He replied, "Ah?" He said to him, "Since I have been sick, until today, you have not come to visit me." He said, "Where can I enter?" He replied, "You only have to walk here and then there, fall into this hole and I will devour you." He said to him, "Hyena, you must be crazy! You will never see me nor will you devour me."

A goat passed by there the next morning. He said to him, "You, Uncle Goat. You are very bad." He replied, "Ah?" He said to him, "I am sick and you haven't visited me." He said, "How can I locate your place?" He said, "If you only pass by here and then pass by there, fall into this hole and I will devour you." He replied, "Stay there because I will not come to visit you."

A bull passed near by there. He called out to him, "Uncle Bull, I know that you are very fat but you are also very bad." He said to him, "Ah?" He said, "I am sick today and you have not visited me." He replied, "Well, tell me how to locate your place." He answered, "When you pass by here and pass by there, fall down into this hole and I will devour you." The bull said to him, "You. You can just stay there!"

The hyena acted that way and acted that way until, you know, he became very thin. Now the hyena's back became just like that of the red and yellow lizard.[2] The hyena became delirious. He no longer knew what he was doing. He began to salivate whenever he looked at his own testicles. He said, "HUMMM it is honey. If I devour you, you will know it." He sat down again for a little while. He paced back and forth in the well. Then he seized them into his mouth and said, "Hai! They are on me . . . they are part of *me!*" He then sat down. Paced around the well. He seized them into his mouth again. He said, "HUMM. They *are* part of me, you know." He stayed like that for a long time until he died. He was very frustrated. What could he do but just hold the testicles in his mouth?[3]

[1]Narrated by Malik Boye in Porli, The Gambia, on October 30 at 2:45 p.m. in the center of the village before 13 men, 9 women and 12 children.

[2]The backs of these lizards are sharply ridged, thin, and protruding. The hyena was so emaciated that his spine resembled that of the lizard.

[3]The patterned structural design of this narrative contrasts the mental capabilities of the hare with those of the hyena. The hare used his knowledge of the world and the beings in it to provide for himself and his family. In the opening episode he turns his awareness of the hyena's greed to his own advantage in securing food for his family. The hyena is perceived as a victim of his own weakness and lack of intelligence. Since he cannot think beyond the immediate circumstances, he invites great hardship to himself and his family. In contrast, when the hare is thrown into the well, he again uses his intelligence to reverse a disastrous situation to a profitable one. His invitations to the sheep, the goat, and the bull are perceived in the same light. Like the hyena, these animals

cannot foresee the logical consequences of the hare's plan. They are too naive and too gullible for their own benefit. This is not a socially approved quality. As the narrative indicates, it is dangerous. When the hyena is placed in the same environment as the hare had been, his lack of intelligence and verbal facility contrast sharply with that of the hare. His stupidity becomes the source of the narrative's humor. The closing image of the hyena holding his own testicles in his mouth plays upon the scorn and ridicule Wolof have for shameful ignorance.

THE HARE MAKES THE HYENA
HIS RIDING HORSE[1]

There was a story . . .
Our legs are crossed . . .
It happened here . . .
It was so . . .

A hyena went out to be a strange-farmer.[2] He walked until he was very far from his own village. There he met up with the hare. He went up to the village square and he met him there. The hare asked him, "Where are you going?" He replied, "I am going to be a strange-farmer." The hare said, "Alright, I will take you on as my strange-farmer." He asked, "Yes?" and the hare replied, "Yes."

So they went to the hare's compound. He gave him some seeds. The hyena shelled them until he was finished. Then he sowed them. He sat down and waited. That is all he did. He stayed there until the plants were almost ready to harvest.

The hare was invited to a naming ceremony.[3] They told him there would be two cows reserved there for him.

The hare brought dinner and they began to eat. The naming ceremony was the next day. They brought the dinner and they began to dine. The hare got up and said, "Oh, I'm satisfied." The hyena said, "My host, what is the problem." He replied, "I am very desperate. My heart feels empty." The hyena asked, "Why is that?" He answered, "Me, they invited me to a naming ceremony where two cows have been reserved for me. If I cannot go, they will not kill the two cows. I cannot walk that far." The hyena said, "Hai, come on, eat until you are satisfied. If that is your only problem, you can drive a cart." He said, "That is right." The hyena asked, "Do you have a cart case?" He replied, "Yes." The hyena said, "Tomorrow you can tie me up and ride me." The hare said, "Alright." The hare ate until he was full.

At night they lay down to sleep. In the middle of the night the hyena got up and knocked on the hare's door. "Host! Host!" The hare said, "Yes!" He said, "Get up, it is dawn." The hare answered, "HA-HA-HA! You, it is not dawn yet. Go back to sleep, it is too early in the morning. Come back later and I will take out the case and tie you up so that we can leave." The hyena said, "Yes." He went back and lay down.

He rested a little while. He got up and struck a match and started his room[4] on fire. He called out, "Host! Host! It is dawn. See the light, it is dawn." He said, "HA-HA-HA! You have only burned down your own room. It is not dawn yet. Go to sleep." The hyena went and slept with the young men at their quarters until it was dawn.

In the morning, he brought a whip and gave it to the host and said, "If I am too slow, just whip me, whip me if I am too slow." The hare said, "Yes." The hare brought out a bridle and tied up the hyena with the case on his back. When it was ready he rode in it.

He whipped and whipped the hyena until they arrived at the naming ceremony.

The people said, "HA-HA-HA! Look at the hare's horse! Look at the hare's horse!" The hare got down from his case and tied the hyena at a tree on the outskirts of the village. Then he went and sat down with the people.

The hyena remained there. He stayed and stayed and stayed but he did not see anything. Then he said, "YAH-YAH-YAH-YAH."[5] The people in the village said, "HA-HA-HA-HA! Is that how the hare's horse brays?" The hare said, "Now you all watch this. Listen to me now. I will soon get rid of him."

When the hare walked towards the hyena he was wearing his gown, adjusting it[6] and saying aloud, "No! I will not do that. Whoever would do that, whoever would do *that* is a bastard. Do you think I would agree to *that*?" He moved towards the hyena. The hyena said, "What is it?" The hare said, "Listen, they say they will kill my horse for the naming ceremony." The hyena said, "Hey, come and untie me." The hare went and untied the hyena, who ran away into the wilderness.[7]

---

[1]Narrated by Alisan Jalo, age 34, in Porli, The Gambia, in the compound of Bessi Njay on November 20 at 9:30 p.m. before 39 men, women and children. This story bears strong resemblance to Antti-Aame's Tale-type 4, "Carrying the Sham-Sick Trickster," and Stith-Thompson's Motif K1241, "Trickster Rides Dupe Horseback."

[2]In Wolof, *navatane*. This term might properly be translated as "migrant farmer." These are most often Fulani, Bambara or Serahuli from up-river locations. The migrant farmer is housed, fed, and allowed to work on his own plot of ground in return for working on his landlord's farm. Migrant farmers are usually hired to increase the production of groundnuts, the main cash crop of the Gambian Wolof.

[3]In Wolof, *ngente*. The naming of a child is scheduled on the eighth day after birth. It will

usually occur at 10:00 in the morning in the compound where the baby was born. If it is a first born child, a great celebration follows where great quantities of food are provided for the guests. As in this narrative, a large animal is killed and prepared, to be consumed throughout the day's and night's festivities. (See David Gamble, *The Wolof of the Senegambia,* for a detailed description of this ritual.)

[4]In Wolof, *neg.* Rural Wolof compounds are composed of several one-room, mud-walled, palm-roofed, non-contiguous buildings. This arrangement allows the room of the hyena to burn independently of that of the hare.

[5]The hyena cries out, repeating the word for bone. Hyenas are scavengers whose powerful jaws enable them to crunch the bones of dried-up carcasses. It is believed that the hyena are so foolish, they love hard bones better than the tender meat.

[6]This is a commonly used literary device which is intended to convey a sense of righteous indignation. The character straightening up or dusting off his/her clothes is indicating through action that he/she is proud and dignified, unworthy of improper conduct. The hare's use of this sign is thus full pretense, for he is the instigator of the entire sham.

[7]The hare's treatment of the hyena is not cruel, unjust nor cunning. This has been the interpretation proposed by previous scholarship (See Emil Magel, "Hare and Hyena, Symbols of Honor and Shame in Wolof Fictional Narratives," unpublished dissertation, University of Wisconsin, August 1977) in an attempt to fit the hare into the West African trickster character-type mold. This is a gross misrepresentation of the hare's role in Wolof oral narratives. From the narratives recorded from the griots of the Saloum, it is more accurate to describe him as socially committed than as anti-social. In this narrative, the "trickery" exhibited is entirely justified. This is an assumption so commonly accepted by Wolof audiences that often material which would obviously support this assumption is omitted by the narrators. In this tale that material is provided, though not elaborately. The initial narrative sequences, identifying the hyena as a strange-farmer for the hare, reveal drastic irregularities of conduct. The hyena agrees to work for the hare according to the commonly accepted terms of these agreements. The hare contracts with the hyena in good faith, accepting his word that he will in fact labor in the groundnut fields. However, hyena does not honor the contract. The narrator states that the hyena shelled the seeds and sowed them. Wolof groundnut farmers immediately recognize that this is hardly enough labor to insure a good crop. The hyena does not properly prepare the soil for planting nor does he constantly cultivate around the tender plants to eliminate weeds competing for the minimal soil moisture. The hyena is therefore not laboring as is expected of strange-farmers. For Wolof audiences, this is to be expected. One of the associations to the symbol of the hyena in fictional narratives is untrustworthiness. He never keeps promises (see "The Hare Saves the Hippopotamus"). When the hyena contracted to be a strange-farmer, the audience was probably already prepared for his renege. The entire following sequence involving the hare's using him as a riding horse is thus seen by the Wolof as just and right. The hyena owed the hare his labor. It is only by manipulating the hyena that the hare can obtain what is contractually his. The positive response of the community at the naming ceremony, furthermore, indicates that his "trickery" is indeed justified and supported.

THE PILGRIMAGE TO MECCA[1]

There was a story . . .
Our legs are crossed . . .
It happened here . . .
It was so . . .

A goat made a pilgrimage to Mecca. When he was on his journey he met up with a hyena in the middle of the wilderness. The hyena greeted him "Hey goat, where are you going?" The goat replied, "I am making my pilgrimage to Mecca." The hyena offered, "Hey, may your pilgrimage be blessed!" But the goat countered, "Uncle Hyena, do not be so quick to help my family. Do not be too eager." The hyena shot back, "Hey, all I said was 'May your trip be blessed.' "

This particular herd of goats numbered 3,333. Their leader was a person who was very grateful to Allah. This man only left his compound on Fridays to pray to Allah. He was the only one who spoke to the hyena.

The hyena questioned the chief goat, "What are you thinking . . . thinking— thinking! 'Don't be too eager to help.' What do you think could possibly save you?" The goat replied, "We are accompanied by our *gewel*.[2] This *gewel* has a very pleasing voice. I know that if he sings for you, you will be satisfied and leave us alone." The hyena said, "Yes. Well, let him begin to sing so that I might know it." The *gewel* began to sing:

> UNCLE HYENA, YOU CAN EAT AT HOME,
> TAKE AN EWE AND FREE US.
> TAKE A RAM AND FREE US.
> THE HYENA SAID, "AT THE EDGE OF THE RIVER, I WILL LOOK FOR A BOAT.
> I WILL GO THERE, AHA.
> AT THE EDGE OF THE RIVER, I WILL LOOK FOR A BOAT, AHA,
> AT THE EDGE OF THE RIVER, I WILL LOOK FOR A BOAT, AHA,
> I WILL GO THERE, AHA." /

At that time the sun was just beginning to set. It descended slowly until it was completely dark. Now you know that the hyena loves meat so much that he has lost his mind. When the *gewel* told him that he could take two goats home to eat them, he became very excited. The goats said to him, "Uncle Hyena, before you take the two goats, find us a boat that is suitable for us. Now you should go and look for the largest *hai*[3] tree that you can find. A tree which, you know, if you carve it out, would hold all of us at one time." The hyena replied, "You speak the truth. That is a very good idea. But first I want to listen to the song. Before it is over, I will have cut down the tree."

UNCLE HYENA, YOU CAN EAT AT HOME,
TAKE AN EWE AND FREE US,
TAKE A RAM AND FREE US,
BUT LOOK FOR AND CONSTRUCT A BOAT, AHA.
HE SAID, "I WILL LOOK FOR A BOAT AND I WILL CARVE IT,
AT THE EDGE OF THE RIVER, I WILL LOOK FOR A BOAT AND CARVE IT,
AHA."

The hyena departed looking for a *hai* tree. A *hai* tree which was very large. When he reached the right location he removed the axe from his shoulders. He chopped seven times and then he said, "I must go and look for a place to hide my cache.[4] This cache is mine. Allah didn't give it to me; his messengers didn't give it to me; my luck didn't give it to me; my mother's hard work didn't give it to me. I gave it to myself. No one gave it to me. Yes, I will eat from it during my lifetime and it will never be all consumed. I will give Toj Geda two goats. I will give Wida Nyamul Saket three. I will give Njonkon Cheli[5] four. I will not allow Dulange[6] to touch any because someday he will inherit everything that I own. For Yaga Yaga[7] I will give nothing.

It happened that, as he turned his back, the goats ran in the opposite direction for about a mile and a half. When they heard the footsteps of the hyena running through the brush, the eldest goat yelled, "All of you stop!" They stopped right there. When the one said stop, the others stopped.

When the hyena arrived he said to them, "AHA! Goat?" The leader replied, "Yes?" He said, "I didn't leave you *here*." "Uncle Hyena, if you look at the position of the moon and then look at our position, you will know that we speak the truth. May we die if we lie. When *we* die, we will die with honor. For here is where you left us." The hyena gazed up at the moon and then down at the goats. He stood there for a while and then he said, "You speak the truth before Allah. You are telling me the truth. I know that you would not lie. But now I am not satisfied. Let me hear some more of that song." The *gewel* sang:

UNCLE HYENA, YOU CAN EAT AT HOME.
TAKE AN EWE AND FREE US,
TAKE A RAM AND FREE US,
BUT FIRST LOOK FOR A BOAT, AHA,
HE SAID, "THERE I WILL LOOK FOR A BOAT, AHA,
I WILL FIND IT THERE, AHA.

AT THE EDGE OF THE RIVER I WILL LOOK FOR A BOAT, AHA,
I WILL CARVE IT THERE, AHA."

As he was giving him the song again, the hyena set off into the brush. The goats left when they saw that he was completely out of sight. It was as if they had gone from our village[8] to Panchang[9] and waited there. They ran there. When the hyena reached the tree, he immediately turned back again and went to where the goats had advanced. When he reached them he said, "You all, now listen! This is not the place where I left you." They replied, "Uncle Hyena, if you look at the position of the moon and then at our position, you will see that you left us here." The hyena said, "HUMMMMM! You speak the truth. But before I leave again, satisfy me with your song." He sang:

UNCLE HYENA, YOU CAN EAT AT HOME,
TAKE AN EWE AND FREE US,
TAKE A RAM AND FREE US,
BUT WHERE WILL YOU LOOK FOR A BOAT TO TRANSPORT US, AHA,
HE SAID, "THERE I WILL LOOK FOR A BOAT, AHA,
I WILL FIND IT THERE, AHA,
AT THE EDGE OF THE RIVER, THERE I WILL LOOK FOR A BOAT, AHA,
I WILL FIND IT THERE, AHA."

When he returned to the *hai* tree the goats left again. They continued to run. By the time the hyena had reached the tree, the goats had arrived at the village of Njau.[10]

The hyena chopped only two times at the *hai* tree with his axe when his thoughts returned again to the goats. He stopped, and then began to run back to them. When he reached the place where he had left them, the goats heard his footsteps and stopped. When the hyena caught sight of them, they were standing still. When he caught up to them he said, "AHA! Honestly now, this is *not* the place where I left you!" They said to him, "Uncle Hyena, look at the moon. You will see that we are in the same position we were when you left us." He agreed then, saying, "You are right. But now I am not satisfied. I must hear the song while I head back to the *hai* tree." The *gewel* sang:

UNCLE HYENA, YOU CAN EAT AT HOME,
TAKE AN EWE AND FREE US,
TAKE A RAM AND FREE US,
BUT FIRST LOOK FOR A BOAT TO TRANSPORT US.
HE SAID, "THERE I WILL LOOK FOR A BOAT,
I WILL FIND IT THERE, AHA,
AT THE EDGE OF THE RIVER, I WILL LOOK FOR A BOAT, AHA,
AT THE EDGE OF THE RIVER, I WILL LOOK FOR A BOAT, AHA."

When he heard this song he left the goats. He returned to the *hai* tree. As soon as he reached there the goats entered Njau. Each one went into his own home and stayed there.

After only two or three chops, the hyena threw down his axe and ran after the goats with very long strides NAR . . . NAR . . . NAR . . . NAR[11] until he arrived at the Njau crossroads. He saw many footprints there in the dirt but he did not know which footprints to follow. He then entered the village of Njau and went up to the center of the village square. There he called out with a very loud voice, "HE CAN EAT AT HOME! HE CAN EAT AT HOME! HE CAN EAT AT HOME!"

Until today, that is why if goats meet the hyena in the fields, they do not travel with him.[12]

[1] Narrated by Bessi Njay in Porli, The Gambia, on October 30 at 2:15 p.m. before 13 men, 9 women and 12 children in the center of the village under the shade of a large tree.

[2] Griot.

[3] A fine-grained, reddish-brown hardwood tree of the bead tree family of trees, having red berries which are used for necklaces. It is significant that the goats send the hyena to this tree, for it indicates that they are outwitting the stronger hyena. It is very difficult to cut such trees down, but the hyena does not know this. They use his ignorance and greed in their plans to escape the danger.

[4] The new-found store of food he envisions to be provided by the goats.

[5] The hyena's wives. (See note no. 3 in "The Hyena Eats the Ostrich's Eggs.")

[6] The hyena's son; "one who is excrement."

[7] The hyena's daughter; "one who has been living at home for a long time."

[8] Porli, The Gambia.

[9] A small village two miles from Porli.

[10] Residence of the District Chief, Alhaji Omar Sise, in the Lower Saloum region of McCarthy Island District, The Gambia.

[11] Ideophonic expression recreating the fast-paced gait of the Mauritanian, *nar.* The hyena here is walking like a Mauritanian.

[12] This narrative focuses on the character of the hyena, his behavior with his own family and the community at large. It provides a good understanding of the basis for his use in the narrative tradition as a symbol of shame. He is consistently presented by *gewel* as a highly individualistic, and thereby anti-social, being. This is dramatically illustrated in his soliloquy regarding his imagined cache. Here he disclaims any linkages with others; neither Allah, his disciples nor his own mother were instrumental in his acquiring this wealth. Thus he claims no need for reciprocity. Although he states that he will give a goat to various family members, their number is insignificant compared to the 3,333 goats that he plans to capture. His apparent generosity conversely highlights his selfishness. These highly individualistic character traits are antithetical to Wolof cultural values.

THE MONKEY WHO CLAIMED
TO BE A GEWEL[1]

There was a story . . .
Our legs are crossed . . .
It happened here . . .
It was so . . .

There was once a monkey who said, "I am a *gewel*. I drum on the *tama.*"

It happened that this monkey left his home one day and approached the village of Njau.[2] The chief organizer for the women of the village became his hostess. She killed a goat for him and cooked him a fine meal.

In the evening all the people assembled at the public square and asked, "Monkey, drum for us so that the young women might dance." So the monkey introduced himself and drummed:

PREPARE TO TREMBLE

They said, "Alright now, monkey, drum and the children will dance." He began to drum. He drummed:

PREPARE TO SHAKE

They said, "Alright now monkey, drum, because it is getting late." He drummed:

PREPARE TO SHAKE

They said, "Monkey, please stop this game." He said, "If that is the way you are going to talk, then I am leaving." He took one step and then left. The dance was ruined and the people were disappointed.

Then he sent a message to the people of Ker Mu Ali.[3] He said, "If you assemble at the compound of Hancha Fana,[4] I will come there tomorrow and spend the day."

Afterwards Hancha Fana called the young girls together and said, "The monkey said that he will spend the day here tomorrow. Let us prepare for him."

They killed a goat for him and cooked it.

The monkey came to the compound and ate until he was satisfied. In the evening they said, "Alright, begin. Monkey, drum for us." He drummed:

PREPARE TO TREMBLE

They said, "Oh, monkey, drum so that we can dance." He drummed:

PREPARE TO SHAKE

They said, "We heard that this is what you did to the people of Njau." He replied, "If that is the way you are going to talk, then I am leaving." He left there immediately.

He sent a message to Jarang[5] that he would spend the next day there.

The chief organizer for the women there said, "I have heard that the monkey is traveling about the country. They kill goats for him and cook them. He eats the food and will not drum for them. But I think that if he comes here, he *will* play." They said, "We have to do something about it."

Thereafter, you understand, they prepared for his arrival. They cooked for him.

When he arrived in the evening, he ate until he was satisfied. The chief organizer for the women called the young people together and said to them, "Now take seven dogs to the public square. When you get there, enclose them in some overturned wooden basins."

So they went and they put the dogs into the basins. Afterwards the dance began. They said, "Monkey begin!" He drummed:

PREPARE TO TREMBLE

They said, "Oh monkey, drum! the children want to dance." He drummed:

PREPARE TO SHAKE

She said, "Monkey, we know you did not play for the people of Njau and Ker Mu Ali." He said, "If that is the way you are going to talk, then I will leave."

He turned his back to go. The woman organizer called out, "Children! Do what I told you to do." Each one got up and opened up one of the basins. The dogs got out and moved towards the monkey. The monkey turned his head and saw the dogs. He turned back and adjusted his drum. Then he knelt down and began to drum:

SELA[6] IS LOOKING AT ME, PREPARE TO TREMBLE.
MBOLOH[7] IS LOOKING AT ME, PREPARE TO SHAKE.
SAFO[8] IS LOOKING AT ME, PREPARE TO QUAKE.

SELA IS LOOKING AT ME, PREPARE TO TREMBLE.
MBOLOH IS LOOKING AT ME, PREPARE TO SHAKE.
SAFO IS LOOKING AT ME, PREPARE TO QUAKE.

THEIR BELLIES ARE EMPTY.

EMPTY . . . EMPTY:
THEIR BELLIES ARE EMPTY?
EMPTY . . . EMPTY.[9]

[1] Narrated by Momadu Njay in Ker Mu Ali, Senegal, on November 16 at 10:30 p.m. in front of the compound of Bukari Fall, a tailor, before 23 men, women and children.

[2] A village only a mile and a half away, but in The Gambia. Most of the people of Ker Mu Ali have relatives living there.

[3] A village where the tale is being narrated.

[4] The organizer for women's social activities in Ker Mu Ali.

[5] A village in Senegal, two miles north from Ker Mu Ali.

[6] "Canine Teeth," one of the dogs' names.

[7] "Loose layer of skin under the neck," another dog's name.

[8] "Satisfaction one obtains from eating," another dog's name.

[9] The monkey in this narrative is an imposter; he has pretended to affiliate with the *gewel* caste. Twice he has taken advantage of the people, first in Njau and then at Ker Mu Ali. He has cheated them, enjoyed their hospitality under false pretenses and failed to perform according to the tenets of the caste. In the final episode the monkey pays for his crime: the hungry dogs will devour him as recompense. The brief flurry of drumming which the monkey used to tempt the people at the other two villages, "Prepare to tremble," takes on a different significance in the third. The focus of its meaning ends with the monkey himself as he is overcome with fear. This ironic twist turns the charade into a disaster. As in the narratives "The Hyena Engages the Hare as a *Gewel*" and "The Passion of the *Gewel*," those who claim other caste membership are inevitably brought to suffer for their pretensions.

A SELECTED BIBLIOGRAPHY

Ames, David. "The Rural Wolof of the Gambia," *Markets in Africa,* ed. by P. Bohannan and G. Dalton, Northwestern University, 1962, 29-60.

_____. "The Selection of Mates, Courtship and Marriage Among the Wolof," *Bulletin I. F. A. N.,* 18 (1956), 156-68.

_____. "Wolof Co-operative Work Groups," *Continuity and Change in African Cultures,* ed. by W. R. Bascom and M. J. Herskovits, Chicago, 1958, 224-37.

Basset, Rene. *Contes Populaires d'Afrique,* 1903.

_____. "Folklore Wolof," *Melusine,* 4 (1888-89), 58-9, 91-4, 132-3, 234-5.

Blair, Dorothy. *African Literature in French,* Cambridge, 1976.

Boilat, Abbe. *Esquisses Sénégalaises,* Paris, 1853.

_____. *Grammaire de la langue woloffe,* Paris, 1858.

Brigaud, F. "Les Contes Senegal," *Notes Africaines* (Jan. 1964), 1-7.

Colardelle-Diarrassouba, Marcell. *Le Liévre et l'Araignée dans les contes de l'ouest africain,* Paris, 1975.

Colvin, Lucie Gallistel. "Wolof Social Structure as Reflected in the Genesis and Content of the Traditional Literature," *African Studies Association Meeting,* October, 1974.

Dadie, Bernard. "Le Role de la léende dans la culture populaire des Noirs d'Afrique," *Présence Africaine* (June-September 1957), 163-74.

Dard, J. *Dictionnarie francais-wolof et francais-bambara, suivi du dictionnaire wolof-francais,* Paris, 1825.

Diop, Birago. *Contes et Lavanes,* Paris, 1963.

_____. *Les Nouveaux contes d'Amadou Koumba,* Paris, 1965.

_____. *Les Contes d'Amadou Koumba,* Paris, 1965.

Equilbecq, F. V. *Contes Indigénes et l'Ouest Africain Francaise,* Vol. II, Paris,

1915.

Faidherbe, Le Général. *Langues Sénégalaises: Wolof, Arabe-Hassania, Soninke, Serer,* Paris, 1887.

Gaden, H. "Legendes et coutoumes Sénégalaises: Cahiers de Yoro Dyao," *Rev. d'Eth. et de Sociologie,* 1912.

Gamble, David. *The Wolof of the Senegambia,* Ethnographic Survey of Africa, Part 14, London, 1967.

_____. *Wolof-English Dictionary,* London, 1958.

Irvine, Judith. "Caste and Communication in a Wolof Village," Unpublished dissertation, University of Pennsylvania, 1973.

Kane, Mohamadou. *Contes d'Amadou Coumba: du conte traditionnel au conte modern d'expression francais,* Dakar, 1968.

Kobes, Mgr. A. *Dictionnarie Volof-Francais revue et considerablement augmentée* par le R.P.O. Abiven, Mission Catholique, Dakar, 1923.

Ly, Boubakar. "L'Honneur dans les societes Ouolof et Toucouleur," *Présence Africaine* (1968), 32-67.

Magel, Emil. "Caste of the Hare in Wolof Oral Narratives," *Research in African Literature,* Spring, 1981.

_____. "Hare and Hyena: Symbols of Honor and Shame in the Oral Narratives of the Wolof of Senegambia," *Essays on African Oral and Written Literatures,* University of Khartoum, Sudan, 1981.

Makward, Edris. "Anchou Thiam and Haja Mbana Diop: Two Griots from Northern Senegal," Modern Language Association Meeting, December, 1974.

_____. "Birago Diop: Storyteller from Senegal," *Kentucky Romance Quarterly,* 16 (1969), 357-74.

_____. "The Contemporary Griot in Senegal," African Studies Association Meeting, 1976.

Mercier, Roger. "Un Conteur d'Afrique Noire: Birago Diop," *Etudes Francaises,* 4 (1968), 119-49.

Pichl, Walter. "Wolof-Sprichworter und Ratsel," *In Afrika and Ubersee,* Bd. XLVI (1961), 93-109, 204-18.

Roger, Baron. *Fables Sénégalaises, recueilles de l'Ouolof et mise en vers francais avec des notes sur la Sénégambie, son climat, ses principales productions, la civilisation et les moeurs des habitants,* Paris, 1828.

Senghor, Leopold, and Sadji, A. *La belle historie de Leuk le lièvre,* 1953.

Senghor, Leopold. "Les Civilisations négro-africaines," *Les plus beaux ecrits de l'UNION Francaise,* Paris, 1947.

_____. Preface to *Les Nouveaux Contes d'Amadou Koumba,* Paris, 1972, 7-22.

Sylla, Ousmane. "Les System des castes dans la Societé Ouolof," *France Eurafrique,* 148 (Jan. 1964), 39-54.

Thiam. "Des Contes et des fables en Afrique noire," *Présence Africaine,* 4 (1948), 667-71.

APPENDIX
Wolof Text of
"The Donkeys of Jolof"

FARI MBAM CI REW I JOLOF

Leb-on . . . lup-on!
Am-on a fi . . . da na am!

   Mbam yoyu len ci rew i Jolof deny fa fal-on bena bur, bur nyu diko wah Fari Mbam. Fari Mbam nak dal di sopale ku nit duga ci rew i Saloum. Di doli ci rew i be dem ci bena deka bu hol a mel ni ki Bati Hai. Mu aksi ken hamu ko. Mu yaga fi lol. Be am fi jurom i dom. Am fi jabar, am fi jurom i dom.

   Bam ame jurom i dom, mboka ya tog ca Jolof nyu ne "Nyun dal suny mboka mu nyu wah Fari Mbam. Suny bur i mbam momu dal, war neny ko uti nkah sarkuna. Ndah bur, ko ham ne danga falu bur warul a dugam rew."

   Bam ko defe nak, mbok am yi dal di daje, nju sopeku nit. Ut seni ndenda, ut seni sabar yep. Dal di joge ko wah Masalan ca Jolof. Biny dike be dig i Kaolack, nyu ne woi dig i rew wi nyu dal di dor ci dig i marse ba. Nyu ne:

     FARI MBAM, MBAM MU RERE, FARI BUR I MBAM.
     MBAM RER NA, FARI BUR I MBAM, FARI MBAM ANGALI?
     MBAM ANGALI? NAXE-NAXE, MBAM MU BAX MU RERE NA.
     FARI MBAM, MBAM MU RERE, FARI BUR I MBAM!

Nyu dal di commasse sen sabar, nyu ne:

     FARI MBAM, MBAM MU RERE, FARI BUR I MBAM
     MBAM RER NA, FARI BUR I MBAM, FARI MBAM ANGALI?
     MBAM ANGALI? NAXE-NAXE, MBAM MU BAX MU RER NA.
     FARI MBAM, MBAM MU RERE, FARI BUR I MBAM!

Nyu tega di feca, di feca bem yaga bena wai dika ne len, "Yen dei wai sen mboka mu gena ut, nyu do deg on ci deka buny nyo wah Bati Hai. Nyun ko i wah Fari Mbab." Nyu ne: "Wos, konak ci jana."

   Nyu taka sen bagage joge Kaolack. Nyow Ndofan. Ca marse ba Ndofan nyu dor nuy ne: "Nyun dei suny mboka len yo set." Bany dore nak comasse sen sabar yi. Gay angi tega, nyungi nan:

     FARI MBAM, MBAM MU RERE, FARI BUR I MBAM.
     MBAM RER NA, FARI BUR I MBAM, FARI MBAM ANGALI?
     MBAM ANGALI? NAXE-NAXE, MBAM MU BAX MU RER NA.

FARI MBAM, MBAM MU RERE, FARI BUR I MBAM!

Nyu comasse sen sabar di fecha bem yaga. Bena wai gena ne len, "Yen dei sen mboka mu gena ut dega neny ko funy wah Bati Hai de." Bam ko defe nyu taka sen i bagage dal di joge ko fa deka Nyoro. Ci dig i mares ba dal di tega sen i ndenda, sabar yi doh nyu nan:

FARI MBAM, MBAM MU RERE, FARI BUR I MBAM.
FARI, MBAM ANGALI? MBAM ANGALI? NAXE-NAXE. MBAM MU BAX MU
    RER NA.
FARI MBAM, MBAM MU RERE, FARI BUR I MBAM!

Bena wai dal di len fenyu. Ne len, "Lu ngen di doh?" Nyu ne, "Nyun dei suny mboka mo nyu rer nyu koi wah Fari Mbam." Mu na, "Wow, nyu dei nyun do dega ca rew i Angale ba." Nyu dal di pak sen yef, nyow Farafeni ci gudi. Nyu dor, nyu ne:

FARI MBAM, MBAM MU REY RERE, FARI BUR I MBAM.
FARI, MBAM ANGALI? MBAM ANGALI? MAXE-NAXE. FARI BUR I MBAM!

Bena wai fenyu len ne len lu ngen di doh. Nyu ne ko, "Nyun dei sen mboka mo ham ne mo don suny bur ca Jolof. Mu sanku duga ci rew mi, nyu di ko set." Yala def waji ku fa ham la. Mu ne len, "Su ngen deme Kaur, ngen lajte fu nyo wah Bati Hai. Fofu la Fari Mbam neka. Borom Banke la fa de." Bam ko defe nyu dal di pack sen i bagage nyow Kaur ca marse ba. Dal di dor, nyu ne:

FARI MBAM, MBAM MU RERE.
FARI MBAM ANGALI? MBAM ANGALI? NAXE-NAXE.
FARI BUR I MBAM!

Dal di ko teka ca marse ba. Nyep daje nyu ne, "Wai boka yile neh li nyu def. Wai funyui jem?" Bena wai gena ne len "Lu ngen di doho?" Nyu ne, "Nyun suny mboka nyu rer mu nyo wah Fari Mbam. Fi ba Jolof moi suny Bur. Wai sopeku nit duga ci bir rew mi. Mom le nyu ut." Gayi ne ko "Konak nangen dem Bati Hai." Nyu dem.

Nyu taka sabar, nyow be Bantak. Nyu lajte kena duga ci dig i gew be ne:

FARI MBAM, MBAM MU RERE, FARI BUR I MBAM.
FARI MBAM ANGALI? MBAM ANGALI? NAXE-NAXE.
FARI BUR I MBAM!

Nyom nyepa woi. Nyu ne wo yen "Lu ngen di doh?" Nyu ne, "Nyun dei suny mboka wo nyu rer. Nyu di ko wah Fari Mbam. Ca Jolof moi suny Bur." Nyu ne, "Nyun dei Fari Mbam nyu ham dei nit la. Mom dei munga Bati Hai." Nyu dal fa baye.

Dal di dika ci dig i pencha mi ci Bati Hai Fari Mbam nak bunta ker angi ak pench mi. Nyo jub lo. Bam ko defe gayi dal di tega. Nyu ne:

FARI MBAM ANGALI? MBAM ANGALI? NAXE-NAXE. MBAM MU BAX MU
    RERE NA.
FARI MBAM, MBAM MU RERE, FARI MBAM!

Bile parti ne:

    FARI MBAM, MBAM MU RERE, FARI BUR I MBAM.

Bele parti ne:

    FARI MBAM ANGALI? MBAM ANGALI? NAXE-NAXE.
    FARI BUR I MBAM!

Bam ko defe nak mu jog. Mu joge ca dig i ker am, wahu be ca bunta mbeda ma. Mu ne jabar am, "Dega nalu ma jahul de. Nyo nyu dei suma mboka leny. Bi ma ko dege, suma kau ak bopa gi dafa de be ci suma weyi tanka yi. Gay yoyule du ma len gama seli." Delu mat ca bir neg ba. Tog. Gayi dorati ne:

    FARI MBAM ANGALI? MBAM ANGALI? NAXE-NAXE!
    FARI BUR I MBAM.

Bale parti ne:

    FARI MBAM ANGALI? MBAM ANGALI? NAXE-NAXE. MBAM MU RER NA.
    FARI BUR I MBAM.

Bam ko defe nak mu dem be ci dig i neg am ne jabar am, "Bah na ci jama."

Mu dal di dem dika be ca dig i gew ba mu teg tank ba ne ko REK-REK-REK dal di gene bena tanka ab mbam. Nyu ne:

    FARI MBAM ANGALI? MBAM ANGALI? NAXE-NAXE MBAM FENY NA.
    FARI MBAM ANGALI? MBAM ANGALI? MBAM FENY NA.
    FARI, MBAM MU RERE, FENY NA. FARI BUR I MBAM.

Gayi ne, "Ndesan, suny mboka feny na." Bam ko defe dom yi jeki tega humba lol. Taw be dika ne, "Suma bay dei ndesan sopeku na mbam. Anda ay bokam?" Yay am ne, "Wow, bugen deme di ngen ma baye ab neg nendi." Bam ko defe taw ba ne:

    FARI MBAM ANGALI? MBAM ANGALI? NAXE-NAXE. FARI MBAM FENY NA.
    FARI BUR I MBAM.

Dal di sopeku mbam mom itam. Mu fob tanka am ne do REK-REK-REK gene tanka mbam, gene nopi mbam, dal di mbam.

Bam ko defe ka topa taw ba ne, "Man dei suma bay di na dem bai de." Yay am ne "Man dei dom, su ngen anda sen bay di naa met. Man au-ma ku di yen." Mu dem be ca dig i gew ba mu ne:

    FARI MBAM ANGALI? MBAM ANGALI? NAXE-NAXE. BUR I MBAM FENY NA.
    FARI BUR I MBAM.

Bam ko defe ham nga ne nyar i dom sopeku mbam yi mel ne Fari. Ba ko nyetel dom dem jabar am mu ne, "Suma yay, bay du dem ba ma de." Mu ne ko, "Wow, bon dei di na met." Mu dem be ca dig i gew ba. Mu sepa tanka ba. Gene tanka ab mbam ne:

    FARI MBAM ANGALI? MBAM ANGALI? NAXE-NAXE. FARI BUR I MBAM.
    FARI MBAM, MBAM FENY NA, FARI BUR I MBAM.

Dal di def REK-REK-REK gene tanka mbam, gene nopi mbam, gene gen u

mbam tahaw fale di mbam. Be mui nyetti dom.
Ba ko nyenental dal di tagu yayi. Yay ne ko, "Man dei kon dei di na met de."
Mu dal didem nyow be ca dig i gew ba. Mu ne:

FARI MBAM ANGALI? MBAM ANGALI? NAXE-NAXE. MBAM FENY NA.
FARI MBAM FENY NA. FARI BUR I MBAM.

Sopeleku ne tanka rek gene tanki mbam, gene nopi mbam gene gen ab mbam
tahaw fela mo itam di mbam.
Bam ko defe gay ya ak sen ndenda ya. Nyom konton nyu. Nyu ne, "Deka
bile, Bati Hai, nyun buga nyen ko lol. Ndah suny mboka mi yena ko ame bem am
fi njebot! Jere gen jef! Nyung len di santa wai nak di neny yobu sunya mboka
mi." Nyu tog ga Bati Hai tuit. Nyu dem, nyu ne:

FARI MBAM ANGALI? MBAM ANGALI? NAXE-NAXE. MBAM FENY NA!
FARI MBAM FENY NA. FARI BUR I MBAM!

Dal di dem andak nyom nak! Leb dohe tabi ajana!